P9-CFY-063

Only Connect
Uniting
Reading and Writing

Only Connect

Uniting Reading and Writing

Edited by
THOMAS NEWKIRK
University of New Hampshire

BOYNTON/COOK PUBLISHERS, INC.
UPPER MONTCLAIR, NEW JERSEY 07043

The editor wishes to express his thanks for permission to use the following work:

"The Span of Life" from *The Poetry of Robert Frost* edited by Edward Connery Lathem. Copyright 1936 by Robert Frost. Copyright © 1964 by Lesley Frost Ballantine. Copyright © 1969 by Holt, Rinehart and Winston. Reprinted by permission of Holt, Rinehart and Winston, Publishers.

Library of Congress Cataloging-in-Publication Data

Main entry under title:

Only Connect.

    1. English language—Rhetoric—Study and teaching—Congresses. 2. Reading (Higher education)—Congresses. I. Newkirk, Thomas.
PE1404.48   1986   808'.042   85-24311
ISBN 0-86709-171-1

For information address Boynton/Cook Publishers, Inc.
52 Upper Montclair Plaza, P.O. Box 860, Upper Montclair, NJ 07043

Printed in the United States of America.

86 87 88 89 10 9 8 7 6 5 4 3 2 1

Acknowledgments

These papers were drawn from talks given at a conference held at the University of New Hampshire from October 12-14, 1984. A grant from the University's Elliott Fund helped underwrite the gathering. The conference itself was planned by an ad hoc committee composed of Lester Fisher, Thomas Carnicelli, Gary Lindberg, Carl Dawson, Donald Murray, and myself. In planning and running the conference I was ably assisted by Peggi McCarthy, Robert Yagelski, and Cindi Gannett.

But no amount of planning could have guaranteed the splendid work of the speakers and presenters. In preparing the book I had useful editorial help from Bob Connors and Gary Lindberg. Bob Boynton and Peter Stillman gave steady support to this project and helped me get distance on the papers in this book. My work with them was one more reminder of our good fortune to have them publishing in the area of composition.

(Note: Citations, end notes, and references herein vary in style from paper to paper; some conform to MLA standrads, others to APA. After considerable fretting, we decided to leave it this way, inasmuch as it works no hardship on the reader. Furthermore, in some cases a restyling would have done violence to the work.)

Contents

Background and Introduction

THOMAS NEWKIRK

In the spring of 1975, James Sledd and Neil Megaw submitted a resolution to the University of Texas English Department that would have required all regular faculty members to teach at least one section of composition every three semesters. It caused an uproar, and while it didn't pass, the resolution did, in Sledd's words, "smoke the bastards out." A number of faculty position papers displayed a striking hostility toward teaching composition (while at the same time acknowledging the economic advantages that a giant "service" course can provide).

Some of the papers were quoted in an article by George Nash (1975), then a Teaching Assistant in the English Department. One faculty member claimed that the teacher of composition " . . . does not need to be as specialized in his training [as the teacher of literature]" (p. 126). This was so because "freshman composition is an elementary course." This theme—the elementary, unchallenging nature of the freshman English course—was repeated in many of the papers. Another stated that

> There is one absolutely central reason why Freshman English is avoided by the regular faculty wherever possible—it involves an overwhelming amount of dull, tedious drudgery. . . . marking the hundreds of pages of essays they write in a semester is a time consuming, boring, uninspiring chore because so much of one's effort is spent correcting mere mechanical errors (p. 127).

On a loftier plane, several argued that if this resolution passed, the central mission of the English Department—the teaching and study of

1

literature—would be seriously compromised. And one concluded apocalyptically that " . . . a breakdown in the hierarchy of courses and the corresponding disregard for the expertise of the faculty blur the important distinction between a department in a junior college and one in a university" (p. 127).

I was a graduate student at Texas during this debate, and though not directly involved, I was aware of the attitude and values expressed in these statements—and I resented them bitterly. I couldn't see how an English Department could presume to take responsibility for a course like Freshman Composition and then play absentee landlord. It struck me as irresponsible and massively uninformed for faculty members to deny writing's central influence in developing thinking abilities, especially during this critical period in students' lives. There was something fundamentally narrow and inhumane in perceiving literary study as the exclusive mission of a hierarchically ordered department. And I knew that as long as attitudes like this dominated such departments, my own career as "composition specialist" was in jeopardy.

Now, ten years later, composition seems to be on surer ground. The Conference on College Composition and Communication has flourished and is now probably the most vibrant part of the NCTE. Publishers like Boynton/Cook, Heinemann, and Southern Illinois University Press have come out with books or series on rhetoric and composition. Even English Departments have begun to seek Ph.D.s in this field. Yet despite these healthy signs, composition remains an imperfectly defined field, and old questions about its place live on; the relationship between reading and writing is still unclear.

Initially, those who did research in composition attempted to define their work in opposition to literary scholarship, and there was no small satisfaction in putting distance between ourselves and the mandarinate that looked upon us with such disdain. In fact, one major book in the field, Mina Shaughnessy's *Errors and Expectations*, dealt with the very errors that literature professors at Texas retreated from in such horror. The book treats with utmost seriousnesss the texts of students who, according to the hierarchical mind-set of most literary "humanists," shouldn't be allowed into the university in the first place (though they might sneak into a junior college). The belief that composition scholarship should pay attention to all students amounts to a rejection of the elitist attitude which Shaughnessy calls "guarding the tower," and it has become a central tenet of composition work. But in other ways, attempts to distance composition scholarship from literary scholarship have been more problematical.

First was the almost overpowering interest in "the writing process," with "process" regularly and emphatically opposed to "product." Products, those artifacts studied by the literary scholar, didn't provide clues about their own production; a sentence doesn't explain how it is written. Or, to use Donald Murray's memorable analogy, it's hard to infer the pig from the sausage. Rather than fixing attention on end products, the composition specialist was encouraged to look at the mental activities—the planning, drafting, revision, editing—that go into the production of the text. Correspondingly, it was argued, students learned how to become writers by experimenting with their own writing process and articulating their own approaches to composing. The reading of finished professional texts figured only marginally in this schema.

It also seemed possible to examine writing in isolation from the reading of finished texts because of certain philosophic orientations of the most influential theorists—particularly Macrorie, Britton, and Elbow. As Burton Hatlen argues herein, the predominant orientation of these theorists was a Romantic Idealism which stressed the "natural" forming powers of the mind itself, our capacity to shape experience, to give form to ideas in the exercise of innate capacities. Furthermore, this capacity is used most successfully if the writer is not bound by the constraints of formal modes of discourse—is free to let meaning seek its own forms. Clearly, the reading of finished products would not figure centrally in a pedagogy built on this view of composing.

A third way in which composition distanced itself from literary studies was with the claim that it was interdisciplinary. It would draw on work in a variety of areas—cognitive science, neurolinguistics, anthropology . . . the list goes on. The most influential advocate of this position is Janet Emig, and she put it forward dramatically at the Ottawa Conference in 1979 in a speech entitled "The Tacit Tradition." In it she identified pivotal work that can and should underlie composition research, and the sources she cited were far from the type signed out by our colleagues in literature. Prominent on Emig's list were scientists—Lenneberg, Luria, Popper, Eccles. And her model for the development of Composition as a discipline relied heavily on Thomas Kuhn's *The Structure of Scientific Revolutions.* Conspicuous by their absence were references to classical rhetoric or literary studies.

I was present for Emig's speech, and I remember particularly the sense of exhilaration I felt, the sense of escaping the domination of Literary Studies and the possibility of building connections outside the English Department. In retrospect, though, I think Emig underestimated the difficulty—even the danger—of the kind of work she was calling composition scholars to do. The disciplines she cites are rooted in research traditions that the composition specialist isn't likely to understand. And unless they are understood, the danger of oversimplification and misuse of research is extreme. (Witness the embarrassing dabbling in brain research that was so common a few years back.)

Not only is the diversity of research traditions a problem, but many work from opposing epistemological traditions. The kind of assertion that appears in *College English* probably wouldn't be accepted by readers of *Cognitive Studies* or *Reading Research Quarterly*. Carl Bereiter is fond of saying that those who do work in composition are not part of the same field—they merely have the same topic. And although they may attend the same conferences, drink at the same bars, the empiricists often have little professional interchange with rhetoricians and ethnographers.

I want to argue—and this book provides supporting evidence— that the embrace of science (a natural way to justify an emerging discipline) may have obscured the powerful link that composition studies have with literary studies. And to explore this point, I want to refer to a dramatic moment of the conference from which these papers are drawn. Paul Mariani, near the end of his paper that examined how Robert Lowell reinterpreted a childhood experience throughout his life, paused and asked,

> Is any of what I have written true? Would Lowell himself, who has disappeared forever from us into the text itself, have recognized himself in this reading?

My first reaction to the question was, Of course he would. But Mariani followed with the answer that was inevitable after this first startlement:

> Who can say? Perhaps the most we can hope for in our post-Kantian, post-Heideggerian moment, is a rhetoric of persuasion, a momentary grammar of assent.

I suspect that those in the area of composition who do empirical research—and clearly the scientists to whom Emig referred—would have little use for a discipline based on a "rhetoric of persuasion, a momentary grammar of assent." To use Kuhn's jargon, they would see papers like those in this book as evidence of the "pre-paradigmatic" stage of work in composition, a stage that would at some point become defined in a way that "normal science" could acknowledge. In other words, the kind of scholarship done now, while it may lead to the more rigorous and systematic research that characterizes a mature discipline, is fundamentally different from the work that will be done in that period of maturity. To the empiricist, speculations such as those in this volume have lasting value insofar as they may lead to more systematically verifiable conclusions. English Departments are suspicious of empiricism because of a deeply-rooted belief in the value of individual interpretation. No one wants Helen Vendler to train raters to classify Keats's odes; it is Helen Vendler reading Keats that we want. She gains our assent through a "rhetoric of persuasion." Empiricism seems to deny a place to the provocative, the idiosyncratic reading that can jar us into new ways of seeing. Once-dominant approaches to literary study lose ground not because they have been "disconfirmed" in Popper's sense, but because they cease to be interesting; New Criticism is now out of favor not because it is "untrue," but because to many it had become mechanical and because it didn't deal with questions scholars wanted to explore.

I'm suggesting, then, that composition studies may share a great deal with literary studies, far more than it shares with the sciences. In my experience, for example, literary scholars who have read *Errors and Expectations* have recognized Shaughnessy's achievement because it is so clearly an act of imaginative reading, of interpretation. The British participants in the Dartmouth Conference—Britton, Barnes, Dixon, Holbrook—were students of F. R. Leavis, and their sensitivity to student texts is hardly unrelated to that training. In this book, I think we see as well the same kind of imaginative reading that characterizes the best work in literary studies.

Since the Sledd-Megaw proposal ten years ago, conditions seem more advantageous for the integration of composition into the English Department. Reader-response theory has stirred interest in the moment-by-moment process of reading, an interest that parallels work in the writing process. Scholars in my own department are examining texts as diverse as gravestone inscriptions and the journals of women who crossed the country in the nineteenth century. To suggest that student texts might profit from the same careful attention doesn't seem as radical as it once did. And James Kinneavy's vision, expressed in the Texas debate a decade ago, may seem a little less remote. He wrote,

> The intent of the Sledd-Megaw proposal, as I see it, is to maintain the English Department as the stronghold of the liberal arts tradition where rhetoric, poetic (and logic also) are respected and maintained in fruitful balance, fruitful for faculty and especially for the student. I can see the intellectual life as a healthy organic whole, not a discrete set of suspicious fragments (Nash, p. 127).

As Richard Ohmann and Robert Connors remind us, the fragmentation Kinneavy deplores has long historical roots in this country, and the hierarchical structure of the English Department is firmly established. But on an Indian Summer weekend at the University of New Hampshire, a group of us joined to inch toward Kinneavy's ideal.

In the first section of the book, Richard Ohmann, Robert Connors, and Burton Hatlen provide a historical and intellectual context for looking at the relationship between reading and writing. Ohmann argues provocatively that the university and the English Department within the university mirror features of the modern corporation: that in fact the emergence of the university department coincides with the rise of the modern corporation where there were similar divisions of labor (management, advertising, labor). English Departments defined their discipline as including literature and composition, but these two components were never in anything like co-equal relationship; composition from the beginning was associated with the "dull, tedious drudgery" noted by the Texas faculty member, while literature was a realm for refinement and leisurely contemplation.

Robert Connors, while not dealing directly with the reading/writing connection, asks why composition—with its clear and honorable connection to classical rhetoric—came to be reduced to an almost neurotic concern for mechanical correctness. Like Ohmann, he shows how cultural and economic forces worked to bring about this trivialization. Connors is especially effective in showing how the "writing crisis" of the late 19th century led to many of the odious mechanical prescriptions (e.g. the mandatory topic sentence) that persist to this day.

Burton Hatlen examines the philosophical roots of composition theory and identifies two major traditions: a "romantic idealism" that, he claims, has dominated the approaches to composing that stress the natural forming powers of the mind, and a "dialectical" tradition which stresses the interaction of socially given forms and personal intentions. Hatlen argues that the "dialectical" tradition offers a more satisfactory explanation of the relationship between reading and writing, and, more particularly, that it can help us understand the ways in which imitation (though not the mechanical form of imitation that characterizes many "models approaches") helps the writer.

The second section, "Reading, Writing, Interpreting" moves into the classroom. David Bartholomae examines student responses to Plato's *Phaedrus* and Richard Rodriguez's *Hunger of Memory* to show what it means to continue a dialogue with a text and how students frequently retreat from it, offering commonplaces as a way of resolving perplexity. His essay illuminates the dilemma of students entering the academic community and being called upon to speak with an authority they do not yet possess. Gary Lindberg and Louise Smith echo many of Bartholomae's observations. Lindberg shows how literature, in particular, resists the "stable, authoritative, pure" kind of generalizations that "hold their shape independent of the biases of individual readers." The act of coming to work, of speaking about our readings, requires, as Bartholomae suggests, a continuing dialogue involving "messier truths that we formulate, undo, and remake again." Smith looks at how students can use writing to ponder the way in which these messier truths are formed by examining the way students use metaphors to make meaning. She claims that the metaphor "is not a perception of truth but a continued dialogue with the knotty particularities of experience."

I have paired the essays by Ann Berthoff and Judith Goleman because each argues for the importance of a particular theorist. Berthoff shows how the principles underlying Paulo Freire's literacy programs can also inform reading and writing instruction at the college level. Berthoff stresses Freire's rejection of instruction that reduces literacy to an atomized skill and stresses the importance of using language to interpret the world—so that naming the world and naming the word are synonymous. Another theme in Freire's (and Berthoff's) pedagogy, the importance of the learner's awareness of learning, is picked up in Goleman's essay. Drawing on the work of the Russian linguist, Mikhail Bakhtin, she shows how a series of reading and writing assignments can bring students to an awareness of the languages—of school, of parents, of the street—which intersect in their lives.

The final three essays in this section focus more specifically on classroom issues. Rosemary Deen replicates a workshop she conducted at the conference where participants both wrote and analyzed very short texts. Like Berthoff, Deen views the mind as particularly attuned to structures, and her exercises assist students in moving to a conscious awareness of structures—in the language they read and in the language they write.

Carol Batker and Charles Moran relate current work in reader response to one of the most intractable problems that faces students in a writing class: Who (really) does he or she write to? Batker and Moran illustrate strategies used at the University of Massachusetts to help students understand the processes that readers of their papers experience. The reader they depict is far more dynamic and versatile than that described by many texts which vaguely urge students to "consider their audience."

Lynn Quitman Troyka also looks at the active, moment-by-moment processes that students go through as readers of their own writing. She identifies a concept "closeness to text" and argues that if students are to make useful predictions—or to help their readers make useful predictions—they need to shift from a tightly focused look at words or parts of words to the movement of ideas, to the ways texts make promises and fulfill them.

The final section, "Fictions," begins with a parable that appears in many composition texts. An Indian sculptor is asked how he carved an elephant, and he replies that he took a block of stone and knocked off everything that didn't look like an elephant. Sarah Sherman contends that the parable misrepresents the act of writing, wherein there is no clear division between elephant and non-elephant. The historian, for example, must pick a perspective that allows her both to intensely consult and to intensely ignore. The interpretation, the history, that emerges is a fiction and not a mirror of "what happened."

Judith Fishman Summerfield makes a case for narratives, noting that the narrative is often thought of as an intellectually substandard kind of writing in composition courses—in some it is outlawed entirely. Borrowing from the work of Barbara Hardy, James Britton and others, she argues that in reading and writing narratives we test and apply systems of values, that narratives allow us to become spectators, and as such we can more fully evaluate human experience—our own and those of people we read about. We are drawn into this act in part because narratives contain gaps—perspectives that are implied but not made explicit. Fishman uses newspaper fillers to show how we can be drawn in to fill these gaps, and in doing so to further apply and reflect on our system of values. Donald Murray picks up on this theme of gaps and shows how the reading of Jayne Ann Phillips's *Machine Dreams* called up a "ghost text," not exactly an imitation of Phillips but writing "ignited" by Phillips's opening.

The book concludes with Paul Mariani's essay, which ostensibly examines the ways Robert Lowell interpreted and reinterpreted a childhood experience. But the essay is about interpretation itself, about why we interpret, and about the impermanence of these interpretations. I'll conclude with his conclusion:

> . . . in hunting Lowell's texts for the spoor of evidence which was the man, I came to understand something about myself as well. Isn't that what we finally write for, for that secret phosphorescence we call the revelations of the self, words framing the figure in the carpet, dust shaping itself into the magnetic figure of the rose? Fictions we call our writing, but they are fictions by which we live. Each of us here tonight, in our own enlightened, troubled, idiosyncratic, fragmented, yet distinctive ways, bears witness by our very presence to the force of words upon our very lives, the words by which we live and which bear evidence of what we make of the as-yet-unfinished text of life itself.

References

Emig, J. (1983). The tacit tradition: The inevitability of a multi-disciplinary approach to writing research. In D. Goswami & M. Butler (Eds.), *The web of meaning: Essays on writing, teaching, learning, and thinking.* (Upper Montclair, NJ: Boynton/Cook, 1983): 145-156.

Nash, G. (1976). Who's minding freshman English at U.T. Austin? *College English, 38*, 125-130.

Perspectives

1

Reading and Writing, Work and Leisure

RICHARD OHMANN

Wesleyan University

A while back, I was seized by a fascination, or maybe an obsession, with the year 1893, plus or minus one. Let me indulge it for a moment, by mentioning first some events that have a close bearing on our topic here, and then some that are farther afield.

1.   Throughout the year 1894, *The Dial* ran a series of articles on programs in English at eighteen American colleges and universities, written in most cases by the heads of the various departments. Imagine such a series appearing today in a national magazine; and imagine a commercial publisher being, as D. C. Heath was, so impressed by "the great interest aroused in education circles" that it decided to bring the articles out in book form. The interest among *English* teachers was understandable. As William Morton Payne, editor of *The Dial* plausibly argued, the articles "must be admitted to establish beyond question the claims of English as a proper subject of university instruction" (1895, p. 20). That "subject," from Harvard to Berkeley, sidelined a number of older disciplines, and embraced primarily the newer ones of composition and literature.

2.   The year before (1893 itself), Harvard University had appointed a Committee on Composition and Rhetoric to examine the writing of its students, and then had published the Committee's report. It deplored the inadequate preparation of these elite students, and backed up its indictment with an appendix full of comically horrendous themes. The report caused the first national scandal of a type with which we've become all too familiar; and according to Payne, it gave the English reform movement "its strongest impulse, and made a

11

burning 'question of the day' out of a matter previously little more than academic in its interest" (1895, p. 12).

3.   In 1892, the National Educational Association appointed a committee of ten prestigious gentlemen to consider what the curriculum of secondary schools should be. Harvard President Charles W. Eliot was in the chair; the Committee also included the U.S. Commissioner of Education, four other college presidents, three school heads, and a professor. The Committee of Ten found a chaos in the schools. It determined that nine subjects should make up the bulk of school work (English was one of them), and appointed a "Conference" to make recommendations for each of the nine areas. The Conference on English—seven professors and three schoolmen—met late in 1892, and formulated an elaborate program in English, from grade one through grade twelve. It prefaced its proposals by stating the two goals of English instruction:

> (1) to enable the pupil to understand the expressed thoughts of others and to give expression to thoughts of his own; and (2) to cultivate a taste for reading, to give the pupil some acquaintance with good literature, and to furnish him with the means of extending that acquaintance. (National Education Association, 1894, p. 86).

It went on to insist, directly, that although these two goals of communication and appreciation—composition and literature—might be separately named, "yet in practice they should never be dissociated in the mind of the teacher and their mutual dependence should be constantly present to the mind of the pupils." Thus they asserted the unity which is the goal of *this* conference, ninety years later. And their assertion came when it counted, for the Report of the Committee of Ten, which appeared in 1894, was probably the most influential one in the history of American education.

4.   In 1893, the various professional societies of engineers (civil, mining, etc.) banded together and founded the Society for the Promotion of Engineering Education, to regularize standards, maintain their rigor, and insist that engineering education for undergraduates emphasize basic principles—e.g., science—thus more than incidentally grounding the field in a body of unified knowledge that would guarantee it a place in the university (Rae, 1967, p. 336).

5.   In early 1893 the economy went into a depression, and then into a panic. By 1894, more than 150 railroads had gone bankrupt; in four years, 800 banks failed. Unemployment rose to an estimated twenty percent (Hession & Sardy, 1969, p. 459).

6.   Companies responded to the depression in one of their customary ways, sharply cutting wages. In 1894 a wave of strikes followed,

surpassing any previous one except perhaps that of 1877. In all, 750,000 workers struck that year, more than half in exceptionally bitter, violent, and protracted actions that nearly shut down the coal mines and the railroads, and left many workers dead, injured, or imprisoned (Brecher, 1972, p. 101).

7.   In the middle of the panic of 1893, S. S. McClure brought out his new "quality" monthly magazine, at the unprecedented low price of fifteen cents. John Brisben Walker, editor of the old *Cosmopolitan*, promptly dropped his price to twelve and a half cents. And in October, with much hoopla, Frank Munsey cut the price of his faltering monthly from a quarter to a dime. Its circulation went from 40,000 that month to 200,000 the following February to 500,000 in April, 1895. No quality monthly had risen much past a circulation of 200,000 before; by the end of the decade several were close to a million. Historians call this the "magazine revolution" of 1893 (Peterson, 1956, pp. 6–11).

8.   In 1893, Sears, Roebuck and Co. was founded; it rapidly became the world's largest merchandiser.

9.   In 1892, both the General Electric Company and the United States Rubber Company were formed, by mergers. They represented a new kind of industrial firm—the modern, integrated, corporation. To give an idea of what that means: a few years later the organizational chart of U.S. Rubber showed over 80 divisions, plants, and sub-companies, comprehending the entire process of production and distribution, from raw materials to the minds of consumers, and rationally arranged in a nine-level tree of command. One of the departments was advertising (Chandler, 1977, pp. 436–437).

You will not be astounded to hear that I plan to argue more than a coincidental relationship among these nine events. I don't claim any inevitability in their all taking place within a three-year period. Nor do I say that some caused the others. Rather, I suggest that we may understand all of them as belonging to a unified process of historical change, one that transformed our society quite dramatically in a few decades, and that reached a peak of intensity in the 1890s. Though the change came close for a moment to revolutionary discontinuity, in the national strikes of 1894, it progressed by evolutionary means, catching up every social group and every activity of life. I admit at the outset that I am not certain just how the separation of reading and writing fit in, but I have some hypotheses—to which I will come after briefly describing the social transformation at its deepest level, the fundamental relations of production and distribution.

In the mid- and late nineteenth century, *competitive* capitalism ran its energetic course, building a huge industrial system with unparalleled speed. The familiar movement from farm and shop to factory, from country to city, can be expressed in any number of statistics. For instance, the value of manufactured goods increased seven-fold in the last four decades of the century, far outdistancing the value of farm products. The number of factories quadrupled, and the number of people working in them tripled. Profits were large, and most of them went into the building of more industrial capacity: industrial capital quadrupled just in the last three decades of the century, and the *rate* of capital formation reached the highest point before or since, in the 1890s.[1] Production changed utterly, and businessmen were in command of the nation's future.

But as they raced ahead, making fortunes and transforming the society, they were experiencing painfully the contradictions of the system they had built. Every decade between 1870 and 1900 brought a major depression, climaxing in the panic of 1893; crises of overproduction were apparently untamable. Within this volatile *system*, individual businesses led precarious existences; competition was fierce, and none of the legal or illegal attempts to restrain it worked. Bankruptcies were endemic. The rate of profit began to decline. And attempts on the part of businessmen to counter these dangers by reducing wages led to all but open class warfare in 1877 (the Great Upheaval), 1885 (Haymarket), 1892 (Homestead), and 1894. (These conflicts, by the way, sponsored a discourse on "dangerous classes," and what to do about them, just as in England the Hyde Park riots provided an impetus for Arnold's *Culture and Anarchy*. I will not return to this subject, but it has something to do with the formation of English as a subject.) By concentrating their energies on production and on price competition, businessmen had built an empire, but one they could not govern, either as a class or individually—one whose anarchy led to great instability, killing risk, falling profits, and social rebellion.

What emerged from this extended crisis—and partially resolved it—was the system I call monopoly capitalism (the adjectives "industrial," "late," and "advanced" point to much the same phenomenon). This is no time to characterize it in detail—it is, in any case, the ocean in which we now swim, as familiar to all of us as our bodies. I will only mention a few of its main features, as they bear on my theme. What I'd like you to hold in mind as I do this is that every aspect of monopoly capitalism was in part a response to the crisis of which I have spoken, and an effort to control and rationalize processes that felt—to businessmen as well as to most other people—chaotic and threatening. In fact, one might characterize monopoly capitalism by its powerful drive toward *planning*, by its attempt to replace Adam Smith's invisible hand with the "visible hand" of management.

That phrase is from the title of a book by Alfred D. Chandler (1977), a classic study of monopoly capitalism's main institutional form, the giant corporation, which emerged in the last two decades of the nineteenth century (General Electric and U.S. Rubber were my examples from 1892). Where before, entrepreneurs had built factories and concentrated on getting out the goods, from the 1880s on, the impersonal corporation became dominant. Characteristically, it brought the entire economic process within its compass, from raw materials through manufacturing through sales. Far too complex for the supervision of a single businessman (and his family), it brought into existence the modern corporate structure, with divisions, sub-divisions, and layers of hired management. It attempted to coordinate every stage of making and distributing, so as to eliminate uncertainty from the process. That project never succeeded entirely, of course, but it did establish an economic order that has proved supple enough, through our century.

I want now to mention two ways in which the new corporations carried out this design, before turning these thoughts back toward universities and English. First, monopoly capital took control of the labor process, far more precisely and intrusively than had been done before. It developed the approach that came to be known as scientific management, following that magical moment in 1899 when Frederick Winslow Taylor oversaw the work of a "Dutchman" named Schmidt at Bethlehem Steel, and got him to move 47 tons of pig iron a day instead of the twelve and a half tons that had previously been standard. Taylor analyzed a job into its minutest components, divided the process among various workers, and created the techniques which culminated in the assembly line. He built on three principles: (1) dissociate the labor process from the vested skills and knowledge of workers; (2) separate conception from execution; and (3) reserve understanding for management, and use it to control each step of the labor process. As Studs Terkel's workers said, one way and another: a robot could do my job. I draw this understanding of modern management from Henry Braverman, who sums up its role:

> to render conscious and systematic, the formerly unconscious tendency of capitalist production. It was to ensure that as craft declined, the worker would sink to the level of general and undifferentiated labor power, adaptable to a large range of simple tasks, while as science grew, it would be concentrated in the hands of management (Braverman, 1974, pp. 120–121).

The second main movement of monopoly capital: to add control of *sales* to control of production. This was a change of great complexity and unevenness, working through the evolution of department stores, chain stores, mail order houses (chiefly Sears, Roebuck and Montgomery Ward), the railroads, the telegraph, and the postal system,

as well as the new corporate structure and its sales division. The outcome was a universal, national market, increasingly managed by the
same corporations that produced the goods. To enter national markets
successfully, they quickly developed a number of new practices: uniform packaging (as opposed to the barrel of anonymous pickles or
crackers); brand names to help form habits of loyalty among buyers;
trade marks to link a *second* sign to the product and enhance its aura;
slogans, jingles, and cartoon characters to penetrate every buyer's mind.
In short, they came to depend on advertising, as a direct channel of instruction from manufacturer to customer. And piggy-back on the new
advertising industry, arose for the first time a national mass culture,
whose main product was not the magazine, the newspaper, the radio
program, or the TV broadcast, but the *attention* of the *audience*, sold
in blocks to advertisers. The magazine revolution of 1893 created the
first really modern channel of mass culture.[2] I can't prove it here, but
will assert that this characteristic feature of modern society and contemporary humanity derives from exactly the same forces that divided
and transformed labor. In fact the two are obverse and reverse, in a
social mode that has polarized production and consumption, worker
and consumer, work and leisure.

Since a society's practices of upbringing and education must somehow mesh with its adult social relations and its productive system,
American schools and colleges naturally changed to fit the new conditions—and also helped bring them about. I have written about this in
English in America (Ohmann, 1976, Chap. 11). There was no university in the country, in the modern sense of the word, until the last
quarter of the nineteenth century, when many sprang up almost simultaneously, as if planned by a national authority—though there was
none, beyond the rather empty authorization of the Morrill Act. The
old classical, "common" curriculum retreated into the corners of the
new institutions, suddenly disestablished by the elective system, and
shoved aside by science, professional training, and specialized studies
of all sorts—including the new field of English. The university was gear-
ing itself up to be a supplier and certifier of the professionals and managers needed by those integrated corporations and by the other institutions that came into being to monitor and service the corporate social
order. In his inaugural address of 1869, Charles William Eliot forecast
the role Harvard and other universities would have in educating specialized *professionals*: "as a people," he lamented, "we do not apply to
mental activities the principle of division of labor; and we have but a
halting faith in special training for high professional employments"
(quoted by Douglas, 1976, p. 126). He proposed to remedy that. As
for *managers*: there were virtually none in 1869, so Eliot could not
have planned for their training, but he understood later that the new

university worked to that purpose too. In 1923 he reminisced, "All along Harvard College has produced among its Bachelors of Arts young men who went out into business . . . but it could hardly be said that it was a distinct object in the University to train them for it. Now it has become so" (quoted by Ohmann, 1976, p. 292).

The new universities came into being along with the professional-managerial class they educated.[3] They developed new structures to accommodate the task: a division between undergraduate and graduate studies; separate "schools" with deans; academic departments, with specialized courses of study that came to be called "majors"; a hierarchy of faculty ranks; administrations above and apart from faculties. (Cf. the structure of the corporation.) Within this format it became crucial for the instructors of any subject that their field be embodied in a department or school, and that it have its own body of systematized knowledge with graduate degrees leading into its particular profession. Some professions, like the engineers, practiced their discipline mainly outside the university, but all legitimized themselves partly through their standing within it. This is why is was so important, in 1894, to those who taught English, that cultural authorities like Payne and the Committee of Ten accepted "the claims of English as a proper subject of university instruction." No department, no subject, no profession.

For that recognition to occur, the subject must seem to have dignity, a body of knowledge, and if possible, utility as well. That is what English professors—and, with their guidance, school teachers—managed to say persuasively in the formative years of the new university. Precisely how that happened is a long story, that others have told. I will just note that English took its modern shape, in the 1890s, by privileging two of its possible contents—composition and literature—and relegating others to archaism, though those others all had longer traditions: rhetoric, grammar, English language, oratory, elocution. The two newcomers had appeared on the scene sporadically through the century, but had begun to assume a central place only about 25 years before the magic year, 1893 plus or minus one.

Eliot spoke of the need for better language training in his Inaugural Address, and in 1872 brought in Adams Sherman Hill to offer that training. Perhaps that's as close as we can come to spotting the entrenchment of modern composition in the curriculum. It spread like kudzu, mainly because its utility was incontestable—in principle, that is: as already noted, composition barely arrived before it began undergoing crises of perceived effectiveness that have persisted until this day. But all agreed that the young *needed* to write better.

English literature had turned up in this or that college and in some schools, at intervals, but did not gain much credibility until after the Civil War, when Professors of English began to be named, and more than a few courses to be offered. One can trace the growing legitimacy of this subject in its emergence as an entrance requirement. Harvard (again) was the first to take an important step, as it proclaimed to the schools in 1873-74 that they should prepare their students in a short list of texts by Shakespeare, Goldsmith, and Scott. But it is important to note that this list appeared under the heading of "English Composition," in the requirements: students were to read literature in order to have a subject for their entrance *essays*. That relationship persisted through various attempts at uniform entrance requirements for colleges, in the various regions and finally in the whole country. Only in 1894 did Yale become the first to have an entrance requirement in literature apart from composition, selecting English classics for "their intrinsic importance" (Applebee, 1974, pp. 31-32).

Meanwhile, though, literature had been gaining advocates and prestige *within* the universities at a far more rapid pace than had its more "useful" partner. Why, since few of these advocates claimed for it the kind of utility—beyond virtues of mental discipline that would earn it a place beside the classics—that might admit it into a curriculum for the professional-managerial class? No small part of the answer is that instructors liked teaching it better than they liked reading themes: what else is new? And doubtless students liked studying it. Furthermore, teachers could through literature stake out the necessary claim to a body of scientific knowledge, thanks to the mediation of German philology. Equally important, the Arnoldian ideal of criticism and Culture gained great authority through this period; particularly attractive was Arnold's vision of class harmony through culture, without equality. Professors of literature appropriated this vision, and not, I think, cynically, though at some level of consciousness they probably sensed its ideological appeal to the patrons and clientele of universities, in a moment when class conflict was more and more visible, and frightening enough. Finally, and in hidden contradiction to the Arnoldian justification, English literature carried with it the prestige of the leisured class for whom it had long been a "natural" accomplishment—including in the colleges, where students had pursued literature as a voluntary activity through clubs and societies. It seemed fitting that the birthright of an old elite should be codified and promoted as cultural validation for the newly *credentialed* professional-managerial class.

A strange mixture of forces, then, behind the dynamic march of literature into university and school curriculum. And an even stranger marriage of useful composition and elevating literature, in the subject known as English. But it worked. Only one task of legitimation remained: to convince colleagues and presidents that English was *one* subject, not two, so that strong cultural forces behind literature as a field of study could join themselves to the articulate demand for practical composition, and not have to depend solely on the disciplinary and spiritual claims of literature.

In 1894, apparently, the moment had come for a public assertion of the unity of reading and writing, the unity of English. The English Conference of the Committee of Ten spoke with resonance, as did Payne and many of the professors in his collection when they stated the goals of their departmental programs. Their claims had the backing of a felt historical rightness that did not really need to be stated, a rightness grounded in an emerging social and economic system, the confident growth of a new class, and the transformation of universities in consonance with the needs of that system and that class. By which I do not mean to say that the annunciation of "English" was no more than an epiphenomenon, or a determined outcome of broader developments. The professors and schoolmen voiced genuine convictions and educational purposes. And they not only articulated a rationale for their subject; they made for it an institutional home that has proved more durable. We are their direct descendants.

I do not mean to suggest, however, that their success drew on a necessary strategy of unification that was easier to achieve in public statements than in educational practice. It would be tempting to take their proclamations at face value, and suppose that English won its place in the curriculum with a unity of purpose and practice from which we have been falling away ever since. But I doubt that such unity existed, even in 1894, except as an ideal and an item of professional ideology.

A look at the programs described in Payne's book reveals something close to chaos. Some colleges had separate departments of rhetoric and literature; many taught composition and literature separately within the same department. The balance of emphasis between the two varied extravagantly, from places like Harvard, Amherst, and Michigan, with something like two-thirds of the enrollments (and faculty time) going to composition; to places like Stanford, Berkeley, and Yale, where composition barely existed (though Yale was about to import it from Columbia). And nowhere that I can see were reading and writing integrated in any way more substantial than the use of literary models for student essays, or of literary works as subjects for students to write about.

More telling still, almost all the programs took composition to be the more elementary study, and literature the more advanced. Composition was often required, literature elective. Freshmen and sophomores studied composition; juniors, seniors, and graduate students studied literature. Stanford and Indiana carried this hierarchical division to an extreme, claiming to admit only those students already qualified in composition, and offering no Freshman English (the term already meant composition) at all. Berkeley was attempting to achieve the same result by riding herd over the state's secondary schools, and insisting on three years of school English as an entrance requirement.

And through most of Payne's reports runs a sharp contrast in tone, evidence of this ranking. Professors talk proudly or ecstatically about their literature offerings, while sounding a note of complaint or contempt as they write of composition. Gayley of Berkeley: the "disgust, that frequently attends prolonged indulgence in the habit of theme-correcting" (Payne, 1895, p. 102). Anderson of Stanford: "the professors were worn out with the drudgery of correcting Freshmen themes,—work really secondary and preparatory, and in no sense forming a proper subject of collegiate instruction" (p. 52). Sampson of Indiana: "the conditioned classes [i.e., remedial composition] make the heaviest drain upon the instructors' time" (p. 93). Small wonder, if the experience of Fred N. Scott at Michigan was typical: he had read more than 3000 themes in the 1893–94 academic year, "most of them written by a class of 216 students" (p. 121). The whole volume reveals less a unity than an unhappy yoking of alienated to unalienated labor. As an anonymous teacher from an Eastern university wrote, "I have never done any rhetorical work at _____ except in connection with my courses in literature, and I thank God I have been delivered from the bondage of theme-work into the glorious liberty of literature" (quoted by Carpenter, Baker, & Scott, 1903, p. 329n).

Or, to see it another way, Payne's collection expresses not an articulation of unity, but a felt division, between work and lesiure. Not that teaching literature involved no work, or that the subject had no practical value; but the *goal* of literary instruction was to improve or perfect a self that could exist only in the realm of leisure. Payne makes the connection precise, alluding to Arnold's estimate that "conduct" is three-fourths of life, and claiming "a considerable share of the remaining fraction" for literature (Payne, 1895, p. 7). A number of the professors tie the function of literature to pleasure, extended over the lives of their students.

Anderson, Stanford: "to cultivate a refined appreciation of what is best, and thus to reveal unfailing sources of pure enjoyment" (p. 50).

March, Lafayette: "students come to rejoice in these noble passages, and remember them forever" (p. 77).

Sampson, Indiana: "to give the student a thorough understanding of what he reads, and the ability to read sympathetically and understandingly in the future" (p. 95).

Tolman, Chicago: "An unfailing source of rest and refreshment, a life-long process of self-education . . . through the study of English literature" (pp. 89-90).

They expect literature to become embedded in the higher reaches of their students' being: it is an "aliment of the spiritual life" (Cook, Yale, p. 39), that can "quicken the spiritual faculties" (Corson, Cornell, p. 61). Clearly it works its benefits in a realm far removed from labor.

Of course these professors were not training a leisure class, by and large. They privilege literature as a spiritual discipline and a mark of cultivation for students who will have a part in the world's work, but whose refined leisure will be in sharp opposition to the struggles of the marketplace. Furthermore, the implied duality of body and spirit hints at another, less philosophical, one: the distinction between those who work with their minds and those who work with their hands. The professors identify their students with the former class, again and again, by speaking of "taste" as a chief goal of literary education. What ladies and gentlemen got from home, tutor, and social milieu, the raw youths of Iowa, Nebraska, and Indiana will get from college instruction in literature.

No such rhetoric springs to the pen when the professors write about the goals of composition. One (Tolson, Chicago) justifies it by the "grace and skill" it can nurture, thus enabling the graduate to "prove" that he is liberally educated (p. 91). A few others point to a much-reduced version of this ideal in stating as a goal the ability to write "correct" English. But most don't even attempt to articulate aims for composition: the social context has provided the aim—composition is useful. Again and again the professors speak of their approach as "practical," and their method as "practice." (Along the way, some denigrate *rhetoric* as abstract and theoretical.) Their silence about higher cultural goals is, I think, a tacit acknowledgement that composition fits into the world's work, and so is necessary training for students qualifying themselves to carry out the tasks of the professional-managerial class.

I'm suggesting that from the beginning of English as a fully certified discipline in college and school, its strategic assertion of unity masked a good deal of internal tension, even while expressing a genuinely felt purpose. There was the understandable preference of teachers for literature, buttressed by the fact that they could ground their would-be profession in a growing body of knowledge about literature and of techniques for its study, while—having discarded the discipline of rhetoric—they had left composition without foundation, an amorphous activity that could only be taught through incessant practice. At a deeper level, somewhere in their bones, they regarded composition as preliminary, juvenile; whereas literature was the arena of full maturity. Finally, their conception of English, like their daily work, was grounded in institutions that were coming to occupy a key position in a new social order, not yet fully understood. Hence the ideological tensions I have been describing, between manual and mental work, between work and leisure, between an old, more gentlemanly ruling class and a new professional-managerial class that gained its power and privilege from the work it performed on the margins of monopoly capital. This class was developing a conception of itself as *both* vigorous, workful, a progressive historical force, *and* qualified for its social position by its cultural attainments and respectable style of life—including the new museums, symphony orchestras, and libraries, as well as genteel homes maintained by the women of the class. The formation of English as a university subject both cast up and built upon a justification that was homologous in its inner tensions to the ideology of the class itself.[4]

This was a poignant moment, with the new profession poised for growth, yet full of unresolved contradictions. These were to break out most sharply in relations between the colleges and the schools. English literature already had a firm position in many schools, but beginning with Harvard's first list of required literary works, in 1874, the colleges came to exercise a strong influence over high school curricula in English, as teachers sought to prepare *some* of their students for admission to the most prestigious colleges, rather than looking directly to the needs of *all* their students. This hegemony expressed itself in the effort to establish uniform entrance requirements, through the last quarter of the century, climaxing in the formation of the College Entrance Examination Board, which administered its first test in 1901. During this period the colleges sent out mixed signals, indeed. Most notably, first, they told schools that composition and literature were equal, and one. In the same breath, the Committee of Ten report recommended twice as much class time for literature as for composition in secondary school. And out of the other side of their mouths, professors were saying: teach your pupils to write correct English, so *we* can teach them the more advanced and elevating subject of literature. Second, the Committee of Ten spoke resoundingly against tracking: *all* students, whether bound for liberal arts or technical education, or for office and shop, should receive the same training in their "mother tongue." Yet the message communicated in every other way was: a *few* of your students will use their mother tongue to manage the others, to certify their own superiority, and to cultivate their spiritual selves.

Futhermore, this divided message came just as the public high school was about to assume an entirely new place in American society. Not until 1888 had the number of students in high school passed the number in preparatory schools and in the academy divisions of colleges and universities. And though the proportions were shifting rapidly, even in 1894 only 40 percent of college students had gone to public high school. Besides, the total numbers involved were small: in 1890 less than seven percent of the age group was in *any* kind of secondary school (Sizer, 1964, pp. 33–35). Not only were colleges, prep schools, and academies elite institutions: the public high school itself represented the aspirations of the professional-managerial class, more than equal opportunity for all classes.

The Committee of Ten framed its policies with an old, aristocratic ideal of the cultivated, unified self in the back of its collective mind. It adapted that ideal to a moment in which college was becoming the central institution for training and promoting a new professional-managerial class. And it proclaimed the idea to high schools that were about to expand into institutions of socialization for everyone, and were inevitably to take on missions of vocational training, Americanization, and class reproduction very different from anything envisioned by the Committee of Ten in 1894.

Ironically, for the nascent high school, the Committee's recommendations carried enormous weight and influence, just when they were about to become archaic. The schools took very seriously this instruction from above (the more so since they had in effect asked for it: the NEA, which created the Committee, was dominated by school superintendents). By 1904, almost all schools required three or four years of work in English. They tried harder than the colleges themselves to achieve a unity of reading and writing. And they struggled to give all of their increasingly diverse students—middle-class children, immigrants, rural youths, rural blacks newly arrived in the city—uniform instruction in their "mother tongue."

Needless to say, the effort could not and did not overcome the reality of new social conditions and new functions for school training. No more could it work in colleges, which expanded in direct proportion with high schools and faced many of the same tensions. And the colleges, apparently, didn't even try so hard, as professional ideology continued to privilege literature and relegate composition and its teachers to second-class status.

Even as books about the teaching of English first began to appear, a note of resignation to this situation also began to sound in them. In 1903, Carpenter and Baker of Columbia and Scott of Michigan (he of the 3000 themes) linked the teaching of speech and writing to "the necessary demands of business, professional, or social life" (p. 59), while they saw literature as on the defensive against that very "world of fact," against business, science, "the practical life surrounding" the student (p. 61). In 1909, Percival Chubb acknowledged a dual role for the school: "preparation for social and personal life," and "aid in the

choice of, and advance toward, a vocation" (p. 240). He admitted the
value of writing in the latter cause ("the practical importance of the
art of the ready writer; its sheer business value" [p. 319]), even while
urging "higher motives" for the teaching of composition.

This division, implicit in social reality, led in time to overt pleas
for the separation of writing and reading in the curriculum. An editorial in *The English Journal* in 1916 *celebrated* this trend. Since I picked
my title many months ago, with little idea of what I might think when
the date of the conference came around, you can imagine the satisfaction with which I came upon the following, the week before the
conference:

> the separation of the teaching of English as a training for work
> from the teaching of it as a preparation for the enjoyment of
> leisure is rapidly growing in favor and will mark the present dec-
> ade, as the union of rhetoric and literary study did that which
> closed the last century (Hosic, 1916, p. 282).

Exactly so; though I've already expressed my skepticism about the
reality of that union in the 1890s.

I will close with two other dicta from this later time. First, on a
lighter note, John B. Opdycke of Julia Richman High School, in New
York City:

> The language of work is to the language of leisure very much as
> labor is to capital. The one serves; the other conserves. The one
> accumulates; the other perpetuates. The one is currency; the
> other is investment. The one is concerned with immediate use,
> more or less regardless of form and feature; the other is always
> conscious of the close relationship between content and form for
> ultimate purpose. As labor creates values for capital to maintain,
> so the language of work crystallizes into beautiful expressional
> forms maintained by the language of literature (1916, p. 392).

And here is the author of a 1919 textbook on expository writing,
Mervin Curl:

> "The Anglo-Saxons," Emerson said, "are the hands of the
> world"—they more than any other people, turn the wheels of
> the world, do its work, keep things moving. . . . [W]e may safely
> assert that Expository Writing is the hands of literature (quoted
> by Connors, 1985, p. 64).

We can't take Opdycke and Curl to represent a professional consensus.
But we might pay some attention to their analogies. Those suggest an
underlying unity of reading and writing that is more dialectical and
truer to our world than what was proposed in the halcyon moment of
1894, and one that will somehow have to be understood if we are to
bring our two practices together again.

Notes

[1] I argue this in a work-in-progress, basing the claim on the research of Simon Kuznets, especially 1961.

[2] I have adapted the preceding six paragraphs from Ohmann, 1981.

[3] I take this term from Barbara and John Ehrenreich (1979), and generally accept their account of the new class.

[4] I have labored, in revising this section of my argument, to respond to careful and helpful criticism by my colleague, Gerald Burns, who will nonetheless still be dissatisfied with the way in which I have conceptualized work and leisure and connected them to composition and literature. Burns' comments also saved me from a number of plain errors.

References

Applebee, A. N. (1974). *Tradition and reform in the teaching of English: A history.* Urbana, IL: NCTE.

Braverman, H. (1974). *Labor and monopoly capital: The degradation of work in the twentieth century.* New York: Monthly Review Press.

Brecher, J. (1972). *STRIKE!* Greenwich, CT: Fawcett.

Carpenter, G. R., Baker, A. M., & Scott, F. N. (1903). *The teaching of English in the elementary and the secondary school.* New York: Longmans, Green.

Chandler, A. D., Jr. (1977). *The visible hand: The managerial revolution in American business.* Cambridge, MA: Harvard University.

Chubb, P. (1909). *The teaching of English in the elementary and the secondary school.* New York: Macmillan.

Connors, R. J. (1985). The rhetoric of explanation: explanatory rhetoric from 1850 to the present. *Written Communication, 2,* 49–72.

Douglas, W. (1976). Rhetoric for the meritocracy. In Ohmann (1976), 97–132.

Ehrenreich, B. and J. (1979). The professional-managerial class. In P. Walker (Ed.), *Between labor and capital.* Boston: South End Press.

Hession, C. H., & Sardy, H. (1969). *Ascent to affluence: a history of American economic development.* Boston: Allyn and Bacon.

Hosic, J. F. (1916). Editorial. *English Journal, 5,* 281–282.

Kuznets, S. (1961). *Capital and the American economy.* New York: National Bureau of Economic Research.

National Educational Association. (1894). *Report of the Committee of Ten on secondary school studies, with the reports of the conferences arranged by the committee.* New York: American Book Company.

Ohmann, R. (1976). *English in America: A radical view of the profession.* New York: Oxford.

Ohmann, R. (1981). Where did mass culture come from? The case of magazines. *Berkshire Review, 16,* 85–101.

Opdycke, J. B. (1916). New wine in old bottles. *English Journal, 5,* 392–400.

Payne, W. M. (Ed.). (1895). *English in American universities.* Boston: D. C. Heath.

Peterson, T. (1956). *Magazines in the twentieth century.* Urbana, IL: University of Illinois Press.

Rae, J. B. (1967). The invention of invention. In M. Kranzberg & C. W. Purcell Jr. (Eds.), *Technology in western civilization, Vol. I.* New York: Oxford.

Sizer, T. R. (1964). *Secondary schools at the turn of the century.* New Haven: Yale University.

2

The Rhetoric of
Mechanical Correctness

ROBERT J. CONNORS

University of New Hampshire

"He that despiseth little things shall perish little by little."
Apocrypha

Throughout most of its history as a college subject, English composition has meant one thing to most people: the single-minded enforcement of standards of mechanical and grammatical correctness in writing. The image of a grim-faced Miss Grundy, besprinkling the essays of her luckless students with scarlet handbook hieroglyphs, is still a common stereotype; it is only in the last twenty-five years that composition instructors have seriously begun to question the priority given to simple correctness in college-level instruction. Most scholars of rhetorical history have wondered at some time about the forces which turned "rhetoric" into "composition," transformed instruction in wide-ranging techniques of persuasion and analysis into a narrow concern for convention on the most basic levels, transmogrified the noble discipline of Aristotle, Cicero, Campbell, into a stultifying error hunt. In this essay I'd like to examine some of those forces, both cultural and pedagogical, which shaped nineteenth-century rhetorical history and resulted in the obsession with mechanical correctness which for so many years defined the college course in written rhetoric.

The required course in English composition is a uniquely American institution. Less than any other college subject has it been informed by a genuine body of knowledge crying out to be disseminated; more than any other subject has it been shaped by perceived social and cultural needs. College writing courses began in the nineteenth century

*A shorter version of Robert Connors' chapter appeared in the February, 1985 issue of *College Composition and Communication*.

27

as rhetoric lectures in the traditional British mold, studying mental faculties, taste, style, and *belles-lettres*. The general spirit of the age, however, was one of radical equalitarianism, and culturally there was little pressure for formal correctness in writing. Only with the beginnings of a structured system of social classes in America—a system based both on wealth and on education—did an ethic of gentility and "correctness" arise in Americans' attitudes toward speaking and writing. Around the same time, new pedagogical techniques in the teaching of vernacular grammar ingrained the habit of scrutinizing sentences for errors. With the growth of a native literary-intellectual culture—in specific, an identifiable college and university culture—linguistic insecurity arose, and it was exacerbated by post-Civil War evidence that the writing abilities of new college freshmen were indeed atrocious. The result: the first "back-to-basics" movement, the first stab at remedial college English. Teachers were swamped with "themes" to "correct," and their overwork created a booming business in supportive educational technology—handbooks, workbooks, etc.—meant to aid them in their drudgery. These tools came all too quickly to control their masters, however, and the subsequent history of composition instruction until recently is a history of poorly trained instructors pressed by overwork and circumstance to enforce the most easily-perceived standards of writing—mechanical standards—while ignoring or shortchanging more difficult and rhetorical elements.

Things are better now, but this is a sad enough story—a story of well-meaning teachers and administrators swept by ignorance and short-sightedness through an eighty-year pedagogical bad dream. To understand how it all began, we must go back to the first third of the nineteenth century and examine the attitudes toward language, culture, and education held at that time.

Attitudes Toward Language in the Early Nineteenth Century

During the first fifty years of the nineteenth century, the new nation of the United States was striving to define itself as a culture. Jeffersonian and then Jacksonian democracy had produced an ethic of equalitarianism that extended into all areas of national life, including education and language. During the earlier part of the century, Americans tended to be almost contentious in their rejection of imposed hierarchies of value; it was a unique cultural situation, and was due partially to the American educational structure. In 1831, when Alexis de Tocqueville made his tour of the United States, he saw thousands of public elementary schools but relatively few colleges.[1] As Tocqueville put it, "there is no other country in the world where, proportionally to population, there are so few ignorant and so few learned individuals as in America. Primary education is within reach of all; higher education is hardly available to anybody."[2]

The equality of prospect which Tocqueville marked as the most obvious feature of American democracy was to have several effects upon the national attitude toward language use. Most people were taught reading and writing in elementary school and emerged at the age of twelve or so with all the schooling they were to see; thus grew up a common denominator of expression. For a time, it seemed that linguistic class distinctions would disappear:

> . . . when men are no longer held to a fixed social position, when
> they continually see one another and talk together, when castes
> are destroyed and classes change and merge, all of the words of
> a language get mixed up too. Those which cannot please the ma-
> jority die; the rest form a common stock from which each man
> chooses at random . . . Not only does everyone use the same words,
> but they get into the habit of using them without discrimination.
> The rules of style are destroyed. Hardly any expressions seem, by
> their nature, vulgar, and hardly any seem refined.[3]

Tocqueville visited a nation in which elementary schools were emphasizing grammar instruction as an abstract "mental discipline" and where only a very few men could aspire to college training—training which led nearly inevitably to the closed circles of pulpit and bar. Such college-educated men were too few and too specialized to provide a real linguistic aristocracy, and thus for a time the common denominator prevailed in language.

Nineteenth-century America, however, was a culture in transition, and the linguistic leveling that Tocqueville reported was beginning to melt away even as he published his first volume of *Democracy in America*. The period 1830–1870 saw the rise of forces that would gradually overcome the equalitarianism of the earlier part of the century. At some point after 1840, the common denominator stopped falling and began to rise as Americans became aware of and concerned about their speaking and writing habits.

The reasons for this awakening interest in correctness of usage and the niceties of grammatical construction are both cultural and pedagogical. Culturally, the period 1820 through 1860 was the "American Renaissance," an era that saw the rise of a secular literary-intellectual culture in America. For the first time, the New World produced writers and poets who could stand with the best of the Old—and who also wished to stand separate from the old. Tocqueville's comment that "American authors may fairly be said to live more in England than in America," might have seemed accurate in 1831, but by 1840 it was

rapidly becoming outdated by such writers as Irving, Hawthorne, Poe,
Emerson, and many others. The "frontier" was being pushed westward,
and Eastern cities were developing cosmopolitan attributes, generating
indigenous intellectual elites and atmospheres far removed from the
rough-and-tumble equalitarianism of the earlier part of the century.
Classes, based both upon wealth and upon education, were beginning
to form—and where there is class distinction, linguistic distinctions are
not far behind.[4]

In addition, the character of school instruction in language was
also changing. As Rollo Lyman has shown, grammar instruction in the
United States became an important aspect of primary education:

> English grammar gained momentum as the hold of Latin Gram-
> mar weakened (during the post-Revolutionary War period), and
> by the end of the first quarter of the nineteenth century it be-
> came so generally taught that the common term grammar school,
> formerly applied to the secondary school of the Latin-grammar
> type, was now by common consent used to designate an inter-
> mediate school with English grammar as its central study. After
> 1825 the prominence of English grammar became gradually more
> marked, until it reached its height about 1850–1875.[5]

Lyman calls the period around 1860 "the heyday of grammar," and it
is no accident that it coincides with the first great period of American
linguistic insecurity.

This rise of interest in vernacular grammar had led by the 1840s
to a new awareness on Americans' parts of the concepts of "correctness" and "grammaticality." In large part, this new awareness resulted
from new instructional methods in grammar classes. Lindley Murray,
whose immensely popular *English Grammar* was the best-selling grammar text in America prior to 1825, utilized a "correct-incorrect" duality borrowed from the pedagogy used to enforce the learning of Latin
grammar, and his approach emphasized a binary, good-or-bad attitude
toward each sentence studied. Samuel Kirkham, whose 1829 *English
Grammar in Familiar Lectures* took up the market as Murray began to
falter, made heavy use of "false-syntax" exercises—lists of sentences
larded with errors in grammar and usage which students were supposed
to identify and correct. These exercises fostered an attitude of suspicion toward everything written, and as Edward Finegan suggests,
Murray and Kirkham have to be held at least partly responsible for
later negativistic and absolutist attitudes toward language.[6]

The age of Victorian gentility was beginning, and in the 1840s we
begin to see a new movement in the United States, a movement whose
desiderata were proper usage and grammatical correctness in speech
and writing. This new interest seems to have sprung from two distinct

proximate causes: the Eastern reaction against the "roughness" and "crudeness" of frontier America, an attitude which wished to set standards of propriety in language as in all other aspects of life; and the desire for self-improvement and "getting ahead," which was an important part of the American mythos during the nineteenth century. These two elements were found mixed into most of the early works on "good language." The first can be seen clearly during the late 1840s in an address given to the Newburyport Girls' High School by Andrew Peabody, chaplain at Harvard College. Peabody spoke to the girls on "Conversation," and the point of his remarks was that his audience should strive to establish a proper and correct linguistic ambience about them, should "raise the tone" where they were:

> Young ladies do more than any other class in the community towards establishing the general tone and standard of social intercourse . . . you are fast approaching an age when you will take prominent places in general society; will be the objects of peculiar regard; and will, in a great measure, determine whether the social converse in your respective circles shall be vulgar or refined. . . .[7]

Peabody goes on to warn against faulty pronunciation, "ungrammatical vulgarisms," and other "untasteful practices" in conversation. His *Handbook of Conversation: Mistakes of Speaking and Writing Corrected* included this address as well as several other short pieces of linguistic prescription, and it remained in print from 1855 through 1882. Peabody's *Handbook* shows how early the cultural lines between "refined" and "vulgar" language were being drawn. His use of "vulgar" is especially noteworthy; it's not a term previously heard very often in America outside of lectures on rhetoric. It's an essentially elitist term foreign to the ethos of Jeffersonian and Jacksonian democracy, but through the forties, fifties, and sixties we will hear it used more and more.

In 1847, the year that Peabody first gave his Newburyport address, there appeared a book less popular but more important as a harbinger of things to come. This was Seth T. Hurd's self-improvement manual, *A Grammatical Corrector*. Between 1826 and 1834, Hurd had spent his winters as a "public lecturer" on English Grammar, probably at the Lyceums then coming to popularity. In his capacity as a traveling lecturer—a sort of early Chautauqua figure—he visited "almost every section of the United States." Hurd explained his method thus: "The common errors and peculiarities of speech, which were found to prevail in different communities, were carefully noted down and preserved, not only as a source of amusement (to myself), but for the purpose of correction and comment in the Lecture-room."[8] Given this *modus operandi*, it is no wonder that Hurd kept moving on. The epigraph on his title page describes the contents of the *Grammatical Corrector* better than anything else:

> Being a collection of nearly two thousand barbarisms, cant phrases, colloquialisms, quaint expressions, provincialisms, false pronunciation, perversions, misapplications of terms and other kindred errors of the English language peculiar to the different States of the Union. The whole explained. corrected, and conveniently arranged for the use of schools and private individuals.

Painful though it might have been for them, Hurd's audiences in the 1830s were interested in having their "barbarisms" corrected, in being told that "done up brown" was *"a very low phrase."* The general audiences at such Lyceum lectures obviously had wider agendas than mere politeness or gentility; theirs was an interest in self-improvement that must have been much concerned with getting ahead as it was with "raising the tone." Hurd was more than an early Victorian John Simon, shaking his readers down while he attacked their language habits as "uneducated," "impolite," "inelegant," and "vulgar"; there are elements of Dale Carnegie's commercial approach to influencing businessmen in his book as well.

Usage, Correctness, and Social Position

These beginnings of linguistic status-anxiety in the 1840s and fifties grew stronger in the 1860s, when much of the American intellectual community was influenced by a small book written by an Englishman. *A Plea for the Queen's English*, by Henry Alford, who was Dean of Westminster and a noted British intellectual, appeared in 1864; it would see eleven British and American printings and remain in print until 1893. In it, "the Dean," as he was called by his opponents and fellow controversialists, attacked much current usage, both literary and popular, striking out at poor pronunciation, wrong words, improper sentence construction, and other "objectionable" misuses of English. The Dean's book raised a number of hackles in England, but to Americans it was a particularly stinging rebuke, for Alford was bitterly anti-American in addition to being a linguistic purist:[9]

> . . . the language of a people is no trifle. The national mind is reflected in the national speech . . . Every important feature in a people's language is reflected in its character and history.
>
> Look, to take one familiar example, at the process of deterioration which our Queen's English has undergone at the hands of the Americans. Look at those phrases which so amuse us in their speech and books; at their reckless imagination, and contempt for congruity; and then compare the character and history of the

nation—its blunted sense of moral obligation and duty to man; its
disregard for conventional right where aggrandizement is to be ob-
tained . . . Such examples as this . . . may serve to show that language is no trifle.[10]

These was fightin' words in 1864, and America was not long in producing champions to field against the Dean. The great prescriptive-usage
war of the Victorian era was on.

Best known of the Dean's antagonists in these debates were
George Washington Moon, an expatriate American living in England,
and Edward S. Gould, a New York journeyman intellectual. Moon
slashingly attacked Alford's own grammar and usage in his *The Dean's
English* of 1865 and *Bad English* of 1867. Gould's contribution was
published in 1867 as *Good English: or Popular Errors in Language*,
and it shows how conscious the American reading public was becoming
of language:

The present age is pre-eminently an age of progress; and, unfortunately, the progress is not limited to "things of good report."
Error follows fast upon the footsteps of truth, and sometimes
truth is left behind in the race.

For example, the English language, within the last quarter of
a century, through the agency of good writers, critics, and lexi-
cographers, has in many respects been greatly improved; but,
through the heedlessness of those who should be its conservators,
and the recklessness of those who have been, and are, its corrup-
tors, it has deteriorated in other respects in a greater proportion.[11]

Dean Alford was wrong about where the deterioration lay, argued
Gould and Moon, but neither argued that it did not exist. In fact, the
deterioration of English at the hands of uneducated frontiersmen was
what these Easterners excoriated most violently. A linguistic base for
class distinctions seems to be the hidden agenda of this debate. Richard
Meade Bache put the case most clearly in the preface to his 1869 *Vulgarisms and Other Errors of Speech:*

Many persons, although they have not enjoyed advantages early
in life, have, through merit combined with the unrivalled opportunities which this country presents, risen to station in society.
Few of them, it must be thought, even if unaware of the extent
of their deficiency in knowledge of their language, are so obtuse
as not to perceive their deficiency at all, and not to know that it
often presents them in an unfavorable light in their association
with the more favoured children of fortune. Few, it must be believed, would not from one motive or the other, from desire for
knowledge, or from dread of ridicule, gladly avail themselves of
opportunities for instruction.[12]

More than any of the other early prescriptive philologists, Bache realized that the changing nature of American society itself was behind the interest in correct speech and writing that sold so many of the nit-picking books of Alford, Moon, and Gould.

The Alford controversy had powerful consequences in an increasingly self-conscious America. As a result of it, William Mathews wrote in 1876, "hundred of persons who before felt a profound indifference to this subject . . . have suddenly found themselves . . . deeply interested in questions of grammar, and now, with their appetites whetted, will continue the study . . . "[13] The 1870s and 1880s saw a spate of non-academic little "manuals of correctness" covering both conversation and writing.[14] The general ethos of these manuals can be summed up by the quote from Swift that Alfred Ayres (Thomas E. Osmun) chose as the epigraph to his *The Verbalist: A Manual*: "As a man is known by his company, so a man's company may be known by his manner of expressing himself." Though we tend today to think of the Gilded Age as a time when wealth, status, and vulgarity combined in an unprecedented way, it was also a time when the concept of "proper society" exerted a powerful conservative influence. Wealth might make vulgarity tolerated, but it could never make *arrivistes* truly acceptable; thus the children of horny-handed "captains of industry" were carefully tutored by hired intellectuals and shipped to Harvard, Yale, and Princeton to be finished off. Propriety—most obviously reflected in a person's way of speaking—was the desire of even the crassest "new money," and true propriety could not be purchased; it had to be learned.

Colleges had always assumed part of that burden of socialization, and during the 1870s they began to react directly to these changing cultural attitudes. This was, of course, a period when American college education was undergoing a number of profound shifts in emphasis. For the first time, the professional aspects of a college education were beginning to rival the social aspects. New sorts of schools were opening, and the older college ideal of classical study and mental discipline was fast retreating as colleges, striving to attract students and meet changing cultural needs, instituted sweeping curricular changes. Their potential clientele, they were discovering, no longer consisted of aspiring lawyers, ministers, and gentlemen; the growth of vocational specialties and of the concept of college as training in social acceptability meant that the purposes behind enrollment were much broader. Students wanted something new after the Civil War, and the colleges scrambled to try to give it to them.[15]

Changes in the College Rhetoric Course

It was impossible that the college course in rhetoric and writing should be unaffected by these shifts, and beginning in the 1870s we see the focus of writing instruction in America undergo a radical change. The forty years 1865–1905 were years of wrenching necessity and desperate invention for rhetoric. Like the rest of the traditional college curriculum, rhetorical instruction was forced to move away from the abstract educational ideal of "mental discipline" and toward more immediate instructional goals.[16] The immediate goals, in this case, came to involve, not more effective written communication, but rather, simple mechanical correctness. Let us examine how this occurred.

First of all, it must be understood that the idea of teaching grammatical or mechanical correctness on the college level does not go farther back than 1870. From the classical period up through 1860 or so, the teaching of rhetoric concentrated on theoretical concerns and contained no mechanical material at all. Usage and style were, of course, major areas of rhetorical consideration, but traditional prescriptive advice in these areas assumed a student able to handle grammatical construction and to produce an acceptable manuscript with complete facility. These were, after all, supposed to be the subjects of students' earlier course, the grammar course taught by the *grammaticus*, or usher, or master in the boys' school. Such elementary skills as handwriting, punctuation, capitalization, and spelling might be critiqued by the professor of rhetoric, but officially they had no place in rhetoric throughout most of history. They were thought to be the domain of pedagogues and pedants; rhetoric was a higher mystery, the domain of dons and professors, and it didn't degrade itself to the level of mere correctness.

In a sense, the history of the college composition course in America is a history of this heretofore "elementary" instruction taking over a commanding place in most teachers' ideas of what rhetoric was. Between 1865 and 1895, such base-level elements of mechanical correctness as grammar, punctuation, spelling, and capitalization, which would never have been found in pre-1850 textbooks, came to usurp much of the time devoted in class to rhetorical instruction and most of the marking of student writing. What came more and more to be taught and enforced was correctness, but as Albert Kitzhaber points out, "the sort of correctness desired was superficial and mechanical."[17] (The very use of the word "correct" changed between 1870 and 1910 from a meaning of "socially acceptable" to one of "formally acceptable.")

We have already examined some of the general causes of this interest in correctness, but for its direct introduction into the rhetoric course we can also identify a proximate cause: in 1874, Harvard University introduced an entrance examination featuring, for the first time, a writing requirement. The reasons for the introduction of this writing requirement were several: a growing awareness of the importance of linguistic class distinctions in the United States; poor showings in written assignments by Harvard undergraduates; a desire to demonstrate that Harvard had the highest standards and deserved its leadership position in American education; a declaration that henceforward writing would be an important element in the college rhetoric course; perhaps a challenge to the academies that supplied the Cambridge institution with raw material.[18] The examination was introduced and given for the first time during the summer of 1874, and, when the English faculty at Harvard received this first test of candidates' writing ability, they were deeply shocked. The scrawled pages revealed that the graduates of the best academies and preparatory schools in America were writing essays filled with formal and mechanical errors of all sorts. Punctuation, capitalization, spelling, syntax—at every level, error abounded. More than half the students taking these early examinations failed to pass. As Adams S. Hill, who took over the administration of the exam in 1876, put it, "the examination makes a poor showing for the schools that furnish the materials whereof the university which professes to set up the highest standard in America, has to make educated men."[19]

Harvard and other colleges strove mightily to pin the blame for poor freshman writing on the preparatory and secondary schools—where, indeed, much of it did lie—but at the same time, colleges found themselves forced to deal somehow with the results of the poor training they were decrying. The errors students made on their exams were beginning to get a good deal of publicity and were even becoming something of a national scandal.[20] This could not be borne, and the seventies and eighties saw a good deal of pedagogical innovation as teachers engaged in the first great wave of college-level remedial English.

It was quickly obvious to writing teachers that the old abstract rhetoric of Blair, Whately, and Day wouldn't solve the problems uncovered by the Harvard examinations. What good, they asked, did knowledge of tropes or amplification do a student who couldn't spell or punctuate? Beginning in the 1870s, college-level teaching tools of a simpler sort began to appear. New texts were published which contained simple right-wrong sentence exercises as well as theoretical advice, and during the late seventies college texts began for the first time to include sections on such simple formal elements of writing as capitalization and punctuation.[21] All sorts of treatments of materials were tried out by teachers, but the most popular was what came to be known to teachers as "grammar." Uncased from its elementary school framework and its general association with abstract mental discipline, grammar began to be introduced to college students in the 1870s in the hope that somehow a theoretical knowledge of the structure of English would act as a prophylaxis against errors in writing.

Thus was born the soulful trust in the powers of "grammar" that still rules the methods of some instructors today. Teaching abstract grammar didn't work in the 1870s as it doesn't work now; college teachers turned to it out of the idea that somehow students' elementary grammar instruction hadn't "taken," and that it needed to be repeated until it did somehow take hold. This was an *essentially* incorrect idea. As A. S. Hill realized, students wrote poorly because they had never been given any practice in composition during their secondary school careers; vernacular composition wasn't taught in most American high schools until the 1880s. Students failed on the Harvard exams because they had never been asked to do much writing, not because they had failed to grasp their elementary grammar lessons. But once the grammar-based college pedagogy became enshrined in textbooks there was no escaping it, as we shall see.

The Harvard exams seemed to pinpoint mechanical problems as the important troubles of freshmen writers, and it was natural that such exams would tend to make "error-free" writing the central definition of "good" writing in many teachers' minds. This conception quickly gained great power, and after 1885 or so, the very nature of the freshman writing course came to be defined by error avoidance rather than by any sort of genuine communicative success. As Kitzhaber points out, this meant in practice that composition had to be taught as series of explicable rules, and that the writing desired from students was writing that violated none of these rules.[22] The rhetorical theory developed between 1865 and 1895 above the sentence level— most importantly, the modes, the paragraph structure, static abstractions, and the methods of development—was all an attempt to rule-govern the written product. The heart of the rules orientation, however, always remained in grammatical and mechanical rule-application at the sentence level.

After the mid-eighties, this rule-and-form orientation constituted a sort of "hidden agenda" in college writing courses. Unlike the rhetorical theory of the period, which was all developed in textbooks, we find relatively little textbook evidence of the mechanical-correctness aspects of the composition courses of the eighties and nineties. The correctness emphasis was there—as we know from non-textbook sources—but texts hardly mention it, concerning themselves with paragraphs, modes, abstractions, etc. The fact that college composition was fast becoming error-obsessed was like a shameful secret during this period, mentioned only obliquely. Of the four great rhetorical

voices of the *fin de siècle* period, only one—John Genung—ever wrote
a college-level textbook dealing with rule-governed formal correctness;
what sketchy treatments there were are found in texts by lesser authors. Albert Kitzhaber infers that this lack of textbook treatment of
lower-level mechanical questions is a result of the "paragraph boom"
of the nineties and of the low opinion of grammar study developing
in the elementary education level.[23] He is undoubtedly correct, but
there is, I believe, a further reason: college teachers were ashamed to
be found professing grammar, punctuation, and lower-level skills (as
many were in 1971 during the second great remedial period, and as
many still are).

Thus, in spite of growing evidence of the poor writing of college
freshmen—especially the evidence presented to the sound of trumpets
by the Harvard Reports of the nineties—the most notable college
teachers of rhetoric refused to admit publicly that they should deal
with the problem, or that they were dealing with it every day. Instead,
they constantly cried out for deliverance by some sort of secondary-
school *deus ex pedagogia*. E. L. Godkin, one of the Harvard Report
authors, was the most outraged spokesman for this Old Guard attitude;
throughout the nineties he urged that college teachers be "delivered,
in large part at least, from the necessity of teaching the rudiments of
the language."[24] Barrett Wendell, that enthusiastic man, dealt not at
all with mechanics in his famous textbook *English Composition*, nor
did A. S. Hill in his college texts (though he had no aversion to including mechanics in his lower-level texts and in his college-level "adjunct materials"). John Genung, in spite of having authored the rules-
oriented *Outlines of Rhetoric* in 1893, drew the line at teaching sentence mechanics, sneering in 1900 that basic-level punctuation elements "belong to grammar; they are no more a part of rhetoric than
is spelling."[25] And Fred N. Scott, the last of Kitzhaber's "Big Four"
rhetoricians (and the most perspicacious), rejected mechanical emphases for somewhat higher reasons: "These matters, after all," he
wrote, "are subsidiary . . . They are means to an end. To treat them
as an end in and for themselves is to turn education in this subject up-
side down."[26] As a result of these attitudes, we see very little mechanical material in the most popular rhetoric texts of the late nineteenth
century.

In this case, however, these major texts are somewhat misleading.
The later 1880s and the 1890s were times of extreme changes in the
way that writing was taught—changes half-obscured, but no less real
for that. The college rhetoric course was being deformed by novel
stresses and was quickly generating new tools to try to solve the problems that were arising. We need now to look more closely at some of
these problems and at the solutions they engendered.

Overwork

First of all, we must understand the most pervasive reality of the rhetoric teachers at nearly all colleges after 1870: gross overwork. We may still have a way to go today before teachers are given realistic teaching loads in composition, but the composition instructors of the nineteenth century faced situations far grimmer. It is difficult for us today to imagine, but the standard practice during the period 1880–1910 was for teachers to be assigned writing courses that were lecture-sized. Most teachers were responsible for teaching between 140 and 200 students. Barrett Wendell at Harvard in 1892 said that he had in his writing class "within one or two of 170 men."[27] This may have been a large class, for Wendell was a popular teacher, but it was by no means extraordinary. (By 1900, Harvard had adopted the policy of hiring non-professorial help to take charge of the freshman course, and there, at least, the average class size dropped to between 60 and 70.)[28] At Yale's Sheffield Scientific School, one professor and one instructor were responsible for 250 students (as well as for three non-freshman courses totaling 306 students).[29] At the University of Iowa, the average class size for freshman and sophomore courses was 80, and again, over 250 students were the responsibility of one professor and one instructor.[30] At Chicago, which prided itself on its small classes, the courses in "required theme-writing" averaged over 65 students per class.[31]

These very large lecture-sized sections were the result of some of the rapid changes taking place in American universities. As Lawrence Veysey says, after 1870 three basic types of instruction came to prominence: the laboratory, the lecture, and the seminar.[32] The laboratory, of course, was conceived as a specialized scientific instructional form, and the labor-intensive seminar (or seminary, as it was referred to) was usually reserved for upperclass and graduate students. This left the lecture-sized section as the form of choice for most freshman and sophomore courses. The large lecture, of course, is a perfectly defensible technique for courses with testable subject-content that might be fashioned into fruitful lecture material. In composition courses, though, its use, though widespread, always presented problems.

Leaving aside the question of the worth of abstract lecture material to the struggling writer, the large class sizes of lecture-organized sections meant two things: first, that the teacher could give little individual attention to students, even if a large course was split into smaller classes; and second, that the number of papers each teacher was expected to read and grade was staggering.

There are few statements extant today recording the effect of having to grade hundreds of papers each week on nineteenth-century teachers, but it must have been exhausting. Most teachers tried to present a "stiff upper lip" about their struggles. Here is Barrett Wendell, who in 1884 pioneered the "daily theme," which spread from trend-setting Harvard to many other schools, on his workload during the 1892–3 school year:

> The daily theme, as it exists at Harvard College, started in one of my courses perhaps eight or nine years ago . . . I introduced in my elective course the practice of requiring from every student a daily theme, which consists of a single page of probably fifty to a hundred words . . . I have at this moment in my class at Harvard College within one or two of 170 men, and they write these themes every day, and it happens this year to be my duty to read those every day and to make some sort of note on them . . . of course, I must do it rather hastily. It is a matter of two or three hours a day.[33]

A little math indicates the extent of Wendell's reading. Assuming a 26-week school year, he read 855 themes weekly, or 22,230 for the year. This was, of course, in addition to Harvard's required fortnightly themes, which were longer and had to be critiqued in more depth. 170 of these every two weeks adds 2,210 additional papers for the year. Even the effervescent Wendell must have been daunted.

The grading load was terribly heavy even at schools that didn't use the daily theme. Fred Newton Scott of the University of Michigan, the greatest rhetorical theorist of the period 1875–1925, was also the most honest and outspoken about the overwork teachers endured:

> . . . I have read and re-read this year something over 3,000 essays, most of them written by a class of 216 students . . . That the instructor should somehow lay hold of the student as an individual is, for successful composition work, simply indispensable . . . But . . . in the larger universities the day of small and cosey classes is long past. Now the hungry generations tread us down. We hardly learn the names and faces of our hundreds of students before they break ranks and go their ways, and then we must resume our Sisyphean labors.[34]

Scott paints a dark picture, but it must be accepted as a true one. The reasons for such conditions are not difficult to infer. Then, as now, teachers of composition were ill-organized and suffered from a code of "professionalism" that frowned upon public complaint about conditions. Many were low in status, unsure about how their courses should be run, unwilling to demand changes in conditions. College administrators, for their part, probably didn't realize that the introductory English course was qualitatively different from the introductory History course; thus both were organized as large lectures. The result, as we have seen, was the destructive overloading of writing teachers. As George R. Carpenter *et al.* put it in 1903, "It is not uncommon for teachers of English . . . who are conducting twenty hours of recitation a week . . . to sit up until twelve o'clock night after night in order to correct the compositions of their pupils." [35] We will never know the degree to which this glut of theme-correcting destroyed rhetoric as a scholarly discipline by driving sensitive scholars into other fields—particularly literature—but it must have been considerable. [36] This situation persisted from around 1880 through the middle part of the 'teens, when conditions slowly began to improve. [37]

Reactions to Overwork:
Assignments, Reading Styles, and Adjunct Technology

Faced with this gross overwork and with growing social and professional pressure to enforce "the basics," teachers were forced to evolve strategies to protect themselves from insanity and to get on with their work. We are still seeing versions today of the strategies, several in nature, evolved by the writing teachers of the late nineteenth century to cope with those conditions.

First of all, teachers moved quickly to scrap the older abstract paper topics that had been popular between 1800 and 1870, substituting instead simpler assignments that could be scanned quickly for obvious flaws. As Kitzhaber shows, the trend was away from assignments requiring special knowledge, complex conceptualizations, or detailed explanations, and toward essays based on personal experience and observation. In terms of the modal division of discourse then popular, it was a switch from an emphasis on exposition (which was more complex in the nineteenth century than it became in the twentieth) and argument to an emphasis on narration and description. Topics such as "Curiosity" or "The Evanescence of Pleasure" were replaced by "Our Newsboy" and "An Early Morning's Fishing" (and eventually by the notorious "How I Spent My Summer Vacation"). [38]

Kitzhaber's contention that this personalization and simplification of theme topics was the result of dissatisfaction with the older abstract topics is certainly true, but he doesn't go into much depth on the reasons for that dissatisfaction. That such topics as "Selfishness" produced bad writing from college freshmen is easy to understand. More important for the current discussion, however, is that such abstract topics produce writing that is *cognitively more demanding and therefore slower to read and grade.* I believe that this is the central reason behind the adoption of narrative and descriptive topics; as every teacher knows, personal-experience writing is the easiest reading we see.

Criteria for judging narratives and simple descriptions are easy to set, paper content often suggests itself, and the organization of such essays is usually simple chronology or spatial reference. Personal-experience papers can be read and evaluated much more quickly and with far fewer difficult judgment calls than the older sort of abstract-analysis papers, and in short, the newer topics took over because grading them was easier work for teachers snowed under by too many themes.

With questions of content and organization radically simplified, the reading and grading of students papers entered a whole new era. At some point between 1870 and 1900, the act of a teacher reading and commenting on the general communicative success of a piece of student writing—form and content—was succeeded by a simplified concept: the teacher as spotter and corrector of formal errors. Student essays ceased to be "literary efforts" and became instead exhibits of rule-worship, to be examined "with a lawyer's eyes," as Mina Shaughnessy tellingly puts it. Skill in writing, which had traditionally meant the ability to manipulate a complex hierarchy of content-based, organizational, and stylistic goals, came to mean but one thing: error avoidance.

This new emphasis upon mechanical correctness grew out of the "illiteracy" furor we have discussed, but more importantly out of the understandable need of teachers to somehow deal with their huge stacks of student themes. As every writing teacher knows, truly reading a paper—any paper—is mentally demanding and time-consuming. It requires complete attention to all levels of style, form, meaning, full presence of mind. Full editorial reading is tiring and cannot be done efficiently for long stretches of time.

On the other hand, merely scanning a paper for formal and syntactic correctness is a rather mechanical act; with practice it can be done with almost as little concentration as riding a bicycle. Far more students' papers can be passed through such a mechanism in a given period of time than can be passed through a full reading. The writing teachers of the 1880s and 1890s, faced with a reading task that was essentially impossible, were forced to cut their losses as best they could; substituting rapid scanning-for-errors in place of full readings, they came to see this simple correcting procedure as what they were expected to do. Yes, they "read" the 170 themes a day or the 216 themes a week—after a fashion. They "corrected" and graded them, and rationalized this sort of reading by claiming that they were giving students what students really needed most. The work was demanding; it took time; it was onerous—but it was not impossible, as genuine reading would have been. Faced with killing work levels, teachers had to give something up; what went, unfortunately, was rhetoric. Real teacher responses to student papers went the same way as complex and challenging assignments.

With primary teacher attention and nearly all paper correction being devoted to the formal aspects of student writing, it was inevitable that the nature of the college composition course should change. During the eighties and nineties we can see the changes slowly taking place, not so much in textbooks as in adjunct technologies. The mechanical grading and evaluation that teachers were being forced into invited mechanical support systems, usually in the form of systems of rules to which students could be referred. These systems of mechanical rules were found in two primary sources: as "composition cards" containing abbreviated rules and correction marks, and later, in specialized textbooks. Let us examine both of these developments.

"Correction Cards," or "Theme Cards," printed on heavy stock and given out to students, were first used in high schools in the 1870s, but their use quickly spread to the college level. The most common sort contained short directions on manuscript preparation and a key to the system of correction marks used by the instructor. Many of these systems of marks were based on the one recommended in E. W. Huffcut's 1887 *English in the Preparatory Schools*, but they varied a good deal from school to school. Some sort of card system of this sort was the rule at most colleges by 1890. Adams S. Hill assembled one for sale at Harvard, and many other colleges followed suit. The rules of "grammar" might not be good enough for a place in rhetoric textbooks, but no teacher could do without some means of referring to them. These cards were highly ephemeral and few have survived; the one reprinted here is a high-school card from 1908.[39] (See Figure One.)

Use of these cards, while better than nothing, presented several problems. First of all, their correction systems were varied and could be confusing to students. More seriously, they couldn't provide enough space for satisfactory explanations of the key correction marks. Teachers clearly felt a need for some sort of bridge between the rhetoric texts—which overwhelmingly rejected syntax, grammar, and form as "baby-work"—and composition cards. Such bridges were slow in appearing. A few rhetorics appeared which contained a page or two of composition-card material, but they were the exception rather than the rule.[40]

The Genesis of the Handbook

The obvious answer to the problem was a new sort of textbook, one that would explain and exemplify the sorts of rules that teachers were increasingly asking their students to learn and practice, and through the last quarter of the nineteenth century several attempts to find the form for such a book were made, none of them completely

"AIM AT UNITY OF THOUGHT AND VARIETY
OF STATEMENT." —Dr. F. N. Scott

. . . .	I. Manuscript	a Legible	1 Letters
			2 Spacing
. . . .			3 i's and t's
		b Capitals	
. . . .		c Hyphens	
		d Italics	
. . . .		e Quotation marks	
		f Punctuation	1 Comma
. . . .			2 Semicolon
			3 Colon
. . . .			4 Period
			5 Question mark
. . . .	II. Words	a Formation	
		b Good use	1 Verb
. . . .			2 Possessive
			3 Spelling
. . . .		c Precision	
		d Simplicity	
. . . .		e Brevity	
		f Variety	
. . . .	III. Sentences	a Correctness	1 Complete
			2 Subject and verb
. . . .			3 Participle and noun
			4 Pronoun and antecedent
. . . .			5 Case
			6 Shall, Should
. . . .			7 Infinitive
		b Unity	
. . . .		c Mass	1 Beginning
			2 End
. . . .		d Coherence	1 Order of words
			2 Parallel construction
. . . .			3 Precise conjunction
. . . .		e Variety	1 Periodic and loose
			2 Long and short
. . . .	IV. Paragraphs	a Unity	1 Topic Sentence
			2 Length moderate
. . . .		b Mass	1 Beginning
			2 End
. . . .			3 Proportion
		c Coherence	1 Order of sentences
. . . .			2 Parallel construction
			3 Precise conjunction
. . . .			4 Tenses
. . . .	V. Theme	a Unity	Summary in one paragraph
		b Mass	1 Beginning
. . . .			2 End
			3 Proportion
. . . .		c Coherence	Order of paragraphs

Based on Barrett Wendell's ENGLISH COMPOSITION

Figure One: A Typical "Correction Card" from the early Twentieth Century

successful. The first and most obvious answer to the problem of teaching students "grammar" (which by 1885 was a sort of catch-all term used by English teachers to mean formal correctness of all kinds) was merely to update the grammar rules taught by elementary schools. This was done by Alonzo Reed and Brainerd Kellogg in their 1877 high school text, *Higher Lessons in English*, and on the college level by Joseph Gilmore in his 1875 text *Outlines of the Art of Expression*, which used a sort of Baltimore Catechism question-and-answer method to inculcate grammatical rules. The book grew, said Gilmore, "in the author's class-room, out of an attempt to supplement the defective early training of his pupils." Gilmore used an expansive definition of grammar: "Grammar," he said, "may be defined as the art of correctly expressing our thoughts. It lays the foundation for rhetoric, which superinduces, upon mere *correctness* of expression, Clearness, Energy, and Elegance . . . "[41] Gilmore went on to deal in such questions as "Define a simple sentence and an act of thought," and "Give the exceptions to the general rules for forming the plurals of English nouns."

Gilmore's book had some initial popularity, but this question-answer format was by necessity abstract and hard to use as a reference. Much more popular than Gilmore's approach was the "rules" approach taken by Edwin A. Abbott in his 1874 manual *How To Write Clearly: Rules and Exercises*. This book, which went through 25 printings between 1874 and 1914, is the earliest recognizable prototype for all the "handbooks of composition" that came after it. "Almost every English boy can be taught to write clearly," said Abbott, "so far at least as clearness depends upon the arrangement of words . . . Clear writing can be reduced to rules."[42] *How To Write Clearly* contains 56 rules, most of them dealing with sentence construction and style, many of them similar to certain of today's handbook prescriptions. Unlike Gilmore's question-answers, Abbott expressed his rules in positive commandments followed by exemplifications: "32. In a long conditional sentence put the 'if-clause' antecedent, or protasis, first," and "41. Antithesis adds force, and often clearness." Abbott covered few questions of usage, no spelling or punctuation, very little basic syntax or grammar; and yet it was in print for over 40 years. Harvard required students to purchase the book through the 1880s, and it also seems to have been required at different times by Oberlin and the Universities of Pennsylvania, Virginia, Michigan, and Colorado.[43] As early as 1880, teachers were casting about for convenient systems of enforceable reference rules.

What is most surprising about Abbott is not that it was fairly popular, but that it wasn't more widely copied. A few texts appeared during the eighties that treated of mechanics—punctuation, usage, etc.—but no American authors seemed willing to write an Abbott-style rule-book treating all of the questions of mechanics. In 1893, John Genung published his *Outlines of Rhetoric*, which was organized according to rules but which is more accurately seen as the first college-level Basic Writing text than as a book in the reference mode. Genung's attitude toward basic-level instruction in the elements of correctness was paradoxical; he was the only one of the "Big Four" to write anything like a remedial-English college text, yet he didn't seem proud of his chosen task: "(Rhetoric) has as its lower and elementary stages, comprising the procedures that lie at the foundation of all composition, things which it is not so much an honor to know as a reproach not to know; these are what the present treatise is mainly concerned with . . . "[44] Genung proposed that these basic areas could be reduced to 73 rules, based on Usage, Phraseology, and Style, which he numbered consecutively and printed as side-headings throughout the text; a digest of them was printed at the end of the book "to facilitate the correction of the student's written work." "By simply writing the number of the rule in the margin of the student's paper," wrote Genung, "the teacher can call his attention to the error involved."

Outlines was another popular success for Genung, who was one of the first English authors to make textbooks financially rewarding, and it remained in use until at least 1915. As mentioned earlier, however, it started no trends, and the influential textbooks of the time remained set against treatments of basic mechanical material. The authors of the eighties and nineties were the last composition teachers trained in the remnants of the great tradition of rhetoric, and they would not recant their beliefs that rhetoric involved higher mysteries than grammatical correctness.

The day of the rhetoricians, however, was passing, and the day of the composition pedagogues was dawning. The spirit of questing experimentation that had fueled composition in the nineties failed after 1900, and as the torch of rhetorical theory guttered, the practical problems of classroom pedagogy came to the fore. By 1905, Hill, Genung, and Endell had all but retired from teaching and writing about composition, and the few rhetorical theorists still active at that time—mainly F. N. Scott and his disciples—were increasingly voices crying in the wilderness. Textbooks at this time became predictable and derivative, unwilling to experiment with new treatments. Materials on mechanical correctness bloomed, and in 1907 there appeared a new sort of textbook, the logical culmination of the move toward rule-governed composition that had been going on since 1875: the modern handbook of composition.[45]

The first handbook was Edwin C. Woolley's *Handbook of Composition: A Compendium of Rules.* Woolley provided in a primitive form nearly all of the elements that make up today's handbooks: it dealt with punctuation, spelling, legibility, sentence structure. The *Handbook* saw no element of writing as beneath its scope; it had no rhetorical pretensions. Woolley himself argued the case for his handbook most succinctly in his 1909 *Mechanics of Writing:*

> The chief benefit derived from theme-writing lies probably in the instructor's indication of errors in the themes and his showing how these errors are to be corrected . . . But . . . how shall the instructor, as he indicates these eight hundred errors (in the fifty themes he must hand back the next day), furnish the information called for by each one? Obviously he must use some kind of shorthand. Suppose, then, that he writes opposite the incorrect "whom" above quoted the expression "Gr." or "b.E." or "case." Do these expressions furnish the student with the information he needs regarding that "whom"? It seems to me that they do not . . .
>
> Yet shorthand must be used in correcting themes. Is there no system of shorthand which conveys to the student the information he should have regarding each error marked in this themes? There is such a system; it consists of references to a book . . . The *Handbook* was designed, and the present book has been designed, to be used in this way.[46]

This was Woolley's credo. And how did teachers react to this new sort of text? With overwhelming approbation. In a representative review in 1909, H. E. Coblentz spoke for most of the college teachers of the day: "This little book deserves the utmost praise . . . Every teacher of English will find this the handiest book of its kind."[47] At last the cat was out of the bag, and teachers of writing no longer tried to hide the primarily mechanical nature of their readings.

With the *Handbook*, Woolley began what would later be referred to as "the Woolley family" of handbooks, a family still represented by the collateral descendant of the 1907 *Handbook*, today's *Heath Handbook*, 10th edition. He also began the handbook era, initiating a new sort of writing text that would quickly come to be at the heart of most college writing courses. Since the first Woolley *Handbook*, composition pedagogy has been transformed. Needs had shaped the texts, and now the texts shaped the writing courses; this was especially true of handbooks, which were always the favorite texts of untrained writing teachers and thus exerted a great, although often hidden, influence.

The twenty years following the Woolley *Handbook* might be called the Great Handbook Boom. Between 1907 and 1927 at least fifteen different handbooks were published.[48] As important as the numbers of handbooks, however, were the changes the handbook form was causing in the rhetoric texts of the period and the broadening of the purposes of the handbooks themselves. Beginning around 1910 we see the rapid crumbling of rhetoric texts' authors' unwillingness to

include mechanical-correctness materials in their books. Clippinger's
Illustrated Lessons, Foerster and Steadman's *Sentences and Thinking,*
Young and Young's *Freshman English* all reflected a novel handbook-
oriented emphasis on lower-level elements of mechanical correctness:
punctuation, spelling, grammar. Clippinger in 1912 actually included
a separate handbook section in his rhetoric—probably the first such
conjunction. During this period the last vestiges of the old abstract-
theory tradition in composition died out, and with it died any sense
of professional history. By 1925 most of the great nineteenth-century
rhetorical theorists had been forgotten, and their doctrines were assumed to have always existed. In the hands of overworked part-timers
and graduate students, Freshman English entered its Dark Ages: unen-
lightened toil, a benighted processing of students through the obstacle
course of mechanical correctness.

In "Handbooks: History of a Genre" I have discussed how
Woolley's home-reference handbook grew first into a book of rules
and exercises and then into a full-scale textbook meant for use both
at home and in class: the rhetoric-handbook. Woolley and Scott's *College Handbook of Composition* in 1928 marked the beginning of this
phase of textbook development, a phase which effectually meant that
the mechanical organization and algorithmic rule-governed approach
of the handbook extended themselves into all aspects of rhetoric. The
predictable result was that the derivative rhetorical theory of the period became even more debased, even more removed from the actual
process of communication. Handbook rhetoric was always the most
reductive form of current-traditional dogma, and by the 1920s there
was little rhetorical theory not influenced by handbook approaches.
Fewer and fewer rhetoric texts were found that didn't incorporate a
handbook or rules-type section, and after 1925 or so it seemed a tacit
assumption that the average composition course was an essentially remedial endeavor. As John French said in his book *Writing* in 1924:
"This book attempts to supply in one volume material adequate for
such a course in English Composition as includes the review of elementary principles and the *anticipation* of mature studies in English and
other subjects. Consequently it gives much space to rules for correctness."[49] For the freshman of 1924, mature writing was something
only anticipated.

Bereft of a theoretical discipline and a professional tradition,
teachers during this period had nothing to turn to for information
about their subject—except their textbooks. It is during the first two
decades of this century that we first see the pattern of writing teachers
as the only college-level instructors who know no more of their discipline than is contained in the texts they assign their students—a sad
pattern that still, alas, continues today at too many schools. And when

we examine the books these teachers of the 1920s depended upon, it is not difficult to see why I. A. Richards called rhetoric "the dreariest part of the waste the unfortunate travel through" during their first year of college. Quite literally, after 1925, handbooks and handbook-rhetorics were in control of composition classes. A survey taken in 1927 showed that of 27 representative colleges in the Midwest, 85% used handbooks in their writing courses—and more importantly, 41% used no texts *but* handbooks.[50] Rhetoric had truly been transmogrified into the dread discipline of "Freshman English."

Remedial Technology

If the period 1875–1900 nurtured the elements leading to an obsession with mechanical correctness and the period 1900–1925 turned composition from a subject (distantly) concerned with communication into an error hunt, the period following 1925 was what might be called the remedial-technology era. It was a time when composition teachers, at their nadir in terms of experience and interest, were lured farther and farther into mechanism by ever-more-sophisticated "classroom aids" put out by textbook firms. Handbooks became the central reference point for teachers who had never studied any rhetorical theory (and no teacher English-trained could have been taught rhetoric between 1915 and 1950); even those whose training in critical reading made them sensitive readers of student writing were too overworked to bring useful criticism to bear on the papers they graded, and these teachers did what they could: they enforced correctness and made it the heart of their demands.

We cannot overestimate the effect of textbooks on the teaching and paper-grading done during this period; it was everything. Especially influential were the handbooks, which after 1930 assumed a larger and larger place in the pedagogical scene and eventually became the single most important element of stability in the entire composition course. Writing in 1941, James McCrimmon identified the reasons behind the growth of popularity of handbooks: their role in transmitting values. "Instructors," said McCrimmon, "not only consult the handbook they are using, they are likely to con it, get it by heart, pledge indiscriminate devotion to it. Herein lies its power . . . for the English handbook is often the teacher's teacher." Since most composition teachers were untrained graduate students without experience, McCrimmon stated, they have no idea what besides the handbook to teach:

> Little wonder that in such a sea of confusion he (the teacher) clings to his handbook as a shipwrecked sailor clings to his raft, and by an interesting human weakness, soon comes to believe

that these rules, which only yesterday were unknown to him, are the sole criteria of good writing.[51]

Forty-three years later, the phenomenon remarked by McCrimmon is still with us.

Handbooks arrived and proliferated because they were tools for the task of enforcing correctness. Their main purpose, in theory at least, was as support systems for instruction that was still supposed to be rhetorical: student essays read by the teacher. Following closely behind handbooks. however, were their dark siblings: drillbooks and workbooks, which introduced completely a-rhetorical practice in error recognition and sentence construction into the college writing course. Beginning in the mid-twenties and becoming a thriving industry by 1935, the "remedial racket," as Porter Perrin called it, introduced high school-level exercises in grammar, punctuation, and usage into college classrooms. Such books as Howard Grose's *Exercises in Everyday Writing*, Dana Jensen's *Corrective English Exercises*, and Easley Jones's *Practical English Drillbook* were selling well by the mid-thirties, and college composition was close to its most mechanistic point. Perrin's voice was one of the few raised in protest against the workbook approach:

> These exercises obviously violate the lone principle that present teachers of composition have salvaged from the 2500 years of the discipline of rhetoric, that one learns to speak and write by speaking and writing. . . . Why do we adopt them? Well, they're easy to handle: like every popular "advance" in pedagogical method, they are ultimately easier for the teacher. . . . We find a comforting certainty in grading exercises in the most elementary conventions of the language that is a great relief in a field where so little is certain, where the real work is eliciting variables in a growth. We may realize that these absolutely certain elements are few and are the least, or at any rate the lowest, factors in style. But we cannot help breathing more freely as we pass from the sand of better-or-worse to the pavement of supposed right-or-wrong.[52]

Perrin could certainly understand the weakness that made teachers turn to drillbooks, but he could not condone it. His was the first voice in a rising chorus of criticism of the status quo in college composition that began in the 1930s.

The Loyal Opposition

It was during this decade that we see the beginnings of the curious schizophrenia that has afflicted college composition since: the split between the scholars and theoreticians of the discipline and the great mass of classroom teachers. The descent into mechanism that occurred in the thirties was a result of the beliefs and activities of the latter group, but we must note that it took place against a background of serious and capable research and even protest from the former. Scholars of language began during this decade to bring together some of the research that had been ongoing since the teens; studies of errors in writing, of remedial techniques, of the efficacy of grammar drill were all scrutinized, and all of them pointed to the conclusion that the popular sorts of classroom grammar drills were essentially futile as attempts to improve student writing.[53] Sterling Leonard's pioneering study, *Current English Usage*, appeared in 1932, striking a powerful blow against the prescriptive-usage doctrines that were part of the mechanical-correctness tradition. The NCTE, which had existed since 1911, truly found its voice during the 1930s and began to declaim a Deweyite gospel of education for social goals, "tying up literature and composition with the business of living."[54] These pragmatic goals usually meant that the organization worked against sterile drills and mechanistic pedagogies. In sum, a motley crowd of linguists, educationists, and rhetoricians began to coalesce during the thirties and to struggle against the overwhelmingly mechanical classroom methods of the time.

It looked at first to be a futile battle. The forces of overwork and professionally-countenanced ignorance were very great. Handbooks, workbooks, drillbooks appeared in larger numbers each year, continuing the feedback loop of mechanical criteria as the only valid criteria of good writing. But the seeds of dissent had been planted, and through the forties and fifties the anti-mechanical reaction to the standard composition course began to grow strong in the profession of English. Rhetoric, which had been dormant within composition since the 1890s, began to make a reappearance after 1944, when the first communications courses were taught at the University of Iowa. Communications courses quickly spread to other schools, bringing together scholars from English and Speech departments for the first time since the tragic split between the disciplines that occurred in 1914, teaching all four of the "communications skills"—reading, writing, speaking, and listening. Rhetoric, which had been in the keeping of Speech departments during the twentieth century, was a vital part of these courses, and many English teachers learned for the first time what some of the alternatives to mechanical correctness might be.

This reintroduction of rhetoric into composition was to prove extremely vivifying. The idea of successful communication and not mere grammatical correctness as the central aim of writing was novel and exciting to English scholars, who once again began to investigate the great traditions of rhetoric; the newly-formed Conference on College Composition and Communication became the professional vehicle for this movement away from composition-as-grammar. It was inevitable that large parts of this emergency scholarship would involve intense self-criticism by English teachers, and indeed, beginning around the late forties, we do hear voices raised in plaintive criticism of the methods of brother teachers both past and present. Porter Perrin, who had been a soldier in the rhetorical trenches for over twenty years, spoke in 1951 of the years 1900–1935 as "a conspicuously narrow era of instruction" which showed "a general surrender of the broad aims that have made the study (of rhetoric) great to a concentration on minutiae of usage (actually a triumph of grammar over rhetoric)."[55]

By this time, however, Perrin's voice was not the only one being raised in criticism of the mechanical-correctness emphasis in writing instruction. Others were coming to the realization that student disgust for the writing course was no irrational response. Ruth Davies in 1950 wrote that "many teachers of freshman English waste much of their energy trying to enforce rules and standards universally ignored . . . While we are engrossed with the scrawny skin and brittle bones of composition, the flesh and blood and heart of the matter are almost forgotten."[56] Jacques Barzun struck out at the hypocrisy of educational systems that claimed to be "progressive" and eschew narrow insistence on formal correctness—but continue to enforce it:

> I know very well that correctness was supposedly given up long ago. The modern teacher does not mention it. But if the teacher marks spelling and grammatical errors and speaks of little else, what is a child to think? . . . Meanwhile the things that are teachable, the ways of translating the flashes of thought into consecutive sentences, are neglected.[57]

And Barriss Mills, in his seminal "Writing as Process" of 1953, strongly condemned the "police-force concept of usage" that still prevailed in most classrooms. 'Nothing is more blighting," wrote Mills, "to natural and functional written communication than an excessive zeal for purity of usage in mechanics."[58]

All of this criticism of the traditional mechanical priorities appeared during the late forties and early fifties in what can only be called a spontaneous reaction to a notably deficient pedagogical paradigm, a revolt against the current-traditional methods of teaching and thinking about composition that took its impetus from the rediscovery of rhetorical issues as they applied to writing. From its beginning in the late 1940s, this revolt gathered strength during the fifties and suddenly burst into full flower during the early sixties. Suddenly theorists and teachers everywhere were actively—and sometimes heatedly—discussing the purposes and methods of teaching composition, and the reign of mechanical correctness, which had largely depended on continued teacher ignorance, was being threatened.

I need not, I think, rehearse here the disputes of the last two decades over such issues as formal marking, theme correction, the nature of revision, the teaching of grammar. These debates can all be viewed as the mechanical-correctness tradition defending itself against attacks made in the name of rhetorical priority. On the one hand are the theorists, the rhetoricians, the proponents of writing as discovery or communication; on the other are the traditionalists, the front-line teachers, the proponents of writing as vocational skill. Both sides make valid points, and if the rhetoricians often get the best of the abstract arguments, the traditionalists can still point to savage overwork as an occupational reality for many writing teachers—a reality that makes real rhetorical instruction difficult or impossible. A teacher with 100 papers to grade in a weekend, say the traditionalists, cannot possibly respond effectively to each one as communication—and they are right.

There is no doubt that the composition-as-mechanical-correctness tradition has suffered serious setbacks during the last thirty years, but it is not a tradition that can be overcome so long as administrative priorities overwork undertrained teachers. There are still too many "four and four" teaching assignments, and such cynical exploitation of the victims of the depressed academic marketplace only creates grist for the mills of mechanism. Of the making of handbooks there is no end— and too many teachers are still given no training beyond their Harbrace charts. Overwork and ignorance have ever been the parents of destructive overemphasis on mechanical correctness, and these are not conditions we can get rid of easily.

We can, however, rejoice in the gains we have made. At last the reductive traditions of the first half of the century are being questioned and challenged. Teachers are better trained every year. Newer textbooks are providing even traditionally-oriented teachers with more defensible course content than the "shall-will" rules. Administrators have gradually been made to understand that 40 students are too many for one class, and most now accept 30 as too many. We may eventually be able to convince them that 25 are too many as well, and that four writing courses per term is too heavy a load for any teacher. We have made strides, and more will be made.

The enforcement of standards of mechanical correctness is not a tradition that can—or should—die out of composition instruction. Mechanical errors, as Mina Shaughnessy says, are "unprofitable intrusions upon the consciousness of the reader" which "demand energy without giving any return in meaning," and helping students overcome their own unintentional sabotage of the process of communicating their thoughts is certainly an important part of our work. But it is not all of our work. Striking a balance between formal and rhetorical considerations is the problem we now face, and it is a delicate one. We cannot escape the fact that in a written text any question of mechanics is also a rhetorical question, and as a discipline we are still trying to understand the meaning of that conjunction. We may spend the rest of our professional lives investigating how the balance between rhetoric and mechanics can best be struck—a difficult question, but one heartening to see asked, for the fact that we are confronting such questions shows that composition studies is once again a genuine discipline and no longer a purblind drifting on the current of unexamined tradition.

Notes

[1] Tewksbury lists 54 American colleges extant in 1831; this was just prior to the great Protestant college-building boom of the period 1830-1850. See Donald G. Tewksbury, *The Founding of American Colleges and Universities Before the Civil War* (New York: Teachers' College, Columbia University, 1932), pp. 32-54.

[2] Alexis de Tocqueville, *Democracy in America*, trans. George Lawrence (Garden City, NY: Doubleday, 1969), p. 55.

[3] Tocqueville, *Democracy in America*, p. 480.

[4] It is no accident that around this time we also see the beginnings of dialect humor in the Sam Slick books, the writings of Artemus Ward, etc.

[5] Rollo LaVerne Lyman, *English Grammar in American Schools Before 1850* (Washington, D.C.: Government Printing Office, 1922), p. 5. As Lyman shows, the period 1820-1850 saw the largest number of new grammar texts appear. Numbers are: 1811-1820—41 texts; 1821-1830—84; 1831-1840—63; 1841-1850—66. (Lyman, p. 80)

[6] Edward Finegan, *Attitudes Toward English Usage: The History of a War of Words* (New York: Teachers' College Press, 1980), pp. 47-54. Another well-written source on certain nineteenth-century language phenomena is Dennis E. Baron, *Grammar and Good Taste: Reforming the American Language* (New Haven: Yale University Press, 1982). Baron concentrates more on linguistic protest and reform movements, Finegan more on the history of usage debates. Both perspectives are useful to anyone studying the development of composition in America.

[7] Andrew Peabody, *Conversation, Its Faults and Its Graces* (Boston: Shepard and Lee, 1867), pp. 10-11.

[8] Seth T. Hurd, *A Grammatical Corrector* (Philadelphia: E. H. Butler and Co., 1847), p. v.

[9] Alford was actually anti-Union (he was an open Confederate sympathizer like many Britons), but he extended his critique to all Americans.

[10] Henry Alford, *A Plea for the Queen's English* (London: Alexander Strahan, 1864), pp. 5-6.

[11] Edward S. Gould, *Good English: or Popular Errors in Language* (New York: W. J. Widdleton, 1867), p. 1.

[12] Richard Meade Bache, *Vulgarisms and Other Errors of Speech* (Philadelphia: Claxton, Remsen, and Haffelfinger, 1869), Preface.

[13] William Mathews, *Words: Their Use and Abuse* (Chicago: S. C. Griggs, 1876), p. 5.

[14] See, for instance, Alfred Ayres (Thomas E. Osmun), *The Verbalist: A Manual* (New York: D. Appleton, 1881), and the Sheperd and Lee series of social-language handbooks, including Samuel Fallows' *Discriminate!* of 1885 and Harlan H. Ballard's *Handbook of Blunders* of the same year. Probably the longest-lived of these handbooks of linguistic *arrivisme* was Oliver Bell Bunce's classic *Don't* (New York: D. Appleton), which appeared in 1883 and was last reprinted in 1921.

[15] A good overview of this period is found in Frederick Rudolph, *The American College and University: A History* (New York: Knopf, 1962).

[16] For information on this movement, see Lawrence R. Veysey, *The Emergence of the American University* (Chicago: University of Chicago Press, 1965), pp. 1-20, 57-118.

[17] Albert R. Kitzhaber, *Rhetoric in American Colleges, 1850-1900* (Dissertation, University of Washington, 1953), p. 312.

[18] The only dependable information we have on the introduction of this examination seems to be in A. S. Hill's essay "An Answer to the Cry for More English," and Hill was not even on the Harvard faculty when the exam was first introduced in 1874. (He took it over two years later.) The essay is found in *Twenty Years of School and College English* (Cambridge: Harvard University Press, 1896).

[19] A. S. Hill, "An Answer to the Cry for More English," p. 11.

[20] They were even provoking scornful laughter from the general public. See Caroline B. Le Row, *English As She Is Taught: Genuine Answers to Examination Questions in our Public Schools* (New York: Cassell, 1887), which prints funny examples of student writing. Example: a definition of "inertia" as "the negative quality of passiveness either in recoverable latency or incipient latescence." The beginning of a long tradition of rather cruel humor.

[21] See, for instance, Henry Jameson, *Rhetorical Method* (St. Louis: G. I. Jones & Co., 1879), and Henry Coppens, *A Practical Introduction to English Rhetoric: Precepts and Exercises* (New York: Catholic School Book Co., 1880).

[22] Kitzhaber, *Rhetoric in American Colleges*, p. 319.

[23] Kitzhaber, p. 306

[24] E. L. Godkin, "The Illiteracy of American Boys," *Educational Review* 8 (1897), 7.

[25] John F. Genung, *The Working Principles of Rhetoric* (Boston: Ginn and Co., 1900), p. 128n.

[26] Fred Newton Scott, "What the West Wants in Preparatory English," *School Review* 17 (1909), 19.

[27] Barrett Wendell, "English Work in the Secondary Schools," *School Review* 1 (1893), 659–660.

[28] C. T. Copeland and H. M. Rideout, *Freshman English and Theme-Correcting in Harvard College* (New York: Silver, Burdett, 1901), p. 1.

[29] William Morton Payne, ed., *English in American Universities* (Boston: D. C. Heath, 1895), p. 30.

[30] Payne, *English in American Universities*, p. 83.

[31] Payne, p. 86.

[32] Veysey, *The Emergence of the American University*, p. 153.

[33] Wendell, "English Work in the Secondary Schools," pp. 659–660.

[34] Fred Newton Scott, in Payne, *English in American Universities*, pp. 121–122.

[35] George R. Carpenter, Franklin T. Baker, and Fred N. Scott, *The Teaching of English in the Elementary and Secondary School* (New York: Longmans, Green, 1903), p. 329.

[36] This is illustrated by "a private letter by a teacher in an Eastern University" quoted in Carpenter *et al.* in which the anonymous author says, "I have never done any rhetorical work at _____ except in connection with my courses in literature, and I thank God I have been delivered from the bondage of theme-work into the glorious liberty of literature" (p. 329n).

[37] It was early obvious that the lecture-sized class was the wrong sort of setting for composition, but nineteenth-century administrators, as many today still do, turned their backs on the obvious evidence of overwork and meditated instead on the bottom line. Seminar-type writing courses seem never to have been considered, but some schools were wealthy enough or had prestigious enough faculty members so that their writing courses were taught as "laboratory" courses. John Genung at Amherst led this movement most obviously. These first lab-type courses were not much different from regular classes except in their numbers—Henry Frink, the freshman teacher at Amherst, had five assistants for a class of 110 students—but numbers were so important that a movement in favor of composition as "laboratory work" became very vocal and had by 1900 gained some power. If composition is truly laboratory work, said Fred Scott in 1895, "why should it not be placed on the same footing as other laboratory work as regards manning and equipment?"

Such support, despite outcries from teachers, was not rapidly forthcoming. In 1911, the NEA and NCTE organized a committee to investigate the labor involved in composition teaching. Edwin M.

Hopkins, chair of this committee, said in his first report that "composition teaching has been described as a 'laboratory subject' for a fairly long time," but that adequate conditions had never been provided for such teaching and only existed, when they did, as "the result of a fortunate chance." The Hopkins Committee Report, issued in 1912, put their findings bluntly:

> Under present average conditions, English teachers are assigned more than twice as much work as they can do. Some of them try to do it by working more than twice as much as other teachers do. This is wrong, because it disables them. Others do only what they reasonably can and let the rest go. This is wrong in another way, because it is an injustice to the pupil and a waste of his time . . . Under present average conditions of teaching English expression, workmen must choose between overwork and bad work; between spoiling their material or killing themselves . . . . (Edwin M. Hopkins, "The Labor and Cost of Composition Teaching: The Present Conditions," *Proceedings of the NEA* 50 [1912], 750.)

This report was the first shot in an NCTE campaign to lower class size in writing courses, a campaign that has lasted into our time. Conditions did improve during the twenties and thirties; by that time, however, teachers had been set in pedagogies shaped by the bad old days.

[38] See Kitzhaber's discussion of this change in *Rhetoric in American Colleges*, pp. 169–177.

[39] This correction card is reprinted from M. Atkinson Williams, *Report on the Teaching of English in the United States* (London: Swan Sonnenschein and Co., 1908). Williams, a young Englishwoman touring the schools and colleges of the U.S. in order to report on their methods to her fellow Britons, says about the use of these cards, "I wish I could be sure that the pupils made as much use of them as the teachers." (p. 52).

[40] See, for instance, William Williams, *Composition and Rhetoric by Practice* (Boston: D. C. Heath & Co., 1890) and Edward R. Shaw, *English Composition by Practice* (New York: Henry Holt & Co., 1892).

[41] Joseph H. Gilmore, *Outlines of the Art of Expression* (Boston: Ginn Bros., 1876), p. 5.

[42] Edwin A. Abbott, *How To Write Clearly: Rules and Exercises on English Composition* (Boston: Roberts Bros., 1874), p. 5.

[43] This is an extrapolation from data in the *National Union Catalog*.

[44] John F. Genung, *Outlines of Rhetoric* (Boston: Ginn & Co., 1893), pp. 3–4.

[45] See my essay-bibliography "Handbooks: History of a Genre" (forthcoming, I hope) for more detailed information on this extremely important textbook form.

[46] Edwin C. Woolley, *The Mechanics of Writing* (Boston: D. C. Heath, 1909), pp. vi–viii.

[47] H. E. Coblentz, review of Edwin C. Woolley, *Handbook of Composition*, *School Review* 17 (1909), 581.

[48] See the bibliography at the end of "Handbooks" for the authors, titles, and dates of these handbooks.

[49] John C. French, *Writing: A Textbook of Structure, Style, and Usage* (New York: Harcourt, Brace & Co., 1924), p. v. Italics are mine.

[50] Ralph L. Henry, "Freshman English in the Middle West," *English Journal* 17 (1928), 302–304.

[51] James M. McCrimmon, "The Importance of the Right Handbook," *College English* 3 (1941), 70–71.

[52] Porter G. Perrin, "The Remedial Racket," *English Journal* 22 (1933), 384–388.

[53] See, for instance, Roy Ivan Johnson, "Persistency of Error in English Composition," *School Review* 25 (1917), 555–580, and William Asker, "Does Knowledge of Formal Grammar Function?" *School and Society* 17 (1923), 109–111.

[54] Stella C. Center, "The Liberalism of the NCTE," *Education* 53 (1932), 164.

[55] Porter G. Perrin, "A Professional Attitude for Teachers of Communication," *Education* 72 (1951), 488.

[56] Ruth Davies, "A Defense of Freshmen," *College English* 12 (1950), 442.

[57] Jacques Barzun, "English As She's Not Taught," *Atlantic Monthly* (December, 1953), pp. 28–29.

[58] Barriss Mills, "Writing as Process," *College English* 15 (1953), 21.

3

Old Wine in New Bottles: A Dialectical Encounter Between the Old Rhetoric and the New

BURTON HATLEN

University of Maine, Orono

In their recent *Rhetorical Traditions and the Teaching of Writing* (1984a), C. H. Knoblauch and Lil Brannon argue that the time has come to bury the "Old Rhetoric"—i.e., the rhetoric whose principles and procedures, first codified by Aristotle, have been passed on from generation to generation down to the twentieth century. According to Knoblauch and Brannon, the Old Rhetoric was grounded on epistemological assumptions that have been obsolete since Descartes. But in our time, these authors propose, a Modern Rhetoric compatible with post-Cartesian epistemological theory has at last found for itself a voice and an audience, thus allowing us to inter the desiccated corpses of Aristotle and Cicero. The scorn which Knoblauch and Brannon heap not only upon the classical rhetoricians but also upon those closet Ciceronians that still, we are asked to believe, skulk about the corridors of English departments may seem to some of us like rhetorical overkill. And even after reading *Rhetorical Traditions and the Teaching of Writing*, I still suspect that the rule-governed pedagogy encoded in almost all twentieth century composition handbooks owes more to the mechanistic psychological theories of Alexander Bain than to the epistemological assumptions of Aristotle. Nevertheless, I also share some of Knoblauch and Brannon's sense that in our time we are seeing a revolution in rhetorical theory and practice: that there is indeed a New Rhetoric which can give—has already given—new hope to the despairing. Further, I share these authors' belief that a satisfactory rhetorical theory must begin, not simply by enumerating the attributes of the ideal text within each available mode of discourse, but rather by examining what is now generally called the "process of writing"—or what I'd rather call, borrowing my terminology from Kenneth Burke, the *act* of writing. Therefore if I sometimes quarrel with the emphases of Knoblauch and Brannon—and, more variously, with those of James Britton, Ann Berthoff, Ken Macrorie, and Peter Elbow—I hope it will always be clear that I am by no means advocating a mere return to Cicero: that I am proposing a correction, not a rejection, of the New Rhetoric.

Nevertheless, Knoblauch and Brannon's insistence that each of us must choose between the Old Rhetoric and the New seems to me unwarranted and unwise. The apostles of the New Rhetoric, even though they have assumed almost total control over the CCCC, still feel embattled, and thus they are prone to exaggerate the differences between themselves and the "traditionalists." There are two dangers here: that we will fail to preserve what is of value in the Old Rhetoric, and that the New Rhetoric itself will congeal into a New Orthodoxy. These dangers can be avoided only if we are willing to cultivate a critical stance toward the New Rhetoric: to see it not as a complete solution to all our problems but as a way of thinking that needs to be tested and refined.

In this paper, accordingly, I propose to test out the New Rhetoric by examining the way it has engaged one key issue: the reading/writing relationship. In such a project the Old Rhetoric can, I believe, still serve a useful purpose, by offering a standard of comparison against which we may assess the assumptions and the consequences of the New Rhetoric. I'll therefore begin by summarizing the Old Rhetoric's conception of the reading/writing relationship. I'll propose that the Old Rhetoric invited the student to read certain texts as models of "correct" compositional structure, and then to write texts in imitation of these models. In its repudiation of the Old Rhetoric, the New Rhetoric has generally rejected the idea that the imitation of "classic" models is the best way of learning how to write. But having rejected Old Rhetoric's text-as-model, the New Rhetoric has found itself uncertain of the role which reading itself—at any rate, the reading of "finished" pieces of work by "established" authors—might play in the writing classroom. This uncertainty points to a fundamental weakness in the theoretic foundations of the New Rhetoric itself, at least as those foundations have been laid out by Knoblauch and Brannon. Accordingly, I'll here attempt to move from a critique of Knoblauch and Brannon's ego-centered rhetoric toward a conception of discourse as a process of social interaction—a view which finds at least as much support in "modern philosophy" as does the philosophical Idealism of Knoblauch and Brannon. Having laid out a philosophic rationale for a socially grounded rhetoric, I'll return to the issue of modeling and will propose that a dialectical conception of the relationship between the ideal model and the concrete utterance might allow us a way beyond the sterile quarrel between Old and New Rhetoric.

I

The Greeks of the classical epoch assumed that we learn principally through imitation of ideal models. Both Plato and Aristotle saw the human creature as impelled by an inherent force to move toward the Good, whether as an object of contemplation (Plato) or as a fulness of being which each person seeks, perhaps blindly, to realize (Aristotle). And both assumed that a primary function of the community should be to guide human beings along this path, by allowing the person whose virtues are still *in potentia* to contemplate examples of people further along in the arduous journey toward a full realization of their human possibilities. Personal acquaintance with such a person may help. Thus in Plato's dialogues Socrates repeatedly offers himself to the youth of Athens as a model of the ideal human being. But the Greeks also saw reading as a way of discovering such models, as Protagoras says in the Platonic dialogue to which he gives his name:

> And when boys have learned their letters . . . they set the works of good poets before them on their desks to read . . . poems containing much admonition and many stories, eulogies, and panegyrics of the good men of old, so that the child may be inspired to imitate them and long to be like them (1963, p. 322).

So too, Plato's Socrates would expel the writings of that liar Homer from his ideal republic, lest young people begin to imitate the scandalous behavior of the Homeric gods. Aristotle carries the quest for ideal models beyong the realm of ethics into a study of the physical world, of the state, of poetry—and of that region of discourse which the Greeks called rhetoric. Thus was born imitation, the central pedagogical principle in all rhetorical instruction down to our century.

The pedagogies born in ancient Greece were redacted and passed on first by Roman and then by Medieval and Renaissance theorists and teachers, and all these heirs of the Greek rhetorical tradition gave imitation a central place. The "high" culture of Rome derived almost entirely from Greece, as Virgil imitated Homer and as Catullus imitated Sappho and as Cicero imitated Plato (in *De Republica)* and Aristotle (in *De Oratore*) and Isocrates and Demosthenes (in his political orations). And with the Renaissance, the emphasis which pedagogical theorists placed on imitation seemed, if anything, to increase. I'll adduce only two cases in point, the first from Erasmus's *De Copia*, one of the most popular rhetorical handbooks of the Renaissance. Erasmus counsels teachers to assign their students

> translation from Greek authors, because the Greek language is especially rich in both word and thought. Moreover, it will occasionally be very useful to emulate them by paraphrasing. It will be of especial help to rewrite the verses of poets in prose: and on the other hand, to bind prose in meter, and put the same theme into first one and then another type of verse. And it will be very helpful for us to emulate and attempt by our own efforts to equal or even to improve upon that passage in any author which appears unusually rich in copia. Moreover, it will be especially useful if we peruse good authors night and day, particularly those who have excelled in copia of speech, such as Cicero, Aulus Gellius, Apuleius; and with vigilant eyes we should note all figures in them, store up in our memory what we have noted, imitate what we have stored up, and by frequent use make it a habit to have them ready at hand (1936, pp. 17–8).

I offer one additional Renaissance defense of imitation, from Sir Thomas Elyot's *The Book Called the Governor* (1531). Elyot advises that students be invited to write both poetry and more public forms of discourse in imitation of classical models:

> And if the child were induced to make verses by the imitation of Virgil and Homer, it should minister to him much delectation and courage to study; ne the making of verses is not discommended in a nobleman . . . (1962, p. 32)

In the writings of Erasmus and Elyot we see the humanist dream of an educational system that would allow all the potentialities of the human creature to unfold fully, through imitation of perfect models. And before we let ourselves sneer at this dream, we should remember that Humanism begat the English Public School, and that the Public School begat the vision of a liberal education expounded by Arnold and Newman, and that from this vision issues whatever traces of a humane love of learning for its own sake may still linger in our universities.

As an example of how imitation worked as a pedagogical method, we should look briefly at the poetry of the seventeenth century, especially the writing of John Milton. As an undergraduate English major, I found it hard to understand how Christian poets like John Donne and Robert Herrick (both Anglican clergymen) and Andrew Marvell (a minor official in the Cromwell government, and a vigorous advocate of the Puritan cause) could write such unabashedly sensual poems as "To His Mistress Going to Bed," "Corinna's Going A-Maying," and "To His Coy Mistress." But when as a graduate student I read Ovid, Catullus, and Horace, I finally understood what was going on in seventeenth century poetry. For these poems at least began as conscious imitations of Latin poems. Imitation, it seems, allowed respectable Christians to write passionately pagan poems—all in the guise of a "mere literary exercise." There are many other instances of imitation as a stimulus for composition during the Renaissance: a major example is the way a whole series of poets imitated the Petrarchan sonnet, testing, stretching, and finally transforming it in the process.

But John Milton was perhaps the supreme example of Imitation as a Way of Life. As Donald Clark long ago demonstrated in *John Milton at St. Paul's School: A Study of Ancient Rhetoric in English Renaissance Education* (1948), Milton's education was grounded upon the Aristotelian principle of learning through precept and imitation: "textbooks" consisted primarily of lists of precepts, and students read classical authors primarily to find models for their own writing. Students were expected to imitate not only the stylistic flourishes of their models but also methods of "proof and structural arrangement" (p. 167), and they were required to memorize, translate, and paraphrase texts in order to absorb the stylistic and structural qualities of these texts.

The effects of this educational system are apparent everywhere in Milton's poetry. His earliest verses are painfully self-conscious imitations not so much of the Latin elegiac poets as of Mantuan's Neo-Latin elegies; and he also wrote, in Italian, equally banal imitations of Petrarch's sonnets. But with "Lycidas" Milton's practice of inscribing his own texts over a series of prior texts became, not a symptom of artistic diffidence, but rather a powerful method of incorporating the past into the present and of making that past new. Indeed, Milton remade the pastoral elegy so completely that his poem has become the nexus of this poetic tradition. So too, Milton's deliberate imitation of Isocrates in his *Areopagitica* is by no means a mere academic affectation. Rather the act of imitation allowed Milton to reconceive the meaning of his own situation in revolutionary seventeenth century England—and indeed, to reconceive the meaning of history itself, for the *Areopagitica* has been a principal source of the characteristic modern vision of human life as a continual questing forward into the unknown. In all of his later poems, finally, we can see Milton consciously selecting a classical form (the Homeric/Virgilian epic in *Paradise Lost*, the "epyllion" in *Paradise Regained*, Sophoclean tragedy in *Samson Agonistes*, the Petrarchan sonnet in "Methought I saw my late espoused saint"), and then radically metamorphosing that form as he tests it against his own perceptions of the world—and, dialectically, also tests his own sense of the world against these formal structures.

The tradition of education-by-imitation survived long after Milton's time, but between the seventeenth and twentieth centuries the sense of imitation as a process of testing one's perceptions against another's model faded away. Rather in the rhetorical handbooks of the last three decades imitation does indeed become, as theorists like Knoblauch and Brannon have complained, a sterile and mechanical procedure. Consider, for example, the 1964 edition of Gerald Levin's once very popular *Prose Models*. Levin's text first surveys the "elements of the essay": "THE SENTENCE," with subsections on "Parallelism," "Balance," "Antithesis," etc., and then "THE PARAGRAPH," with subsections on the "Topic Sentence," "Main and Subordinate Ideas," "Definition," "Division and Classification," etc.—fourteen subsections in all, with each subsection including a brief example or two or three, usually fairly short paragraphs, followed by some "questions," then a writing assignment which asks the student to imitate the form of the paragraph or paragraphs that she has just read. For example, after reading passages by Francis Bacon, Sidney Hook, and Leslie White, which presumably illustrate the process of "Division and Classification," the student is told to "Write an essay discussing the different classifications under which Shakespeare's *Hamlet* or the gyroscope or Akron, Ohio, might be placed. Be sure that your classifications are mutually exclusive" (p. 76). Only now, after working through the various "elements" of the essay, does Levin's book finally arrive at "THE WHOLE ESSAY," where we learn of the "implicit" and the "explicit" thesis, etc., and where the student is invited to write imitations of these longer units of discourse.

Just down the shelf from Levin's book, I find Randall Decker's *Patterns of Exposition* (1966). Decker's book is a little more restrained than Levin's, for Decker focuses exclusively on "the whole essay": finds ten basic types of them, ranging from those that "illustrate ideas by use of Example," through those that "explain through Process Analysis" to . . . well, you can guess; asks the student a series of questions about these texts; and then mandates a composition using the "pattern of exposition" illustrated. The tone of these textbooks is a good bit grimmer than that of *De Copia*, for Erasmus apparently wants his students to play with words, while there isn't much sense of play in either Levin or Decker. But if the moderns see the goals of imitation somewhat differently than did the ancients, still ancients and moderns alike seem convinced of the efficacy of imitation as a pedagogical method.

Before this essay ends, I'll propose that all of us still have something to learn from the Aristotelian tradition. But if we are to recover what is of value in this tradition, we must first recognize that books like Levin's and Decker's, while preserving the mechanical procedures of an imitative pedagogy, have entirely lost touch with the spirit that impelled Milton to try to shape his own experience into the "classical" forms of epic, ode, etc.—and impelled him also to reshape these forms, to make the old new. There are dozens more of "rhetorics" designed more or less like *Prose Models* and *Patterns of Exposition.* Some begin with "the whole essay" and then work down to the sentence; others limit themselves to the various "types" of essays—"definition," "comparison and contrast," etc. But these variations are incidental, for all share three common qualities. First, all of them see the process of composition as essentially mechanical, a matter of selecting certain appropriate parts and putting them together in accordance with the "rules" of composition. Second, all of them see the choices which the writer makes as "value-free"; neither the commitments of the writer nor the values and beliefs of the audience should, these textbooks assume, affect the process of composition. (The silly "division and classification" assignment quoted above suggests the end result of this conception of discourse as "value-free.") Finally, all of the texts in question see the act of imitation as also mechanical: the values, beliefs, and commitments of the writers imitated are irrelevant: for it is the "form" of the exemplary texts, not their "content," that the student is asked to imitate—what Bacon or Sidney Hook says is, the student is told implicitly and sometimes explicitly, irrelevant. There is a direct line of descent from the imitative rhetoric of Aristotle to the imitative rhetoric of Levin and Decker. Yet Aristotle and Milton, both of them passionately concerned with the moral development of the human creature, would have found these technocratic twentieth century models of imitation impoverished if not positively vicious. Thus it is important to recognize that the rhetoric handbooks with which most of us grew up represent, not the triumph, but the ultimate decadence of the Aristotelian tradition.

II

Having withered into sterility, the imitative tradition has apparently, over the last two decades, quietly expired, for not many books like *Prose Models* have found their way into my mailbox during the last ten years. Something seems to have changed, and I think I know what. During the last twenty years, the precept-cum-example instructional methods which we see in the kind of handbook I've described above have come under vigorous attack from the New Rhetoricians, and the insurgents have routed Levin and Co., so that nowadays only very old-fashioned, habit-bound teachers are assigning books like *Prose Models.* Here as on many other issues Knoblauch and Brannon make explicit certain attitudes which in the writings of other New Rhetoricians sometimes remain implicit. Thus in *Rhetorical Traditions and the Teaching of Writing* Knoblauch and Brannon dismiss imitation

as one of the emptiest pedagogical procedures promulgated by the
Old Rhetoric:

> Just as there is no persuasion essay, no ideal text that all readers
> would characterize as persuasive on the basis of its properties,
> neither is there a a ready-made strategy for making writing per-
> suasive. . . . Both errors derive from the ancient habit of looking
> at existing texts, a collection of venerated works by poets,
> tragedians, great orators, and others, and then describing their
> characteristics in ways which implied that other writers should
> produce similar-looking discourses (1984a, p. 28).

And in a letter published in the October, 1984, issue of *College English*,
Knoblauch and Brannon suggest that the issue of modeling lies at the
heart of the struggle between the Old Rhetoric and the New. The pedagogy of the Old Rhetoric, they state,

> implies that form is a preconception, and that an inventory of
> suitable forms exists which writers learn as technical constraints
> and then apply, as ready-made structures, during the process of
> writing. The perspective [of the New Rhetoric] suggests that form
> is an achievement of the search for meaning, that it manifests the
> ability to think well in language . . . but does not precede the ef-
> fort to discover the intellectual and imaginative connections ar-
> ticulated as discourse. Two wholly distinct instructional emphases
> have evolved in response to these epistemological starting-points. . . .
> (1984b, p. 620).

The notion that there exist certain ideal forms of discourse and that
writers should be encouraged to shape their own discourse into accordance with these ideal patterns here becomes the central principle of
the Old Rhetoric. Conversely, for Knoblauch and Brannon at least, a
commitment to the New Rhetoric means, *ipso facto*, a rejection of
imitation as a pedagogical method.

In explicitly rejecting imitation as a pedagogical method, Knoblauch and Brannon carry to an extreme a widespread tendency among
the principal spokespersons for the New Rhetoric. Macrorie and Elbow,
for example, have never to my knowledge openly attacked imitation;
but neither do they discuss the potential uses of models in the writing
classroom, and almost all the pedagogical procedures which they recommend begin, not with the reading of exemplary texts, but with
free-writing. (A significant exception is the teaching of poetry, where
Elbow does recommend beginning with a model [1981, p. 112].) More
than Macrorie or Elbow, Ann Berthoff, whose pedagogy is philosophically the richest of the New Rhetorics, consistently emphasizes the relationship between reading and writing. Yet Berthoff too seems very

uneasy about imitation. In the last few pages of *Forming/Thinking/ Writing* (1978), Berthoff suggests that a student who has become "tired" of her own "voice" might try imitation. Berthoff then acknowledges that "the traditional way of teaching composition was to set a certain theme or topic and require students to compose in the manner of a master stylist whose essay on the same topic had been painstakingly analyzed," and she grants that this practice might have had some instructional value. But she immediately adds that "the topics were generally banal or 'irrelevant' and the distance between the student writer and Francis Bacon or Thomas Carlyle was often felt as a shameful fact" (pp. 222–223). The tone of this short paragraph, the only discussion of imitation I've found in Berthoff's writings, seems distinctly ambivalent, suggesting that this theorist, like other New Rhetoricians, sees imitation as belonging to an older pedagogy which she has rejected.

There are, it must be added, several modern rhetorical theorists who have spoken out in defense of imitation. Both Edward P. J. Corbett (1965) and Frank D'Angelo (1983) have attempted to reconceive classical rhetoric in such as way as to make it functional within the modern classroom, and in these neo-classical rhetorics imitation continues to occupy an honored place. For my purposes, however, it seems more significant that at least two well-known New Rhetoricians also seem willing to give imitation a significant role within their pedagogies. James Moffett hasn't said very much about the pros or cons of imitation, but his *Active Voice: A Writing Program Across the Curriculum* (1981) incorporates "collateral readings" along with every writing assignment, and these readings are chosen to give students examples of the kinds of writing that they are being asked to do. And William Coles also makes intermittent use of imitation in his *Composing* books (1974, 1981). Yet Moffett and Coles are, I think, the exceptions that prove the rule: and in this case the rule is that New Rhetoricians are generally very suspicious of imitation as a pedagogical method.

Why is the New Rhetoric so suspicious of imitation? The answer, I believe, lies in certain common assumptions generally shared by the New Rhetoricians. Some key terms of the New Rhetoric offer a useful clue to these assumptions. The first such term is "process"—along with its inevitable antithesis, "product." "Process" suggests change, fluidity, indeterminacy: all positive values in a society that has prided itself on its presumed freedom from fixed hierarchies, which admires "self-made" people, and which has throughout its history hymned the open road. "Product," on the other hand, connotes finality, determinacy: not an opening toward infinite possibility, but rather a search for prior "causes" which made just this outcome "inevitable." We don't want

our students to think of themselves as trapped—"finished," for better
or for worse. So we ask them to regard both themselves and their
writing as "on the road," "in process." In contrast, any exemplary text
that we offer them must necessarily be finished. Indeed, that's why
we are offering it to them. Here, we are implicitly saying, is where
a piece of writing can get to, here is a goal toward which you too
might strive. Insofar as the exemplary text is necessarily a "product,"
there would seem to be an inevitable tension between a process-
centered pedagogy and a reliance on imitation as a primary method
of instruction.

An examination of some other key terms of the New Rhetoric
carries us toward a similar conclusion. The New Rhetoric has generally
tried to turn "composition" back into a verb; thus Coles's "composing," or even—here is a phrase that tries to capitalize on a galaxy of
positive associations—the much discussed "composing process." The
New Rhetoric also likes to speak of writing as a process of "discovery"—as, in Ann Berthoff's memorable title, a "making of meaning."
Composing, making, discovery—all these words again emphasize action,
an unfolding of something still *in potentia*, a movement into the unknown. And once again the exemplary text at least seems to be finished, an object rather than an act, and—especially if it has become a
"classic"—all too well known. The insistence of Knoblauch and Brannon that the Old and New Rhetorics are fundamentally incompatible
thus may seem justified. If we celebrate "discovery," we must, it might
seem, reject "imitation." Conversely, to defend imitation is to reveal
oneself, it would seem, not merely as a closet Ciceronian, but as an
enemy of all green and growing things. And indeed, if the only alternative to Knoblauch and Brannon's version of the New Rhetoric is a
return to *Prose Models*, few of us would want to mount the barricades
in defense of the pedagogy of imitation. And yet . . . and yet . . . Is it
really that simple? Or is it possible that there are some other alternatives that we haven't yet recognized?

Like thousands of American writing teachers, I abandoned the
instructional methods encoded in books like *Prose Models* because I
was appalled by the empty, thoughtless writing which these methods
seemed not merely to permit but to encourage. It was, then, a failure
in my classroom practice which impelled me in search of an alternative
rhetorical theory, which I discovered in the writing of Peter Elbow
(the strongest personal influence on my teaching), Ann Berthoff (the
strongest theoretician among the New Rhetoricians), etc. Guided by
these mentors, I gladly learned to think of writing as a process of discovery, a making of meaning. And this way of thinking about writing
has in turn led me to develop some innovative pedagogical procedures
of my own, such as "loop-writing" sequences (Elbow) and "re-seeing"

exercises (Berthoff) for use in upper level and even graduate level literature classes. Nevertheless, I have not been able to forget how powerful a stimulus to literary invention the struggle to imitate ideal models proved to be, for writers like Milton and Shakespeare and Donne and Wordsworth and . . . . My lingering interest in imitation as a pedagogical procedure eventually led me to try out some imitation exercises in my writing classes, and they proved remarkably successful. The writing of students both in my composition and introductory creative writing classes regularly took on a new force and focus when I began the writing sequence by reading with them a powerful exemplary text. At this point I found myself in a state of cognitive dissonance, for the rhetorical theory which I had espoused apparently couldn't account for the success of this new (to me, but of course actually very old) pedagogical procedure. Indeed, this entire essay might be read as an attempt on my part to work through this dissonance. As I struggled with this issue, old certainties began to dissolve into questions, and I found that I could answer these questions only by rethinking the theoretic foundations of the pedagogies which I had learned from Elbow, Berthoff, and company.

III

Theoretic exploration, Kant and Marx agree, must begin with critique. And so I begin by asking a question of the New Rhetoric. What are we actually saying, if we declare that the student does not need an already written exemplary text, to guide her in her own writing? In effect, I think we are saying that the student already has within her everything she needs in order to write powerfully: that her intuitive powers will enable her to make the connections among the disjunct parts of her experience necessary to give her "something to say," and that her inherent impulse toward form will guide her to create a structure adequate to the meaning that she is trying to make. This vision of the writer seems to me noble, attractive, and liberating in many ways, but is also seems to be (and I am not using this word as a derogatory label, for I mean something quite specific by the term) profoundly *romantic. Rhetorical Traditions and the Teaching of Writing* spells out the romantic vision of the writer-at-work more explicitly than any other text I've read. Repeatedly, Knoblauch and Brannon contrast the New Rhetoric's conception of writing as a "creative activity" with the Old Rhetoric's obsession with "ceremonial decorum" (p. 57). The New Rhetoric conveys, they contend,

> as ancient rhetoric could not, a portrait of the mind in process, coming to understand its experience, and of composing as a process, manifesting the mind at work (p. 52).

Knoblauch and Brannon quote Cassirer at length, to buttress their argument that "discourse enacts the world: its knowledge is not 'about' the world but is rather constitutive of the world, the substance of experience, an explanation of the self" (p. 60). All writing, they declare, is a "making of meaning" (p. 60), a process which is "purposeful but unbounded" (p. 62), "not just a complex reciprocity among discrete operations, but an organic wholeness" (p. 64):

> Making verbal discourse, then, is a process of asserting connections among the ideas, impressions, images, bits and pieces of recollection or research, insights, fragmentary lines of reasoning, feelings, intuitions, and scraps of knowledge that comprise a person's experience of some subject (pp. 68-69).

*   *   *

> In other words, the central problem of composing is never finding something to say but rather finding a means of regulating, and eventually halting, the process of making connections (p. 69).

This process is constrained only by "the limits of a writer's intent and the increasingly insistent, emerging shape of the discourse" (p. 71). In sum, writing is "a vehicle for discovering new knowledge and thereby promoting personal growth" (p. 73). (Note the order of priorities here: even "new knowledge" exists to promote "personal growth.") I label Knoblauch and Brannon's vision of writing as "romantic" because it sees discourse as issuing out of an essentially autonomous self. Discourse "constitutes" the world, but it issues "from" a self which is, as it discourses, connecting its fragmented experiences into a whole that will be "organic," even as the self is "organic." And ultimately all discourse moves toward one goal: "personal growth." For to Knoblauch and Brannon, as to all romantics, the self constitutes the ultimate ground of being, the only certainty in a treacherous world, and the continuing growth of that self is the only absolute imperative.

Knoblauch and Brannon seek to ground their romantic vision of writing in certain "profound reorientations in Western epistemology" which have occurred "over the past 400 years" (p. 4). This reorientation began, they propose, with Descartes, and it has come to fulfillment in

> the gradual articulation of the concept of "symbolic representation," the organic coalescence of mind and nature through symbols, which began in Kant's *Critique of Pure Reason* and which has culminated in such generative twentieth-century statements as Ernst Cassirer's *Philosophy of Symbolic Forms*, Ferdinand de Saussure's *Course in General Linguistics*, and Alfred North Whitehead's *Process and Reality*, all arguing a way of thinking

about language, discourse, and knowledge which Susanne K. Langer, herself a major contributor to the theory of symbolic forms, has memorably termed "philosophy in a new key" (p. 51).

This is, beyond question, a resounding list of names. Yet in fact Knoblauch and Brannon have nothing much to say about Saussure or Whitehead, and I question whether these two names actually belong on this list. For Saussure's sense that language "speaks us" implies, as the Structuralists and Post-structuralists have agreed, a "decentering" of that very self which Knoblauch and Brannon treat as an absolute. And I am convinced (although some philosophers would disagree) that Whitehead's conception of each Nexus as constituted by the sum total of its relationships with a network of other Nexūs is also incompatible with a view of the self as an absolute ground of being.

We are thus left with Descartes, Kant, Cassirer, and Langer. I believe that Knoblauch and Brannon are quite correct in seeing the New Rhetoric as grounded in a tradition of thought represented by these four philosophers. At best, however, the thinkers in this list represent only half of the modern philosophical tradition. The usual name for this Cartesian/Kantian tradition is "Idealism." This term seems appropriate because all the philosophers in question inherit from Descartes an assumption that the "thinking self" constitutes an unquestionable "given," while everything else in the world is subject to doubt; and all these philosophers see the "real" as in some way constituted by the mind—in Kant by a universal "human" mind (for Kant is a child of the Enlightenment) and in Cassirer (for he was struggling to come to terms with history) by a mind that constitutes itself in culturally contingent forms. But in any case, all (and now I'll link and capitalize my two key terms) Romantic Idealists share a conviction that the "real" is constituted out of what Coleridge called the "shaping spirit" of the human mind.

And Kant begat Coleridge, and Coleridge begat I. A. Richards, and Richards begat Ann Berthoff. Berthoff seems to me far and away the subtlest, most philosophical of the New Rhetoricians. And reading Berthoff I am reminded on almost every page how profoundly Kantian and Neo-Kantian idealism has influenced the terms of discussion within the New Rhetoric. Berthoff begins by turning "form" into a verb; and "forming," the first term in Berthoff's rhetoric, is also the first term in Kantian epistemology. And when, at the end of the first chapter of *Forming/Thinking/Writing* (1978), Berthoff sums up the "philosophical foundations" of her pedagogy, her commitment to Kantian principles is clear:

> *The composing process by which we make meanings is a continuum. We don't take in the world like a camera or a set of recording*

devices. The mind is an agent, not a passive receiver; experience isn't poured into it. The active mind is a composer and everything we respond to, we compose (p. 43).

I don't find in the writings of Macrorie and Elbow equivalent statements of philosophic conviction, but in various ways these rhetoricians too reveal themselves to be Romantic Idealists. Both Macrorie and Elbow give free-writing a central place in their pedagogies; both also display a tendency to regard what students have learned from books as likely to prevent them from finding their own voices; and both find in free-writing a kind of energy (if often "raw" or "unfocused") generally lacking in the more "formal" writing their students produce. There are some differences between the two also—Elbow's pedagogy seems to me consistently more dialectical than Macrorie's. But the similarities I've enumerated suggest an admiration for untutored spontaneity that seems distinctly "Romantic." Further, Elbow and Macrorie share the "Idealist" assumption that there is a "natural" shaping power within the human mind. Free-writing, both rhetoricians assume, liberates this power, thereby allowing us to make organic connections between the disparate parts of our experience, connections that are somehow "truer" than the more mechanical linkages created by the conscious mind. Thus free-writing enables us to discover what we "really" want to say. Free-writing also, especially for Elbow, allows the voice of the "true" self to break through layers of false acculturation. Elbow's centering of "voice" in his most recent work (1981, pp. 281–313) clearly demonstrates the degree to which the assumptions of Romantic Idealism have pervaded the New Rhetoric. For what is the source of this "voice," if not some "deeper," more "authentic" self that is for Elbow, as for the New Rhetoric generally, the only ultimate certainty in a world of shifting appearances?

James Britton, perhaps the most influential rhetorical theorist now alive, provides my final example of the degree to which Romantic Idealism has shaped the thinking of the New Rhetoricians. Let us look first at the opening sentences of Britton's essay on "Language and Representation":

> From many diverse sources has come the idea, the hypothesis, that the importance of language to mankind lies not so much in the fact that it is the means by which we co-operate and communicate with each other as in the fact that it enables each of us, as individuals and in co-operation, to represent the world to ourselves as we encounter it: and so to construct—moment by moment and year after year—a cumulative representation of 'the world as I have known it' (1982, p. 88).

The either/or that Britton here sets up—communication or representation—seems to me neither necessary nor accurate. Rather, we might perhaps say that even as we communicate with one another, we are creating a collective representation of the world. Britton edges toward this position when he admits that we sometimes "represent" the world "as individuals and in co-operation." Yet even in this phrase he gives precedence to the "individual" representation. And in privileging representation over communication, he reveals his persistent tendency to see the personal and "inner" world as primary, the social and the public as secondary. Britton, furthermore, has encoded all the basic assumptions of Romantic Idealism into his famous model of the universe of discourse:

Transactional   Expressive   Poetic

The "expressive" mode, Britton tells us, stands in the middle because it is the matrix out of which the other two functions emerge (1975, p. 83). This privileging of the "expressive" makes clear Britton's assumption that human experience is first of all private, unformed. Further, this three-cell model again separates the "merely" instrumental modes (like the "essay") from the "poetic" modes which, unlike the "expressive," are "formed"—but which are formed, as Britton tells us elsewhere, "simply to please" the writer (p. 32), rather than to effect some change in the reader or in the writer/reader relationship. Language as a means of social interaction clearly is of secondary interest to Britton. And at many points in his writings Britton states the Romantic Idealist assumptions which lie behind his bias in favor of the personal. Here is an example, from "Shaping at the Point of Utterance":

> I want to associate spontaneous shaping, whether in speech or in writing, with the moment by moment interpretive process by which we make sense of what is happening around us; to see each as an instance of the pattern-forming propensity of man's mental processes. Thus, when we come to write, what is delivered to the pen is in part already shaped, stamped with the image of our own ways of perceiving. But the intention to share, inherent in spontaneous utterance, sets up a demand for further shaping (1982, p. 141).

The belief in a "pattern-forming propensity" inherent in the human mind stems, it should by now be clear, from Kant, perhaps by way of Langer. What makes Britton not only an Idealist but specifically a Romantic Idealist is his belief that this "pattern-forming propensity" works most freely and most creatively, "expresses" the individual's uniqueness most completely, when it operates "spontaneously," uncontaminated by any formal constraints or any concern with the needs of an audience. Britton is by no means indifferent to forms or to audience. He recognizes that an awareness of audience leads to "further shaping," and elsewhere in this same essay he states that once the child's creativity is at work, "his progress as a writer depends thereafter, to a considerable degree, on his increasing familiarity with forms of the written language, the enlargement of his stock of 'internalised' written forms through reading and *being read to*" (1982, p. 143). Yet, to Britton, the spontaneous "shaping power" of the human mind, a power most fully apparent in the child, is the foundation upon which all else rises; and this belief marks Britton too as a Romantic Idealist.

IV

The thinkers who have contributed to the development of the Romantic Idealist tradition in philosophy and rhetorical theory offer us much of practical value. However, it seems to me imperative that we see these thinkers as representing, not Philosophy Itself or Rhetoric Itself or Truth Itself, but rather one particular philosophical and/or rhetorical perspective. A discipline which has a lively tradition of theoretical discourse must at least tacitly recognize that each theoretical perspective constitutes a lens through which we may see the world. A theory is useful to the degree that it brings certain phenomena into focus, but in doing so any theory must inevitably leave other phenomena blurred, out of focus. At this point, therefore, having traced the history of the Aristotelian pedagogy of imitation through to its ultimate decadence, and having acknowledged the validity of the New Rhetoric's critique of that pedagogy, and then having defined the theoretic limits of the New Rhetoric itself, I'd now like to move toward a transcendance of the opposition between the Old Rhetoric and the New. What lies beyond the limits of Romantic Idealism? Is there an alternative to this tradition, other than a return to Aristotle?

I'd like to begin by invoking and placing myself within a tradition of modern thought which seems significantly richer than the Romantic Idealist tradition: the tradition of dialectical reflection which issues from Hegel, Kierkegaard, and Marx, and which has been carried on into the twentieth century by the American pragmatists (Mead and Dewey especially, but in many ways Burke himself belongs here), by successive generations of phenomenologists and phenomenological existentialists (Nietzsche, Husserl, Heidegger, Merleau-Ponty, Sartre, Ricoeur), by at least some Marxists (Vygotsky, Bakhtin, Lukacs, Adorno, Habermas), and by the French Structuralists and Post-Structuralists (Levi-Strauss, Lacan, Derrida). What do the thinkers in this dialectical tradition have in common, and how do they differ from the spokespersons for the Romantic Idealist tradition? First, the three founders of the dialectical line positioned themselves either in opposition to the static, ahistorical character of Kantian idealism (Hegel) or they rejected idealism itself (Kierkegaard, Marx). Instead these seminal thinkers saw the self and its shaping powers as grounded in something larger than itself: either in the dialectical processes of history (Hegel, Marx) or in an "existence" that refuses to be reduced to the categories of human reason (Kierkegaard).

Obviously there are some enormous differences among the three founders of the dialectical line, for both Kierkegaard and Marx began with vigorous critiques of Hegel, and many people in the 1950s saw Kierkegaard as representing an affirmation of "individualism" over against the "collectivism" of Marx. Yet the very act of critique implies a willingness to build upon the work of one's predecessors, and one crucial thread links Hegel to Kierkegaard and Marx and links all three to the various currents in twentieth century thought that I have alluded to: the dialectical method itself, a method which insists that we can never understand a phenomenon until we see it in relationship to and even in terms of its "other"; that "identity" is always "deferred," always a function of context and of process; that there is no absolute, no stable set of first principles upon which we can ground our thinking; and that if discourse is to be "true" it must of necessity be ironic (Kierkegaard, Marx, and Nietzsche are all constantly ironic writers, and Burke is our greatest twentieth century American ironist), thereby tacitly acknowledging its own limits, the ways in which it is grounded in all those "opposing" discourses which our own discourse has, for the moment, displaced.

In these respects this tradition of dialectical reflection and discourse stands in sharp opposition to the Romantic Idealist tradition, which would establish the Ego as an absolute: self-creating, self-grounded, and autonomous. Indeed, one of the major projects of the dialectical line, especially in recent years, has been a deliberate "decentering" of the self, a "deconstruction" of the self's claims to an absolute, "originary" "authenticity." These terms are all buzz-words of Structuralism and Post-Structuralism, but in committing themselves to such a decentering, these fashionable modern movements have only been continuing a project that began in the work of Hegel, Kierkegaard, and Marx.

If modern philosophy offers us an alternative (indeed, a whole galaxy of them) to Romantic Idealism, in rhetorical theory too we are by no means limited to a choice between an Old Rhetoric which would require us to swallow Aristotle whole and a New Rhetoric which would require us to see the autonomous individual as our only absolute. For example, Chaim Perelman's *The New Rhetoric* (1969) systematically attempts to redefine rhetoric not simply as a set of techniques for organizing our discourse but as a dynamic process of social interaction. Both Perelman and Stephen Toulmin (1964), furthermore, have tried to stake out a territory within which reasoned debate conducted according to socially sanctioned rules (both use the courtroom as a model) will be recognized as a valid means (indeed as our only available means) of arriving at truth. In this territory, as Toulmin in particular has demonstrated, we may observe how various "fields" of study establish—are, indeed, constituted by—an evolving consensus as to what constitutes a significant question or a persuasive argument. Discourse itself thus becomes, for Toulmin, essentially field-specific, rather than a product of autonomous individuals releasing their "innate" "shaping" powers.

Drawing on some of the same sources (Wittgenstein, Austin, Searle) which have shaped Toulmin's conception of argument, Stanley Fish (1980) has pressed the notion of a "community of discourse" about as far as it will go, arguing that any principle which the members of such a community can be persuaded to accept as true *is* true for that community, and that such context-specific truths are the only kind that we can know. Finally, and in many ways most usefully of all, Wayne Booth (1974), alarmed by what he saw as a breakdown of the rules of reasoned debate, and drawing in significant measure on Mead and Dewey (both of them in turn direct heirs of Hegel), has argued that the very concept of "rhetoric" implies a definition of the human being as above all a social creature. Booth, like Perelman, would go back to Descartes as the *fons et origo*—not of a "modern epistemology" which has, as Knoblauch and Brannon propose, rescued us from Aristotle—but rather of a dangerously misleading idea of the self. And for Booth, a redefinition of the human creature as "the rhetorical animal" offers us our best hope of salvation from the philosophical relativism and the moral egoism into which the Cartesian tradition has, in our time, finally degenerated (p. 134). From Booth's perspective, to speak at all is to admit one's membership in a community, and to accept the responsibility of speaking in a way that will sustain and advance that community. Given this tacit commitment to the community, we are free to disagree and debate, but always within limits established by that common commitment.

The rhetoric formulations of Perelman, Toulmin, Fish, and Booth all help to support the position I'm attempting to establish, insofar as all of them see discourse as first of all a social process, and individual creativity as occurring not in some magical place both logically and developmentally prior to our participation in the process of social interchange, but rather in the moment when an individual questions some communal consensus and then attempts to persuade the community to move toward this new way of looking at the matter at hand. However, while the general model of the interaction between the individual and the community that Booth *et al.* have sketched is acceptable, it has only a limited applicability to my own teaching. For these rhetoricians are chiefly concerned with the way interpretive questions get posed and debated, while as a teacher of writing, I'm more concerned with the way certain *forms* of discourse take on an aura of authority within a given discourse community, and the ways in which individual writers challenge and transform such normative structures.

I thus turn now from these implicitly dialectical thinkers to an explicitly dialectical thinker: Kenneth Burke, who has, I believe, come closer than anyone else to creating an adequate account of the ways in which our systems for encoding the world (whether formal structures or philosophical systems) pattern and constrain our discourse, and of the forces that cause one such symbol system to metamorphose into another, sometimes totally opposite, such system. In *Counter-Statement* (1931, rpt. 1968), Burke's first and most formalist book, he defines "form in literature" as "an arousing and fulfillment of desires" (p. 124). There are, he assumes, certain "invariant" patterns in human experience, and the pleasure we take in a literary text comes from living through one of these patterns as it is enacted, symbolically, by the movement of the text. However, in his next two books, *Permanence and Change* (1935, rpt. 1984) and *Attitudes Toward History* (1937, rpt. 1984), Burke tilted away from Freud toward Marx, and away from a formalist model of the way symbol systems work toward a dialectical model. As he did so, Burke became less interested in "eternal" patterns of experience and more interested in the ways in which "orientations" (*Permanence and Change*) or "acceptance frames" (*Attitudes*) emerge at certain historical moments out of our attempts to resolve the contradictions within those moments, and in the reasons why one such "orientation" or "frame" gives way to another, whether in one person's life or in the history of a civilization.

Burke's reflections on these issues assumed a definitive form in his great *A Grammar of Motives* (1945, prt. 1968), where he seeks to classify all possible formal structures and/or ideological systems as "featuring" one or another of the five terms in his "dramatistic pentad" ("act," for example, would be foregrounded in tragedy [p. 38] and in the great philosopher of tragedy, Aristotle [p. 227 ff.]): and where he proposes a theory of "dialectic in general" to explain how the very excesses of one orientation inevitably evoke a counter-orientation as a corrective. So a Romantic Idealism which foregrounded the agent (Kant in philosophy, the Wordsworthian lyric in literature) gave

way to a materialism which foregrounded the "scene" (Darwin, the
naturalistic novel). In the *Grammar*, Burke also proposes his own
dramatistic orientation as an ultimate "frame of frames," in that it
allows him to describe and accept the ongoing interplay of acceptance
frames and to relish the high comedy of it all—however momentarily
tragic the Death of God or of Communism or of "serious literature"
may feel to people who have invested their deepest commitments in
one or another of these ideologies or aesthetic structures.

Can we, building primarily on Burke's model of how symbol
structures emerge and pass away within history, develop a "Dialectical
Rhetoric" that will be faithful both to the ways in which the historical
moments into which we are born determine the symbol systems
through which we understand ourselves, and to the power of the individual human beings to unmake and remake these symbol systems?
I'd like to think that we can.* On the one hand, such a Dialectical
Rhetoric would reject the Old Rhetoric's insistence on seeing the forms
of discourse as eternal, ideal structures. Rather a Dialectical Rhetoric
will see such forms as historical phenomena, issuing out of specific historical circumstances and changing as those circumstances change: so,
for example, the romance and the confessional narrative merged at the
beginning of the bourgeois era, to give birth to the novel. Further, a
Dialectical Rhetoric will recognize that the forms of discourse are not
neutral "containers" into which any sort of content can be poured;
that rather, these forms are inherently ideological, encoding very particular stances toward the world.

On the other hand, a Dialectical Rhetoric will also reject both the
dream of recovering an "authentic," pre-social language which has
haunted our current New Rhetoric since its inception in the 1960s,
and the considerably older heritage of Romantic Idealism which has
consistently tried to find in the Self an unconditioned ground of being.
When Ann Berthoff observes that students should be allowed to "make
meaning" by linking the disparate parts of their lives, I'm willing to
agree. But a Dialectical Rhetoric allows me to see the forms in terms
of which my students "make meaning" as issuing, not out of some
"shaping" power presumed to be inherent in the human mind, but
rather out of the give and take of social interaction. Yes, the self forms
a world. But the self itself is formed by the world in which it finds

---

*Discussing some of these same tensions in contemporary rhetorical theory,
Richard Young (1980) has proposed that today "two conflicting conceptions" of rhetoric, one "classical" and the other "romantic," are available
to us, and he proposes that we must find some way of honoring the "deep
truths" in both these ways of thinking about rhetoric (pp. 59–60). I agree,
and I would also argue that a Dialectical Rhetoric offers us our best hope of
synthesizing the "classical" and the "romantic" strains in rhetorical theory.

itself. And this "world" in turn consists, not simply of "nature," but of a vast sea of symbol systems which have been collectively created by all the human beings who have preceded us upon this earth. Therefore I propose a *via media*: a rhetoric which will see the relationship between the antecedent form and the individual act of creation as truly dialectical, a breathing in of one or more exemplary texts, and a breathing out of something new, remade. In such a Dialectical Rhetoric the issue of imitation will obviously occupy a central place.

V

A dialectical perspective allows us to see imitation not simply as a mechanical reproduction of certain external patterns of organization but as a dynamic process in which the writer introjects and remakes formal structures. The moments of radical historical rupture, when an old form (like the Renaissance romance) metamorphoses into a new way of seeing and structuring the world (like the novel) are relatively rare. But even in a "normal" discourse situation (analogous to Kuhn's [1962] "normal science"), all writing enacts a tension between an internalized ideal model and the specific concerns working in the writer, and this tension shapes the specific form (as distinct from the generic "kind") of what that writer makes.

Evidence for this statement comes in part from literary history. Aristotle promulgated certain "rules" for the composition of a tragedy, based largely on a description of Sophocles' *Oedipus Rex*. And every subsequent writer of tragedy has had some knowledge of this Aristotelian model. Yet the post-Greek tragedies that still compel our interest—the Renaissance plays of Marlowe, Shakespeare, Webster, Corneille, and Racine, *Samson Agonistes*, a scattering of modern plays like *Death of a Salesman*—all depart in more or less extreme ways from the Aristotelian norm. Those Neoclassic critics who condemned Shakespeare and Co. for their "failure" to reproduce the ideal model are now universally recognized as foolish; yet it would be no less foolish to conclude (as some Neoromantic critics would like to do) that each text created by these playwrights is *sui generis*, and that the general label "tragedy" is merely a convenience. For what *King Lear*, for example, "is" emerges directly out of the tension between, on the one hand, a model of tragedy that filtered down to Shakespeare from translations of Seneca and from the plays of Marlowe and from whatever bits of critical writing he may have read and, on the other hand, the specific public and private motives that impelled him to write.

So too for those of us who aren't Shakespeare. Every time we set pen to paper we have some sense of what kinds of things it is possible for us to make, and usually we have some sense of what we want (or think we *should* want) to make. We have, that is, a model in our heads. I can't offer any empirical proof of this premise, any more than the New Rhetoricians can "Prove" that the human mind spontaneously "makes meaning." However, I can offer some introspective evidence in support of this premise, for I can say flatly that I have never engaged in "formless" writing which then turned into something "formed." Rather every poem or essay has first manifested itself as a "poem-intentionality" or an "essay-intentionality" which was present in my mind from the moment I started to write. Indeed I always start to write with an intent to make a certain *kind* of poem or essay—an "elegy," or a "dramatic monologue," or a "theoretic essay" like this one. Further, I would challenge any teacher to give me a truly "form-less" piece of student writing, or one in which the forming principles can be demonstrated to be purely intuitive—i.e., in which it can be proved that the writer had no previous experiential knowledge of any text in which these forming principles were operating. (Note: even "free-writing" is a form governed by certain rules, and people can "learn how to do it.")

I'm proposing, then, that none of us could write at all without having some sort of notion, however inchoate, of what sort of thing we are setting out to make. Yet I'm also proposing (and here is the wonder and joy of writing) that none of us ever actually makes that thing which we imagined that we were setting out to make. Once the pen is in motion, the pressures of the concrete situation in which we find ourselves, of our personal hopes and fears, begin to distort and expand or even explode that ideal text, transforming it (when we're lucky) into something rich and strange—or at any rate into the specific shape which it is possible for us to make, at that moment in our personal lives and in our collective history. Certainly this essay has a very different shape than it originally had in my mind. Such is, furthermore, what I see happening again and again in my students' writing.

If I am correct that when we set pen to paper we are always initially trying to write something which we have previously read, then perhaps some of the problems which we see in the classroom stem less from the perverse efforts of teachers to superimpose an "ideal text" on the work of their students than from the efforts of the students themselves to write in accordance with inappropriate or empty models. For example, I came to the New Rhetoric primarily because of the appalling amount of "Engfish" that my students were generating Macrorie and Elbow offered an initially plausible explanation of this phenomenon. My students were writing Engfish because I was forcing them to conform to mechanical models of "correct" structure, rather than inviting them to make their own connections and to generate their own forms out of these connections. And indeed, when I encouraged my students to free-write, they *did* write more fluently and with more verve than previously.

Yet their free-writing didn't evolve "naturally" toward forceful, lively essays. On the contrary, when I suggested that a student might turn this or that collection of free-written bits into an essay, she would almost always revert to Engfish. (The ones who didn't weren't writing Engfish in the first place.) When I asked my students why they reverted to such empty, stilted modes of discourse, I learned that they believed that essays *should* sound like they had been written by someone two hundred years old and fifty feet tall (Coles, more or less). Since I hadn't told my students anything of the sort, I found myself wondering where they had picked up their presuppositions about "essays." Well, I have learned from experience that if you ask a college freshman to write a poem, she will write something that sounds like the only sort of poetry she has internalized: i.e., the lyrics of the pop/rock songs she has been listening to. And if you ask her to write a story, she will probably try to write something more or less like the TV shows she has been watching. And if you ask a student to write an essay, she will imitate . . . what? Usually, I suspect, she will model her writing on the kind of expository prose that she knows best: the language of the textbooks that her teachers have been handing her for twelve years or so. (Many of my students have, quite literally, never read anything but such textbooks.) Engfish, it seems, is what happens when students try to sound like textbooks.

We all have a pretty good idea of the kind of writing we'd like to get from our students: we want writing that will be analytically rigorous yet specific, firmly grounded in personal experience yet able to move out toward general inferences. Yet shouldn't we consider the very real probability—at least this is true of us who teach in public universities—that *most of our students have never read writing like that*? So when we moan, "Be more concrete," they really don't know what we're talking about, for they certainly haven't read any writing in their textbooks that is "concrete," in our sense of the word. Of course, they've read a few short stories in their English classes. But we're not asking for stories: we're asking for essays, and the very word itself seems to invite a kind of language that derives, I suspect, mostly from a seventh grade social studies textbook. If so, then we get Engfish from our students not because we've given them too many models but because we haven't given them *enough* models, or because we've given them the wrong *kinds*. It would follow that if we are going to get our students to stop writing Engfish, we need to give them lots more models—models that will open up their sense of the formal possibilities available to them when they sit down to write.

In accordance with the principle here proposed—i.e., that all writing begins as an attempt to create something more or less like something the writer has read—I now try in my own classes to begin each
writing sequence by reading with my students (usually aloud) a text
or two which can serve as models of the kind of writing that I am asking them to do. The texts I select are models not so much of "correct"
"patterns" of "organization" as of certain ways of engaging experience.
For instance, in the freshman level Introduction to Creative Writing
class, the semester begins with the assignment of an autobiographical
narrative about "an experience which changed my view of the world
or of myself." On the day this is assigned, I bring to class xeroxed
copies of George Orwell's "Shooting an Elephant" and Maya Angelou's
"Graduation Day." We read these texts aloud, going slowly around the
circle, each student in turn reading a paragraph. My goal here is simply
to give the students an opportunity to absorb the amplitude of these
texts, the way they evoke a sense of place and of character through
the sheer number of details they offer us. I also want the students to
experience a sense of anticipation and suspense: that odd combination
of hunger for the climax and love of the journey for its own sake which
all good narrative evokes. After we finish reading, students are encouraged to abstract some usable principles from these narratives: the ways
Orwell and Angelou establish a context and then focus on a brief (a
few hours at most) period of time; the ways in which the authors with-
hold information to build suspense; the ways they articulate the
"themes" of their stories; etc. All this usually takes a full class period.
At the end of the period I invite the students to set to work on their
own narratives, urging them to use Orwell and Angelou not only as
examples of "how to do it" but also as standards of a serious *engage-
ment* with a subject.

In this same class, I also begin each poetry writing sequence by
asking the students to read aloud an exemplary poem. For example,
we will hear three or four readings of Pound's "The River Merchant's
Wife: A Letter," and then I'll invite the students to write a letter poem.
Here again the point isn't to ask students to imitate a specific organizational structure—the sonnet or whatever. I'm more concerned with
helping them grasp what I would call "rhetorical forms" (such as the
personal letter, which encodes a certain specific kind of reader/writer
relationship) and with recognizing possibilities that may not have previously occurred to them (that a "poem" can also be a "letter"). But
I don't limit this practice of "writing from models" to the creative
writing class. In teaching composition, I use model essays selected by
the same criteria and presented in much the same way as the model
texts in the creative writing class. And even in upper level and graduate
literature classes, I have recently resolved never to assign a "critical

essay" without first giving the students some examples of powerful writing about literature. I incorporate models in all of these classes because I have come to recognize that even in a graduate literature class my students have often *never seen* an example of the kind of writing that I'm asking them to do, and so are mystified (though they don't dare say it, for fear of sounding stupid) when they're asked to write a "critical essay," or whatever.

I don't claim any particular originality for any of the writing assignments described above. Yet I will claim that they work: I could, if space permitted, offer dozens of examples of exciting student prose elicited by these assignments, all of them rich in "voice," all of them both shapely and inventive. Further, I don't find in recent discussions of rhetorical theory a satisfactory explanation of why such assignments work: thus the decision to write this essay. And I also suspect that many other writing teachers currently find themselves in a situation rather like mine: these teachers have been using assignments like the ones described above, but they haven't had a theoretic rationale for what they were doing, and therefore they have often felt uneasy— especially when confronted by passionate advocates of the New Rhetoric. Actually, teachers who use models have ample precedent on their side, for the life history of every writer that we know anything about suggests that we all learn to write primarily through the kind of imitation described here. So Milton found his voice by imitating Virgil, and Keats by imitating Spenser and Milton, and William Carlos Williams by imitating Keats, and Emily Dickinson by imitating Protestant hymns and Emerson's essays, and Willa Cather by imitating Sarah Orne Jewett, etc., etc.

But in the absence of an adequate theory to explain why imitation is such a powerful tool or how it works, we have in recent years oscillated between the Scylla of a decadent Aristotelianism which tells us that we should be giving our students models of texts that exemplify certain presumably all-purpose "rules" of composition, and the Charybdis of a Romantic Idealism which has been telling us that the "natural" shaping powers of our students give them everything they need to write. I hope that the Dialectical Rhetoric sketched out here will encourage teachers to resist those voices of dogmatism that surround us on all sides. For as teachers, we have a professional responsibility to deny our students neither the exemplary texts they need to start them on their way nor the freedom to reform these models into shapes which will allow these young writers to say what needs to be said, here, now.

Finally, a Dialectical Rhetoric should allow us to preserve what is still of value both from the Old Rhetoric and from the New. As a theory, as is probably clear by now, the Old Rhetoric seems to me indefensible, not only because it saw the forms of discourse as static and eternally frozen, but also because it established hierarchies of discourse forms (privileging epic over romance, tragedy over comedy, the essay over the letter and the journal) which were implicitly elitist, sexist, and racist. Yet the Old Rhetoric did at least insist that the genres of discourse have a social import: that they are in effect the verbal counterparts of social institutions, structuring our verbal actions in the same way that social institutions structure other kinds of actions; and that such social and verbal forms are *real*, pre-existing our short lives and remaining after we are gone. And if we judge the Old Rhetoric less by what its advocates thought they were doing—training people to reproduce those "perfect" formal patterns—than by the way their pedagogical practice actually affected the writing of people like Shakespeare and Milton, then maybe it wasn't so destructive after all.

On the other hand, while as a theory Romantic Idealism also seems to me impoverished and ultimately untenable, I believe that many of the specific strategies and techniques developed by the New Rhetoricians can find a place within a Dialectical Rhetoric. For instance, I continue to use free-writing in all of my classes, although I have come to believe that free-writing is of most value to experienced writers who have deeply internalized certain rigid formal patterns such as the five paragraph theme, and who need to loosen up these structures. Further, the concern of the New Rhetoricians with small group work and other interactive pedagogical strategies seems to me fully compatible with a Dialectical Rhetoric. I also continue to find much of value in Peter Elbow's sense of a dialogic relation between an inner voice (which "generates") and a socially shaped voice (which "edits"), although I would see that "inner" voice as no less a product of social experience than the "editing" voice. I would also like to preserve Ann Berthoff's conception of revision as a process of reseeing and reshaping, although I would want to open out this process beyond the individual's progressive "reseeing" of her personal world, to encompass the ongoing, collective reseeing in which we are cooperatively engaged. My admiration for the pedagogical inventiveness of Elbow and Berthoff, indeed, remains boundless.

But in the end, if our pedagogy is to remain flexible and inventive we must be willing to "resee" our own theories too. Thus I hope that the Dialectical Rhetoric proposed in this essay will help us to accept the historically contingent character of our thinking, to recognize that even the best of theories is only a sandbar in the river of time: even as we cling there hoping for a moment of rest, history is already eroding our most certain truths. And with this recognition, as Kenneth Burke has known best of all, epistemology and metaphysics must themselves give way to rhetoric, which is, we are again and again forced to recognize, the vehicle of the only truth we can know.

References

Aristotle. [*The rhetoric of Aristotle.*] (1932). (L. Cooper, Ed. and Trans.) Englewood Clifs, NJ: Prentice-Hall.

Berthoff, A. E. (1978). *Forming/thinking/writing: The composing imagination.* Rochelle Park, NJ: Hayden.

Booth, W. C. (1974). *Modern dogma and the rhetoric of assent.* Notre Dame: University of Notre Dame Press.

Britton, J. (1975). *The development of writing abilities (11–18).* London: Macmillan.

_____. (1982). *Prospect and retrospect.* Montclair, NJ: Boynton/Cook.

Burke, K. (1968). *Counter-statement.* Berkeley: University of California Press.

_____. (1968). *A grammar of motives.* Berkeley: University of California Press.

_____. (1984). *Attitudes toward history* (3rd ed.). Berkeley: University of California Press.

_____. (1984) *Permanence and change* (3rd ed.). Berkeley: University of California Press.

Coles, W. E. (1964). *Composing.* Rochelle Park, NJ: Hayden.

_____. (1981). *Composing II.* Rochelle Park, NJ: Hayden.

Corbett, E. P. J. (1971). *Classical rhetoric for the modern student* (2nd ed.). New York: Oxford University Press.

D'Angelo, F. J. (1983). Imitation and the teaching of style. In P. L. Stock (Ed.), *fforum.* Upper Montclair, NJ: Boynton/Cook.

Decker, R. E. (1966). *Patterns of exposition.* Boston: Little, Brown.

Elbow, P. (1981). *Writing without teachers.* New York: Oxford University Press.

_____. (1981). *Writing with power.* New York: Oxford University Press.

Elyot, T. (1962). *The book called the governor.* New York: Dutton.

Erasmus, D. [*On copia of words and things*] (1963). (D. B. King and H. D. Rix, Eds. and Trans.) Milwaukee: Marquette University Press.

Fish, S. (1980). *Is there a text in this class?* Cambridge: Harvard University Press.

Knoblauch, C. H. & Brannon, L. (1984). *Rhetorical traditions and the teaching of writing.*

_____. (1984). C. H. Knoblauch and Lil Brannon respond. *College English, 46,* 618–620.

Kuhn, T. (1962). *The structure of scientific revolutions.* Chicago: University of Chicago Press.

Levin, G. (1964). *Prose models: An inductive approach to writing.* New York: Harcourt, Brace.

Macrorie, K. (1976). *Telling writing* (2nd ed.). Rochelle Park, NJ: Hayden.

Moffett, J. (1981). *Active voice: A writing program across the curriculum.* Montclair, NJ: Boynton/Cook.

Perelman, C. & Olbrechts-Tyteca, L. (1969). *The new rhetoric: A treatise on argumentation.* Notre Dame: University of Notre Dame Press.

Plato. [*The Collected Dialogues*] (E. Hamilton and H. Cairns, Eds.). Princeton, NJ: Princeton University Press.

Toulmin, S. E. (1958). *The uses of argument.* Cambridge: Cambridge University Press.

Young, R. (1980). Arts, crafts, gifts, and knacks: Some disharmonies in the new rhetoric. In A. Freeman and I. Pringle (Eds.), *Reinventing the rhetorical tradition.* Conway, AR: University of Central Arkansas (L and S Books).

Reading, Writing, Interpreting

4

Wandering: Misreadings, Miswritings, Misunderstandings

DAVID BARTHOLOMAE

University of Pittsburgh

To read is to play the role of a reader and to interpret is to posit an experience of reading. This is something that beginning literature students know quite well but have forgotten by the time they get to graduate school and begin teaching literature. When student papers refer to what "the reader feels here" or what "the reader then understands," teachers often take this as a spurious objectivity, a disguised form of "I feel" or "I understand," and urge their charges either to be honest or to omit such references. But students know better than their teachers here. They know it is not a matter of honesty. They have understood that to read and interpret literary works is precisely to imagine what "a reader" would feel and understand. To read is to operate with the hypothesis of a reader, and there is always a gap or division within reading.

Jonathan Culler

But learning is not, of course, merely a matter of learning about, nor is it simply a process whereby a student becomes assimilated into his culture. It is primarily the action whereby a student learns who he is in relation to something outside himself.

Roger Sale

I

Let me begin with an anecdote, a cautionary tale. I walk into my class, an entry-level reading and writing class, and begin with what has become a standard exercise by turning to a book I have assigned, in this case Richard Rodriguez's *Hunger of Memory*. This is a very teachable book—well-suited, in its way, for a composition class. Rodriguez

89

becomes himself a metaphor through which my students can organize and think about their own experience with education, moving from one world to another, finding in the contradictions of his experience a way of talking about, of inventing even, the contradictions in their own.[1] It's a teachable book also, however, because Rodriguez's prose resists quick summation or any easy reduction to a "main idea." It requires application, extension, interpretation—not just summary. It has the grace to ask more of a reader, that is, than assent or affirmation. There is more for a reader to do than admire the author's wit and wisdom. It doesn't propose answers to all the questions it raises. It poses problems that the author has not already solved. It's a hesitant, tentative, contradictory text and, as such, it posits a role for a reader or writer that my students would not (or could not) imagine on their own.

I walk into my class, ask my students to turn to a passage I've chosen the night before, and I read it to them aloud. It's a difficult passage because it pushes against the available language of daily life— it talks about a moment when Rodriguez read Hoggart's *The Uses of Literacy,* cites a passage from that book, and talks about how that reading (Rodriguez's reading of Hoggart) gave a "shape to desire." I read the passage aloud and ask my students, "What does this say?" Not, "What does this mean?" but "What does this say?" And there is silence. I wait, as I have learned to do, since this is not a silence, I think, that a teacher should fill, not if he wants to teach composition. I wait until I pick one student from the class: "Kevin, what does this say?" And again there is silence. Although this time the student is looking at the passage, reading it over and over to himself, as if waiting for it to speak. I wait again until Kevin is forced to speak himself for the passage, and he says what he can, beginning first, however, by reading part of the passage verbatim out loud, reading back to me what I have already read to him.

I'm interested in this silence and what it can be said to represent, and I'm interested in the moment when a student breaks that silence to speak. Gadamer, in *Philosophical Hermeneutics,* said that

> The understanding of a text has not begun as long as the text remains mute. But a text can begin to speak. (We are not discussing here the conditions that must be given for this actually to occur.) When it does begin to speak, however, it does not simply speak its word, always the same, in lifeless rigidity, but gives ever new answers to the person who questions it and poses ever new questions to him who answers it. To understand a text is to come to understand oneself in a kind of dialogue. This contention is confirmed by the fact that the concrete dealing with a text yields understanding only when what is said in the text begins to find

expression in the interpreter's own language. Interpretation belongs to the essential unity of understanding. One must take up
into himself what is said to him in such a fashion that it speaks
and finds an answer in the words of his own language.[2]

To read this passage as I would read it (and as I present it to begin a
discussion of the conditions that must be given for understanding to
occur), you have to take the "answer" in the last sentence—that answer a student finds in the words of his own language—as the answer
in a dialogue (where someone speaks and another "answers") and not
as the "answer" to a question or a problem, the answer to a question
like, "What does this passage mean?" Understanding, then, is not an
act of recognition but something that is initiated by a response and
justified by the elaboration or extension of that response.

The textbooks say, "Find the author's main idea, look to see how
he supports it, look for transitions, look up the difficult words." But
this advice has little bearing on Kevin's problem. Kevin, I think, felt
more like a trespasser than a trailblazer, so it isn't much use to tell
him to think of reading as an organized search in difficult terrain. The
"real event of understanding," to return to Gadamer's words, "goes
beyond . . . methodical effort and critical self-control." It isn't really
we ourselves who understand, he says, "it is always a past that allows
us to say, 'I have understood.'" The real event of understanding, in
other words, is the effort to justify or account for (and usually by
speaking or writing) a position we have taken by speaking over or
against the words of an author who gave us our beginning. Kevin's
problem, in a sense, comes when he must put that passage aside and
speak in turn, not when he looks at it and reviews the words on the
page. At the end of his silence, Kevin says to me in class:

> It's like when Rodriguez knew that he was like a scholarship boy,
> like Hoggart says he was, reading all those books and doing good
> in school to please his teachers and not for himself. And he thinks
> Hoggart is wrong because it was more then that but when he
> thinks about himself as a scholarship boy he gets that part of
> himself fenced in. Hoggart is right but Rodriguez has to figure
> out how he's wrong.

And it is my job, then, to resist any desire I might have to say, "Yes,
that's right," or "No, that's not it," and to answer only with one of
the classroom versions of "So what?": "So why is this interesting?"
"So what does this have to do with the 'shape of desire'?" "Why
'fenced in'?" "What can you make of the fact that you say Hoggart
was both right and wrong for Rodriguez?" "So what can you say, then,
about *Hunger of Memory* or about education or about teachers or
about Rodriguez's relations with his parents or about Rodriguez as a
reader?"

My role as a teacher, in other words, is to insist that the student re-imagine a past that will allow him to say, "I have understood." Gadamer says that this experience of reading is felt as enrichment and not as a loss of self-possession. I'm not so sure. Even if we both respect it, I think Kevin and I are aware of the violence in what we have done.

II

One must take up into himself what is said to him in such a fashion that it speaks. I want to insist in my paper that the act of interpretation begins in that first act of speaking—speaking for a text—and that the problems of interpretation can be represented by the problems represented in that initial act of aggression and translation, the moment when a student breaks the silence and gives priority to his words over the words spoken by another, in this case Richard Rodriguez, a man who speaks very well, who has written a book, a book that was assigned in a class, a book whose priority, whose right to speak, has been well established. To speak, then, my student Kevin had to do what by rights he knew he shouldn't do; he had to assume an authority that wasn't his—at least not yet.

The silence, then, could be said to be an act of respect, not a failure of understanding or an inability to comprehend, but a clear and subtle understanding of a difficult and problematic situation. For my student to speak, he would have to replace or displace the language of the text with his own language. His first response was to give the text back to me verbatim—in other words, to give me a *literal* reading (and this is the only way I can understand the concept of a literal reading, as a literal re-speaking of the words on the page—any other act of speech would be an interpretation, a recomposition of what Rodriguez had to say about Hoggart and the "shape of desire"). And if he could not give me back the words he was hesitant to displace, what could he give me? The silence, I suspect, was an attempt to find that language as well, a language that was not immediately available to him. Gadamer would say that this language was his, but I think it is more likely mine or his freshman's version of my language, or the language of the institution I represent, the sanctioned, official discourse that speaks through me, try as I might to displace it when I speak for Rodriguez. That is the language Kevin could not find ready-made, although he showed that he could appropriate a version of it, an approximation. And that was what I was insisting on when I waited and wouldn't let the class progress until he spoke. When he spoke he offered what he could—a misreading. The version of Rodriguez he offered was not what Rodriguez wrote, just as his version of my language for Rodriguez was not what I would have said.

Interpretation thus begins with an act of aggression, a displacement, an attempt to speak before one is authorized to speak, and it begins with a misreading—a recomposition of a text that can never be the text itself speaking. If you accept this scenario, then the problems for a student reader are considerable—and they are not, or at least not solely, cognitive. I am presenting reading and writing as a struggle within the languages of our contemporary life. A classroom performance represents a moment in which, by speaking or writing, a student must enter into a closed community, with its secrets, codes and rituals, and the drama of this is as intense and telling as the drama of a student's internal cognitive processes. The student has to appropriate or be appropriated by a specialized discourse, and he has to do this as though he were easily and comfortably one with his audience, as though he were a member of the academy and, of course, he is not. He has to invent himself as a reader and he has to invent an act of reading, by assembling a language to make a reader and a reading possible, finding some compromise between idiosyncracy, a personal history, and the requirements of convention, the history of an institution. George Steiner said,

Through language, so much of which is focused inward to our private selves, we reject the empirical inevitability of the world. Through language, we construct what I have called "alternities of being." To the extent that every individual speaker uses an idiolect, the problem of Babel is, quite simply, that of human individuation. But different tongues give to the mechanism of "alternity" a dynamic, transferable enactment. They realize a need of privacy and territoriality vital to our identity. To a greater or lesser degree, every language offers its own reading of life. To move between languages, to translate . . . is to experience the almost bewildering bias of the human spirit towards freedom.[3]

While I want Steiner to speak for me here, I would have to put freedom in brackets in that last sentence, since it could be argued, and I think in the same spirit of hope, that the experience of translation is the experience of the "bewildering bias of the human spirit" towards captivity. A translation is also a loss, a displacement of the original, a definition of oneself in terms of another or in another's terms. Or, as Culler said in the passage from *On Deconstruction* that stands at the head of this essay, "To read is to operate with the hypothesis of a reader, and there is always a gap or division within reading."[4]

I'll turn soon to some essays students have written in response to *Hunger of Memory* and Plato's *Phaedrus*. All of these will be essays from the beginning of a semester. My goal, that is, will be to look over

the terrain and not to defend a curriculum or to celebrate its heroes.[5]
I'll be arguing that these essays, as they represent readings, are neither
right or wrong but approximate. They are, that is, evidence of a discourse that lies between what I might call the students' primary discourse (what they might write about *Hunger of Memory* were they
not in my class, or any class, and were they not imagining that they
were in my class, or any class—if you can imagine any student doing
any such thing) and the language of the official, English class essay
(which is imaginable but impossible to find). The students' essays are
evidence of a discourse that lies between these two hypothetical poles.
The writing is limited as much by the students' ability to imagine
"what might be said" as it is by a lack of information or anything
that could be identified solely as a "reading" problem. The act of
writing takes students from where they are and allows them to imagine something and somewhere else. The approximate discourse, then,
is evidence of change, a change that, because we are teachers, we call
"development" or "growth." I wouldn't want to suggest that it is
progress toward Truth or Reason or a clearer mind.

The systems we produce, teachers as well as students, are all
always approximate. I never say, alas, what I would hope to say—or
to put it another way, everything I write suggests its own possibilities
for revision. Nor can I say at any point with precision what belongs to
me and what belongs to my branch of the profession—or to put *this*
another way, the use of quotation marks and the placement of foot-
notes is arbitrary. I know, because I know the rhetoric, what I can
offer as mine and what I must attribute to someone else or place in
some context other than my own sentence, but these lines of demar-
cation are part of the fiction of scholarship and the rules that govern
these decisions are mysterious and unspoken, which is why beginning
students have such a terrible problem with citation, quotation and
paraphrase. One way of describing our students' need is to say that
they are people who need to learn to extend themselves, by successive
approximation, into the commonplaces, set phrases, rituals and gestures,
habits of mind, tricks of persuasion, obligatory conclusions and necessary connections that determine "what might be said" and constitute
knowledge within the various branches of our academic community.
This, at least, would make them citizens in good standing.

Some students can take their place with little pushing and shoving.
When Jonathan Culler says, "the possibility of bringing someone to see
that a particular interpretation is a good one assumes shared points of
departure and common notions of how to read," he is acknowledging
that teaching has had to assume that students, to be students, were already to some degree participating in the structures of reading and
writing that constitute (here) English Studies.[6] Stanley Fish tells us

"not to worry" that students will violate our enterprise by offering idiosyncratic readings of standard texts:

> The fear of solipsism, of the imposition by the unconstrained self of its own prejudices, is unfounded because the self does not exist apart from the communal or conventional categories of thought that enable its operations (of thinking, seeing, reading). Once we realize that the conceptions that fill consciousness, including any conception of its own status, are culturally derived, the very notion of an unconstrained self, or a consciousness wholly and dangerously free, becomes incomprehensible.[7]

He, too, is assuming that students, to be students (and not "dangerously free") must be members in good standing of the community whose immediate head is the English teacher. It is interesting that his parenthetical catalogue of the "operations" of thought ("thinking, seeing, reading") excludes writing, since it is only through written records that we have any real indication of how a student thinks, sees and reads. Perhaps "real" is an inappropriate word to use here, since there is certainly a "real" intellectual life that goes on independent of writing. Let me say that thinking, seeing and reading are valued in the academic community only as they are represented by extended, elaborate written records. (Class participation, in other words, will get you little more than a plus or a minus.)

Writing, I presume, is a given for Fish. It is the card of entry into the closed community that constrains and excludes dangerous characters. The real danger, of course, is not to the English profession but to its students, those whose "communal or conventional" habits of thought threaten to keep them on the outside, somewhere in the borderland between home and school. We can improve education if we put our critical skills to the test and learn to pay attention to those acts of reading and writing that are neither here nor there.

Let me return, for the last time, to my opening anecdote. I have another way of accounting for Kevin's silence—this time to say that it represents shame. Kevin, like all of my students, equates comprehension with memory, and he is haunted, as they are haunted, by the recognition that he cannot remember all of what he has read, whether it be a passage of half a page or a book of 300 pages. And if he cannot remember it all, what he does remember, he suspects, is the very stuff he should have forgotten—material remembered arbitrarily, by chance, or perversely, because he was paying attention to the wrong things.

Frank Kermode, in *The Genesis of Secrecy*, speaks of forgetfulness, but he speaks of it as an inevitable element in a successful reading—inevitable in that we all must forget, and successful in that it puts the burden of coherence—of accounting for the appropriateness of what we remember—where it belongs, on the person who is recomposing the text. The desire to remember everything is not only obsessive, if achieved it would be madness. "A text with all its wits about it would see and hear and remember too much."[8] And a reader with "all his dull wits about him," the reader who would literally recall a text, would never be able to misread and would therefore be able to speak only the same text back to itself. The concern for getting the right meaning, for memory, a concern at the center of most reading labs and study skills centers, puts students in an impossible position.

To be a good reader is to misread. The paradox is more than an amusing puzzle. Our students are bound by the model of reading they carry to the act of reading. It's the metaphors that a teacher should pay attention to, not reading "skills" (whatever they might be). Their obsessive concern over the fact that they don't remember everything they read, their concern to dig out the right answers, their despair over passages that seem difficult or ambiguous, all of these are symptoms of a misunderstanding of the nature of texts and the nature of reading that must be overcome if students are to begin to take charge of the roles they might play in a university classroom.

The language of reading instruction, like the language of writing instruction, is loaded with images of mastery and control. A writer begins with a controlling idea. A reader finds a main idea and follows it. The practice of reading and writing, however, is nothing like this. Mastery and control, if they come at all, come late in the game. We never know what we've read until we are forced to perform as readers—as though we know what we've read—and we face all those occasions (lectures, tests, papers) with that sense of anxiety, that doubt whether we can pull it off, that is evidence of the fact that comprehension isn't something we possess but something we perform.

When I began studying the problem of student reading by looking at student writing, I was concerned with two things: with the ways students textually established their authority as readers—their right to speak—and with the ways they located, arranged and accounted for the points they were willing to call "significant" in what they read. The assigning of significance is, in a sense, an act of naming, perhaps the most basic act of naming for any reader, since it precedes any attempt to describe, categorize, elaborate or generalize. Significance may be attributed to a text ("What would you say is the central point in this chapter?" or "What point is the author making?"), to an individual reader ("What strikes you as significant in what you've read?"), or to a situation or a project ("Given the essays you've read and the essays you've written on what happens when a person becomes 'educated,' what strikes you as significant in *Hunger of Memory*?") Each act organizes a text in a different way, causes passages that were silent to suddenly speak, or passages that spoke loudly to move into the general undersound of a chapter. It is the place where the press of the competing demands of convention and idiosyncracy are most strongly and illustratively felt.

When I talk about locating significance, then, I'm not talking about a student's ability to find a topic sentence. Nor am I talking about memory, at least not a memory for what a text said. It is more a matter of remembering what was not there, or remembering an agenda that exists functionally only after its opening stages have been revealed—an agenda that accounts for and is revealed by the check marks we put on the page, the books we pulled from the shelves while wandering around the stacks in the library, the passage that caught our eye as we leafed through the *Phaedrus*.

III

Let me look now at some written records of students' reading. As I said earlier, these essays were written in response to the *Phaedrus* and to *Hunger of Memory*. In every case these are students who would not be said to be "good readers." They don't, that is, step easily into the conventional discourse that characterizes good reading in a university class. If we look patiently and sympathetically at what they do—at their version of a reader reading—we can get a better sense of the nature of the task that is expected of them and at the problems of transition that are, at once, problems of reading, writing and teaching.

I'm interested in those moments in a text that students take to be significant and I'm interested in the ways they establish their authority to speak. A student, I've said, must act to displace the words of a text with his own. Let me put this in more immediate terms: a student must find a way of writing about the *Phaedrus* to put Socrates aside, to put him on hold, to make him silent while another speaks. (In most cases, it is Socrates they have to put aside and not Plato. They seldom read the dialogue as a text orchestrated and written by Plato, a person at a level of control beyond Socrates. Their own participation in the dialogue is at the level of dialogue. They hear Socrates speaking in the louder voice and it is to him that they respond.)

Let me look at some examples:

In the *Phaedrus*, Socrates discusses his rules of rhetoric. On the whole, these rules are in agreement with my personal rules. For example, I agree that it is essential to know the truth about one's subject in order to make a good presentation. Also, the concept of classification is vital to see the underlying properties of the subject at hand. However, I do not agree that writing is a less noble art. I believe that writing is vital to the dissemination of information to a wide and varied audience.

The student can speak here because Socrates can speak through him, and when Socrates can't (when Socrates would say that writing is less noble) he's abandoned altogether. This is not summary, in other words, but a kind of triumphantly Emersonian appropriation of the wisdom of the ages. (Socrates has said just what I would say.) Here's the other side of this:

There are some problems with Socrates' theories about rhetoric and dialectic, both from a practical standpoint and from within the *Phaedrus* itself. To begin with, Socrates believes that a person must know all about a subject before hand. How is this done? It is not easy to understand and use everything about a subject. For example, in the second speech Socrates states that "but about its [the soul's] form, the following must be stated: To tell what it really is would be a theme for a divine discourse . . . what it resembles, however, may be expressed more briefly in human language." He is saying that it would take a god to explain what a soul really is; therefore he must do the best he can to explain what it resembles. This conflicts with his idea of knowing everything. I think Socrates should change his statement, saying that it is necessary to know what is needed to talk or write about a subject; this simplifies things more and makes them more practical.

There is a wonderful chutzpah in both of these. Both students, clearly, are working to preserve their right to speak, but in what context? The context they imagine provides some insight into the role they can imagine a reader playing and into the model for the act of reading that enables each to write. In the first example, a reader is a person who agrees or disagrees, confers praise or blame. It is this act that establishes the reader's priority, that sets the text aside and gives him room to speak: Some of Socrates' rules agree with mine, some don't. For example, I too agree that it is essential to know the truth.

In its broad outlines, this would frame what I think we could call a successful reading. But the performance of this act of agreement, of what, for example, it might mean to know the truth—for Socrates, in the *Phaedrus*, for this student, in his experience as a reader and a writer (or, in the dialogue, through his counterpart, Phaedrus)—all of this is unspoken, taken for granted. This performance is, we are asked to believe, beyond saying. A reader is a person with opinions and his only requirement is to state what they are and how they correspond to the opinions in the text. Thus it's as easy for this student to disagree with Socrates as it is for him to agree. In fact, in the passage above, Socrates' argument is replaced by a single sentence, "I believe that writing is vital to the dissemination of information to a wide and varied audience." It's a sentence delivered in "topic sentence" language, the strongest voice the student can bring forward, but also one that is comically inappropriate. (Who cares what this kid has to say about writing? And besides, he talks like a jerk.) By silencing Socrates he acts as though he can speak in his place, appropriate his authority, and of course he can't. The student is doing his best, but he has been betrayed by his training in a situation that calls for more than topic sentence prose, one where he is asked to write as a reader.

Likewise, in the second example, the student has identified a problem that can give her a way of establishing her priority over Socrates—there is a contradiction. Socrates says that a speaker must know the truth and yet he says that there are truths that only belong to the gods. As I read the *Phaedrus*, this is, in fact, a key to finding a way to speak back to Socrates (as Phaedrus, our counterpart, does not.) And this, in fact, was the frame given to this student in the assignment—an offering which, because she is a skillful writer, she turns into her own act of invention. The problem comes when it is her turn to speak, when she can appropriate neither Socrates' words nor the assignments'. The crux comes at the moment of translation, when the student says of Socrates, "He is saying that . . . ." Here she casts the original in terms she can use: Socrates cannot speak like a god, therefore he must do the best he can and speak through resemblances. The project that is announced by this translation would have a reader examining the limits of Socrates' language and his use of metaphor and myth.

At this point, however, the student fails to begin the act of writing that could enact an understanding and account for the significance of this particular passage. I'm not sure I can explain why she failed, however. It could be that she failed to attend to the agenda implicit in her own reading (or writing—the distinction no longer serves here) or that she had not yet learned to adequately monitor the process while it was unfolding. It could be that she saw what she had to do but didn't know how to begin. Or it could be that she had not learned to respect that habit of mind that takes delight in such problems and spends time on them. Whatever the case, it is at this moment that the student becomes silent again. But then not completely, since she does say that she wishes Socrates would change his mind, revise his words, and make the contradictions (and the assignment) go away, so that total silence would, in fact, be appropriate and all she would have to do is admire the *Phaedrus* and pay it a quiet respect.

She begins by identifying a problem in the text that is both practical and internal ("within the *Phaedrus* itself"). This is, in a sense, her moment of access into the conversation. But once the conversation has begun, her only move is to wish Socrates would go back and revise his speech so that Socrates could speak (without gap or division) through the student. For this student, as for the student who summarizes and re-states, a reader is a person through whom an author speaks.

For some students the pressure of hearing a strong, powerful presence speak through them (particularly in Socrates' tone of voice), combined with the scholarly requirement to displace that presence, is cause for little else but despair. Listen in the following passage to the counterpoint of summary and commentary (to the counterpoint of the text and the student speaking in turn):

> When we examine *Phaedrus* for Socrates' argument on the inferiority of written speech, we find it steeped in mythology. The written word was invented by the Egyptian god Theuth. When Theuth gave this gift to man, King Thamus criticized it as more of a bane than the first step toward civilization. He believed it would weaken mens minds and memories and cause men to become conceited know-it-alls, incapable of real judgment. As if the point weren't clear enough, Socrates bludgeons the point by saying, "Then any man who imagines that he has bequeathed an art to posterity because he puts his views in writing, and also anyone who inherits such an 'art' in the belief that any subject will be clear or certain because it is couched in writing—such men will be utterly simple-minded." These are strong words and convictions, but for the life of me I cannot resolve them. Are we all idiots for engaging in the lowly act of writing? I guess so! Socrates had a few points which are true, but seem totally ridiculous.

The idea of a ridiculous truth, although nowhere else so succinctly stated, was common in the papers I read on the *Phaedrus*. It is a student's way of defining a conversational moment in reading, one usually represented dispassionately in a syntax like the following: "While Socrates argues . . . , it seems that . . . ." In the latter, a reader has learned to see that the power of even a powerful text can be accounted for as something other than the power of truth, and he has learned to see re-reading as something other than a ridiculous act. For this learning to take place, students need a curriculum that dramatizes the politics of reading and writing.

The *Phaedrus* is an exemplary text in this regard. There is a telling moment in the dialogue, after Socrates has done his best to woo Phaedrus away from his other teacher, Lysias. Socrates offers a summary of all that has gone on in his conversation with Phaedrus. At the end, he turns to Phaedrus and says, "And now, what about the question of whether it is honorable or disgraceful to write and deliver speeches? Under what circumstances may this properly involve reproach? Wasn't this made clear a little while ago when we said . . ." And he pauses. And Phaedrus, his student, says, "What did we say?" And Socrates goes on like a freight train, without missing a stroke, to tell him what "we" said. Socrates' "we" presents a peculiar but predictable use of the pronoun. It is all too often a teacher's we, one that can never include two "I's," never include a student except as a silent partner—someone who speaks only when a teacher speaks through him.

About Socrates as a teacher, one student wrote:

> Socrates follows his rules of rhetoric, I feel, very well. He breaks things down into parts and knows the truth before he speaks. I also feel that he treats Phaedrus like a lover because Phaedrus wants to learn the truth. Socrates tries to show how important truth is when he tries to convince Phaedrus that a donkey is as good as a horse. Through the whole dialogue Phaedrus agrees, but really never learns nothing.

The opening sentences of this passage—and they are dutiful sentences, to be sure—are phrased in terms of what the student "felt" to be true about the *Phaedrus*. It is a classic example of the student reader Culler talks about.[9] The student reads and interprets by imagining what "a reader" should feel and understand. This performance is broken by the last sentence where another set of "feelings" about the dialogue comes through. I don't want to romanticize the double negative. It is tempting to say that *there*, at that point, the student moves to assert his priority and speak for himself, but it is followed by silence. There is no further discussion of what Phaedrus does and doesn't learn. The point is not what the final phrase *is*, however, but what it can be made to be. By focusing on this statement for a revision of this essay, a teacher could make it part of a past that would allow a student to say that he has understood the *Phaedrus*.

If Socrates failed Phaedrus, it wasn't because he didn't let him speak, or because he listened to Phaedrus only to the degree that his words could serve his own agenda. He failed him because he was more interested in his performance than Phaedrus's. Phaedrus is never allowed to act on his own authority. The student above could best begin a revision of his paper by throwing everything away but that last sentence and addressing the question it asks: How is it that all this teaching goes on, and by a famous and intelligent teacher, and yet Phaedrus never learns nothing? The student would be helped here by being given a moment, a project, a beginning one that violates the conventional habit of mind that is dutiful and pious, one that turns the text back on itself, and one that could provide a working metaphor for the act of reading. This is a project a teacher would have to set for the student, though. He would not come to it on his own.

The students who were "better" readers at the beginning of the semester were students who were able to cast themselves into a more seamless classroom role. They could read successfully, that is, because they had learned a way of writing, a way of composing an "act of reading" that they brought with them to a book and that they used to complete their classroom requirements. Their readings were dutiful and pious—there was none of the subversion of the papers above: no suggestions that Socrates is ridiculous or that he ought to revise his ideas or that he was a failure as a teacher—but they were complete and therefore had an authority those other, marginal readings lacked. There were no obvious gaps or moments of disintegration, no places where the mask would fall away to reveal an 18-year-old kid who was puzzled, bored, lost or confused. I'm less interested in talking about them at length, partly because these papers were less interesting and partly because I have no desire to make a case for their achievement. What they do and fail to do will be immediately familiar to anyone who's spent time in an English class. I'm more interested in what they could be said to represent. I think they represent students who have learned the "topic sentence" versions of reading, school routines that are as set and conventional as their composition counterparts, even if they are not spelled out as clearly in textbooks or handbooks. (I don't think they should be belittled as monkey work, nor do I think they should be cited as examples of clear or reasonable minds at work. They are evidence of students who have learned a routine that they believe will enable them to do the work of a college classroom. The question for a college or university teacher should be What comes next?)

Here are two examples of more successful papers to represent two familiar tropes for the act of reading: "charting main ideas" and "discovering hidden meanings." Both these students, I would argue, give convincing, if not graceful, performances. While they write as Sheridan Baker would have students write, these are not cases where students first had ideas and then cast them into order on the page. They had a form, rather, and read accordingly. The roles they were able to imagine enabled their readings. For the first reader, reading is the celebration of what is clear, predictable, even obvious. He has found, and can speak for, the ostensible argument of the text. Whatever Socrates has "appeared" to say this writer can translate into what Socrates "clearly" said. In fact, his successful pantomime of a way of reading tends to obscure the fact that he has little to say that is not direct restatement. (I suspect that the hidden drama in this argument is the student's attempt to *not* say that Socrates has a sexual interest in Phaedrus. He is silently arguing against a subversive reading.) His style of presentation, I think we can believe, is in imitation of Socrates':

First, it must be established what sort of man Socrates was. He claims that he is a "lover of words," but this fact is useless unless it is understood what is meant by the word "lover." Socrates appears to have defined a lover as one whose "search for love has involved the search for wisdom."

Next, Socrates' reason for conducting this conversation with Phaedrus must be considered. "As for me, I'll cross the stream and go away before you put any greater compulsion on me," states Socrates, arousing Phaedrus's interest. Predictably, Phaedrus replies, "Not yet, Socrates, till the heat has gone. Don't you see that it's nearly high noon, as they call it. Let's wait and talk about what's been said." Socrates has obviously set Phaedrus up for his second speech. Clearly, Socrates was intent on trying to get a message across to Phaedrus. Socrates, a lover of words, is trying to express this sort of love to his friend Phaedrus.

Next to this, I'll place the reader who pursues the hidden, the secrets of a text, and celebrates buried rather than ostensible meanings. This is the reader set against plain wisdom, who announces that she looks beyond or more deeply—all moves in a set performance, an elaborate fiction, that enables a reader to carry out an act of reading:

In reading the *Phaedrus* for the first time, I was struck by a certain sense of ambiguity, as if there were hidden meanings in Socrates' dealing with Phaedrus. Much of what Socrates states in his speeches is plainly his wisdom that can either be taken at face value and will still be meaningful or looked into a little more deeply for more value. In the *Phaedrus* Plato seems to be pointing out the difference between a truly wise man and a typical man. Even beyond this, he tells us about the "real" nature of man, in other words, what constitutes a man.

To other students, these two paragraphs open essays that would seem correct, exemplary, unquestionable. There is power in these performances, and it resides not so much in what the essays say, or in how they would enable another reader to go back to the *Phaedrus* with interest, but in the pat authority represented by these structures of reading. The earlier essays I've cited would be easier for students to critique because they have obvious problems in them—gaps or discontinuities between the reader and conventional classroom readings. These essays, however, seem to show a perfect fit between a reader and reading.

The last of the essays presented above makes its own argument about the politics of reading, about the way status is distributed between those who have access to secrets and those who don't. It's not really a matter of finding hidden meanings at all, however. The "secrets" she has to tell of the *Phaedrus* are stated later in her paper and

they turn out not to be secrets at all but to be plain, cultural commonplaces: "man is capable of becoming wise if taught correctly by men
who not only tell him certain things but show him things indirectly
also." A classroom provides the occasion for an 18-year-old to speak
these words, words she knows to be common, generally true, recognizable, intelligent, and yet to speak them as though they were her
own discovery. Her authority as a reader is realized when she can speak
the words of (what she takes to be) the adult community of readers
back to that community. Within the fiction of this act of reading, however, what distinguishes the occasion is not that she has thought to say
them but that she has found them "hidden" in a book, where others
couldn't find them or couldn't find them quite so well. This right of
privilege (to find secrets) both preceded and enabled her reading and,
she believes, it establishes her position in the classroom over and
against others:

> Socrates is a teacher to Phaedrus and to us, but we must be wise
> enough to find the value in his lessons. And everyone can find
> some value—some can find deeper meaning if they are capable of
> seeing it, but those that can't see quite so deeply will still gain
> something towards wisdom.

Both this student and the student who said "I believe that writing
is vital to the dissemination of information to a wide and varied audience" establish their right to speak by taking as their own a general,
cultural commonplace. By classroom measures, however, the first student was a failure and he was a failure because he didn't know how to
act like a reader, how to frame this moment in a dramatic representation of a reader at work.

IV

I have been looking at bits and pieces—cameos—from student essays in order to highlight student approximation of the act of reading.
I have been looking at student essays as metaphors for reading (or the
reader), and, I believe, by unpacking those metaphors we can better
imagine the work before us as teachers. This is a different view of the
process of reading than that given to us by studies in the psychology
of reading. The process I have been outlining is not an internal psychological process but a rhetorical act of placement, a way of writing that
locates a reader and a text within an institutional setting. The key dialectic in the process as I see it is historical (what a student can understand about the contours and implications of the roles available to her
as a reader, and the ways she can move within and against those roles)
and not to say that beginning students cannot or can never test

Socrates' argument against other possible counter-arguments or counter-examples; it is to say that, in my experience, they do not and, furthermore, they do not do it with any style or hope of gain until they've received some fairly clever teaching, which in many schools goes under the name of composition. They do not have those counter-arguments or counter-examples until they have been located, as writers, in a context that makes those arguments and examples possible.

In talking about his own teaching, Stanley Fish said that,

we are not to imagine a moment when my students "simply see" a physical configuration of atoms and *then* assign that configuration a significance, according to the situation they happen to be in. To be in the situation (this or any other) is to "see" with the eyes of its interests, its goals, its understood practices, values, and norms, and so to be conferring significance by seeing, not after it. The categories of my students' vision are the categories by which they understand themselves to be functioning as students (what Sacks might term "doing studenting"), and objects will appear to them in forms related to that way of functioning rather than in some objective or preinterpretive form.[10]

I think there are finer distinctions to be made here. I think there are degrees in students' abilities to "function" as students, just as I think there are degrees to which students can be shown to *understand themselves to be* functioning as students. And I think both of the above—the ability to perform and the ability to understand the conventions governing performance—are most available when students "confer significance" textually—when they show a way of reading by writing it down; when they don't just "notice," but speak as well. And I don't think that the differences are trivial; the differences, that is, between students who are "inside" the system of classroom reading and writing and those who are outside. I think the moment of transition from the outside to the inside, where the habits of one community are privileged and the habits of another become taboo, is the key moment in undergraduate education. We are a far way, now, from "discovering new ideas" or "independent reading" or the language of any of a number of liberation pedagogies. The burden of teaching, I think, is that we can never totally free ourselves or our students from conventional ways of reading, writing and thinking. We can, however, teach students what's at stake and what's going on.

Let me turn to my last set of examples. These will all be longer pieces—in two cases complete essays. I want to examine, in these, the larger drama of a student's reading. I'll begin with another example of silence:

In this chapter, I see the author comparing himself to Hoggarts theory of the "scholarship boy." It seems as though the story

doesn't do a thing for Rodriguez. It leaves us with mixed ideas
and emotions about Rodriguez's theory. When Rodriguez says
he was a "scholarship boy," a certain kind of scholarship boy,
"always successful, and always portraying no confidence." He
says he was exhilerated by his progress. Yet sad, I can't really
understand why he says he's sad, even though he thinks so highly
of the progress that he has made.

There is a big gap between the "I see" of the first sentence and
the "it seems" (which I take as *it seems to me*) in the second. The first
demonstrates the easy appropriation of the frame set up by an assignment (which asked students to look at how Rodriguez read and used
Hoggart's discussion of the "scholarship boy"). The student begins to
speak, in other words, by locating himself initially within the context
of the assigned exercise. He "sees" a comparison but then goes on to
demonstrate that there is nothing to be seen in the text at all. This is
the dark version of Fish's happy student who sees what he is supposed
to see because of his ability to function as a student (to "do studenting"). This student can make the opening move, but then he is abandoned by the discourse he has called up. For him, the text says
nothing. Or, more properly, what it does say—that Rodriguez is both
exhilarated and saddened by what happened to him—allows only for
silence. "I can't really understand why he's sad, even though he thinks
so highly of the progress that he has made."

The paradox—it seems to say something but it doesn't say anything—is repeated in the second paragraph of the essay:

Rodriguez seems to charish or idolize Hoggart and his theory
about the scholarship boy. I believe this theory does help him,
it seems like a type of incentive for him. He often relates himself
with this scholarship boy that Hoggart so often speaks of. I feel
that it is a sign of both a loss and a gain. I say this because he
often refers back to the days when he was not as educated, they
seemed like happy memories for him. But when he talks about
how much he's learned he is very proud.

In the first paragraph, the student wrote that Hoggart's "story doesn't
do a thing for" Rodriguez. Now for this he substitutes, "I believe this
theory does help him" and tries to find a set of terms that will allow
him to talk about the role the Hoggart passage played for Rodriguez.
It's a "help" and "incentive." He can "relate himself" to what Hoggart said. Hoggart can speak to Rodriguez in this student's account
only as a boy's father might speak to his son as he heads off for school.
(Rodriguez could be seen to be much more feisty in this exchange. I
think he could also be seen to be saying that Hoggart has got the experience of the "scholarship boy" wrong in significant ways.)

The strong statement, "I feel that it is a sign of both a loss and a gain" is appropriated from the assignment ("what did he lose? what did he gain?") and isn't so much a strong statement as it is a way out of the contradictions the student (rightly) finds in Rodriguez's attitudes toward his education. These terms, even as they are taken as a statement of what I (he) felt, cannot operate to organize the reading. The "but" of the last sentence—"they seemed like happy memories for him, but when he talks about how much he's learned he is very proud"—stands for an opposition he still cannot resolve. He has worked himself back into the language of the project that he imagines the assignment has called for, but he cannot make the language work for him. And the reason is evident from the ending of the paper.

> When looking at the aspects of education, I would say in the situation that Rodriguez faces that it was good for a wide variety of different things. He truely needed to be educated, his parents knew it and he eventually realized it. Education in my opinion is good for everything, no one should be denied an education. It is alot of long hours and hard work along with frustration, but in the end, when your education is completed, it all pays off.

What this student "would say" about *Hunger of Memory* makes a good part of the book disappear. The argument of the book is that education is also violation and loss, that the pay-off is equivocal, that it is not good for all things—that, in fact, for some things it is death. The student who is writing this paper, a student who is also a scholarship boy, translates Rodriguez's story into terms consistent with the necessary belief that the long hours and hard work *will* all pay off, that education *is* good for everything. The question of Rodriguez's "sadness" had to be put aside for this reading to complete itself.

This is not, I would argue, a case of ego-centrism or of a student who could not read beyond his own identity themes. I don't think this student believes that education is good for everything. I don't think this is a student who had so much invested in his own hard work that he could not look at or "see" Rodriguez's sadness. I do, however, think that this is the fiction that the student wrote through; its part of the communal fantasy, a way of talking that enables this reading, with its concerns, perplexities, moments of significance and conclusions. This essay presents the case of a student who, when he imagines himself as a reader, comes to imagine a reader who must turn away from perplexity (from questions that don't begin to speak their own answers: "I can't really understand why he's sad") to speak with authority, and the voice of authority that is most readily available to him is the voice of conventional wisdom, the voice that speaks the commonplace, "Hard work pays off in the end." And in our community that way of speaking is taboo: clichéd, trite, predictable (as predictable, in fact, as our responses would be, but here predicting the wrong sort of habit of mind).

You see a similar process at work in the following excerpts from other student papers. Notice in the following paragraph how the student begins with quotation or paraphrase, an example of Rodriguez's "significant" words, and translates them into available commonplaces:

> Mr. Rodriguez writes that education is not an inevitable or natural step in growing up and that one chooses to become a student (p. 48). This is very important and something we tend to forget in the era of mandatory education. If someone does not want to learn and invariably tunes himself out it is almost impossible to teach this individual. In another passage (p. 55), Mr. Rodriguez points out how he "wanted to be like his teachers, to posses their knowledge, assume their authority, their confidence and persona." This is an example of how the student imitates the teacher in hopes of acquiring the teacher's traits. In yet another passage (p. 64), he writes, "I vacuumed books for epigrams, scraps of information, ideas, themes—anything to fill the hollow within me and make me feel educated." Here Mr. Rodriguez seems to be wondering if feeling educated is the same as being educated. "He read to acquire a point of view." Mr. Rodriguez seems to say that education in the sense that he acquired it is a collection of facts and ideas of other men."

The problem here is not, at least not immediately, that the student fails to connect up these various statements and observations, but with the essential act of translation itself. The counterpoint here—quotation and commentary—shows the student translating statements that break the pattern of conventional wisdom back into conventional wisdom. The gap between saying that education isn't natural and saying that students who tune out are impossible to teach is a way of showing that Rodriguez is a better writer than my student. It is also, however, a way of showing how each understands the situation of the writer—one trying to push against the ready-made language for describing education (to whom education is an unnatural act, a loss of something as well as a benefit); the other trying to find a place of authority, a place to enable an utterance that can stand next to Rodriguez, by putting himself within the language that speaks the received wisdom of the community. To speak, one must imagine or write one's way into a privileged discourse and for students—outside the closed discourse of the university—the privileged discourse they can immediately imagine is the wisdom of the community and its elders. Students work to locate themselves within a commonplace where, as Aristotle says, they can find a stock of arguments to which they may turn for a particular need. The difficulty for such students is that the university is a place where common wisdom is only of negative value—or, perhaps, more properly, where students go to have one set of commonplaces replaced with another.

The writer of the passage above concluded his essay by turning to the commonplace that sets originality against imitation (we, of course, would have him use those terms oxymoronically—original imitation, imitative originality—to talk about the role books played early on in Rodriguez's education):

> I suppose this type of education has its merits but it is not origi-
> nal though and therefor this type of education has limited uses.
> Many supposedly educated people can sit around and quote
> other's works, but the true test of an education comes when one
> is asked to sit down and compose an original symphony, design
> a new form of architecture, or write a novel that is truely novel.

This is one of those passages that, if you present them to a class, appears seamless, perfectly complete and self-contained, unassailable. The power of a commonplace has little to do, in other words, with whether it rings true to experience or not. It provides a set of terms within which one can control difficult or problematic information and its power to do so determines its merit. Students, at least my students, will be quick to admire the way that conclusion speaks with power and authority—even with art ("novels that are truely novel"). And they will continue to speak of its power even after I puncture it and make them laugh by asking how many of them would pass an exit exam that required them to compose an original symphony, design a new form of architecture or write a novel that is truly novel. A passage like this is more powerful than a teacher. A teacher can displace it, to be sure, but only by the most overt act of aggression. It is a passage beyond laughter or parody, which is one of the things that makes teaching such a funny business.

The student above was trying to locate himself within a discourse that would work, that would enable the work of a reader in my course. In the paper that follows you'll see a student who does this more gracefully, but who gets stuck trying to figure out whose turn it is to speak: the text's or the reader's. I'll divide this essay into three sections. The first introduces the essentials: a reader, a book and a project or agenda.

> Throughout the book the author is frequently alluding to his true
> feelings for his family. This is best represented by the last chapter
> entitled Mr. Secrets. It is here that Rodriguez talks specifically
> about his family. He deals with the fact that his parents have al-
> ways and continue to separate themselves from a public identity.

Rodriguez explains that his parents see only the family as their private society. He also mentions the fact that no matter how well they act in public, there is always the every present distinction between public and private. This distinction between public and private is shown by the high-pitched voice his mother uses with those who are not relatives. Rodriguez's mother also used this voice with his own friends. It always made Rodriguez feel badly that she could never adjust herself to be as friendly as his friend's parents were to him.

I am trusting that this passage will have a familiar ring to it. This student's performance does not seem unusual the way the earlier student's did (that is, the student who confessed he could not figure out why Rodriguez would be sad). The student here steps more easily into the role of a reader. I'd like to look at what this reader is (or does).

The reader in this first paragraph is a person who sets the stage ("Throughout the book the author is frequently alluding to his true feelings for his family."), warms up the audience ("This is best represented by the last chapter entitled Mr. Secrets."), and then points to passages in the text so that they may speak for themselves ("He deals . . . ," "Rodriguez explains . . . ," "He also mentions . . ." "This distinction is shown by . . ."). In fact, the metaphor of "showing" is dominant here. The reader makes certain decisions about where to look or where to point, but the text then shows or displays what it says. It speaks through the reader, who has decided that she had best remain silent, organizing Rodriguez's words into thesis and example but without speaking herself. She has nothing to add after the presentation of the example. What the example says, how it might be read, all of this goes without saying. It is the structure that speaks here and not the words or bits and pieces from the text—or, for that matter, the historical drama reenacted in this presentation, a drama that plays itself out in the present by telling this girl to keep quiet. It plays itself out in my classroom by telling students there to keep quiet too. It is the rare student who would see anything troubling in this reading— troubling in either what it says about the act of reading and the role of the reader, or troubling in the way it talks about *Hunger of Memory*. (For example, you could read the book to argue that Rodriguez's distinction between public and private is challenged, not "shown," through the example of his mother speaking to his friends as though they were strangers.) The reading may not be graceful but it seems complete.

The second paragraph reproduces the drama of the first until here, after the presentation of the "best" example (to best "show" what the the text says), the reader speaks in turn:

This feeling of separation also blocked family unity and is shown by their holiday dinners. Everyone would be gathered around the table eating and talking but there was something missing. Rodriguez easily talks to his family but he leaves the reader with the feeling that his family members are just saying meaningless words. Examples of this are shown in the types of conversations the family engage. Rodriguez sits next to his youngest sister and they gossip and talk about mutual friends. The reader never gets the impression that the family talks intimately. It is Rodriguez who states that he is the one who does most of the talking. The best example of this is seen when he says "I talk having learned from hundreds of cocktail parties and dinner parties how to talk with great animation about nothing especially." (p. 191–2) This is a rather odd comment about one's own family. Although the reader does sense that they could all be close. If they did not care about one another and their parents, they would never come to the family gatherings anyway. I felt that they all had very different lives. Their education and their parents' feeling of isolation kept distance between family unity. The family's public identify was carried over into their private lives.

The single channel of this discussion is broken, or interrupted, at the point at which she introduces the example of Rodriguez saying, "I talk having learned from hundreds of cocktail parties and dinner parties how to talk with great animation about nothing especially." It's not that the example has nothing to do with the discussion it is meant to serve; it's that it is too good or too big for the kind of discussion we've been hearing. It's a bit like saying, "King Lear is an example of a man with a bad temper." I don't, in other words, think that the writer pulled out this example to serve her discussion. I think this was one of the moments in a text that stuck with her, or stuck out as she was paging through the book looking for an example and, even though it was generally appropriate, it would not fit into the performance she had underway. It is, then, an "odd comment" because it belongs to a way of talking about (of reading) the relationships between public life and private life that stands outside of the project or agenda begun in this essay.

I want to resist the notion that this is a moment where the student's feelings broke in and therefore she was compelled to speak. The feeling that families get together because they care about one another is no more *her* feeling than it is the Hallmark Card Corporation's or the producers of *The Waltons*. I think the oddness of the moment she recalled and then let speak in her essay created a problem she felt interested in solving and that she turned to even though she did not have ready access to the words that would make the problem manageable. She moves from the language of family sentiment to the strange syntax of the final two sentences, where she tries to put together the key words of her discussion: public, private, distance, unity, education, and identity.

The next paragraph in the paper draws out more examples of the "emptiness" of the family Christmas dinner. And at one point the student writes, "It is here that I felt a loneliness for Rodriguez." It's an interesting sentence. It still does more pointing than talking, but it places her in a new relation to Rodriguez—not so much feeling his loneliness, letting him speak through her, but feeling it for him, casting an interpretation on a text that does not announce, "Rodriguez felt lonely."

And this is the final section of the final paragraph:

> The parents who were the force behind the family gatherings were unable to bring the family together. In their alienation from a public society they alienated themselves from their children. There were family gatherings but not familial ties. This produced in each a longing for unity that could not be attained, resulting in a search for this comfort in other areas. For Rodriguez, it seems to be achieved in the writing of *Hunger of Memory* and for his brothers and sisters in their childrens' acceptance into the public society. It is for the parents that there seems to be no relief, only yearning.

I have no interest in offering this as a right reading or a good reading of *Hunger of Memory*. I think it is an interesting answer to the question, "What's wrong with this family?" It's a good question to ask of this book, since it is a question with many rich examples and no set answers. And I think it is the question this writer set for herself once she shook herself free from an earlier agenda and its way of reading. Perhaps the most noticeable difference in this final paragraph is its air of authority. The writer plays against the "naive" language of family life ("There were family gatherings but not familial ties"), she appropriates key terms ("alienation," "public society") and makes them counters in sentences where it is the reader, rather than the text or its author, who is speaking. What the reader has to say is clearly more important than what Rodriguez has to say. She provides a commentary that he could not provide—or so the fiction behind this reading would require us to believe. I could imagine, in fact, that a later step in this reader's education would have her considering this way of reading (now felt, I imagine, as achievement) as a way of unnecessarily limiting what Rodriguez can be shown to know and understand and, therefore, of unnecessarily limiting her own performance in an act of understanding.

This is a mid-term issue, however. For the moment I suspect that the key pedagogical question for this paper is how it might be revised. I think, and I think I have shown, that it would be a mistake to try to work on the "writing" in this paper—to work on its unity, to add or subtract examples, or to "re-see" its ideas. I think it would be a mistake unless the writing of the paper can be represented to the student as the same thing as a reading, for I think that the first thing she must do is to consider what she is doing in this assignment as a reader and why.

Recent literary criticism has celebrated misreading as an achievement, as an occasion for the individual reader to break free from the tyranny of a text or the prison house of institutionally sanctioned procedures for reading, re-presenting and thereby understanding texts. The reader is cast, then, neither as an empty vessel to be filled with the authoritative readings of his teachers or the ostensible wisdom of the text, nor is he cast as a good citizen, carrying on the work of his elders and his community. He is cast, rather, in an agonistic role, struggling against teachers and canonical interpretations—or, in my account of student readers, struggling to find teachers and interpretive procedures that will enable the work of the classroom.

In *Beginnings*, Edward Said gives an account of the problems facing the modern writer that reminds me of the problems facing my students. He says that while there may have been a time when readers and writers saw a text as a "system of boundaries and inner constraints held intact by successive generations (a heritage passed on through time)," for the modern writer a text is "an invitation to unforeseen estrangements from the habitual." He says

> The problem we face today when we study Joyce, or when, untrained in classics or religion, we read Hooker, or when we deploy psychology in the study of a literary text, is a problem of irregularity, or discontinuity. That is, less background, less formal training, less prescribed and systematic information, is assumed before one begins to read, write, or work. Thus when one begins to write today one is necessarily more of an autodidact, gathering or making up knowledge one needs in the course of creating.[11]

Said is not making an appeal to tired notions of creativity—where, on the boundaries of culture, the scholar makes up new ideas. He is talking about the academic version of street knowledge, about a willed, brash toughness of mind that enables a writer to bluff his way into a high stakes struggle for turf, for priority, without knowing all the rules or what moves will work, and without knowing beforehand whether he can carry it off should he win in the end.

The power of this metaphor is the way it enables us to frame the work of a student writer. For me it is poised against the metaphor of the student with a purpose or with a controlling idea. It is important to know, as a teacher, that when a student is making it up as he goes along he may very well be carrying out the essential work of the imagination, the very work that will enable him to move from one end of the block to the other, from the outside in. For this writer, Said also offers the metaphor of the wanderer.

It is less permissible today to imagine oneself as writing within a tradition when one writes literary criticism. This is not to say, however, that every critic is now a revolutionist destroying the canon in order to replace it with his own. A better image is that of a wanderer, going from place to place for his material, but remaining a man essentially *between* homes. In the process, what is taken from a place ultimately violates its habitual way of being: there is a constant transposition . . . .[12]

For an expert writer, this wandering is a willed condition, something one achieves by writing and not a function of one's high school education or socio-economic status. Said's metaphor, however, also describes the students I teach, wandering between the old neighborhood and the university, belonging to neither, and left to invent academic expertise everytime they sit down to write. Misreading, for my students, is no easy route to academic status, and not even in my classroom (and even though I think the students who have trouble with college reading and writing are often in a better position to be students than those who are confident that they know how to "do English"). The misreadings we honor push against conventional systems, our conventional systems, and these readings are different from the misreadings that push against the habits of home or neighborhood or that seek to approximate the imagined requirements of the classroom. Education in the midst of this is push and tug, it is a scramble for power and for violation; it is not the transfer of reading or writing "skills" in a reading or writing laboratory.

At least that's how it has always felt to me—now, as a teacher, and before, as a student. Harold Bloom speaks eloquently of the violent dynamics of the classroom, with its struggle for authority, its necessary appeasements and its shocking violations of identity, when he talks about the dialectics of tradition and influence.

Influence, as I conceive it, means that there are *no* texts, but only relationships *between* texts. These relationships depend upon a critical act, a misreading or misprision, that one poet performs upon another, and that does not differ in kind from the necessary critical acts performed by every strong reader upon every text he encounters. The influence-relation governs reading as it governs writing, and reading is therefore a miswriting just as writing is a misreading.[13]

The force of Bloom's argument for me is the way he places influence functionally in the imagined presence of a single person, a teacher or an author whose presence cannot be ignored or easily categorized, whose writing a student cannot help but imitate and whose presence, then, becomes both an inspiration and a burden. It is through such encounters that we place ourselves in and thereby invent a cultural, intellectual history. Bloom says, in *A Map of Misreading*, "You cannot write or teach or think or even read without imitation, and what you imitate is what another person has done, that person's writing or teaching or thinking or reading."[14]

This is no simple matter, however, since the young poet/student (like Bloom's Shelley) faced with the older poet/teacher (like his Milton) struggles to assert his own presence or priority in the very text that the older figure made possible. Or, as Bloom says, "A poet . . . is not so much a man speaking to men as a man rebelling against being spoken to by a dead man (the precursor) outrageously more alive than himself."[15]

My own experience as a student tells me that I have learned more, or perhaps learned more deeply through these encounters than through a regular exposure to books and ideas and classes. The most dramatic educational experience I had was my contact with Richard Poirier in my first year of graduate school. The first three years of my graduate training were driven by a desire to be able to do what he did— to be able to read and speak and write like him. I would, for example, copy out difficult or impressive sentences he had written in order to get the feel of them. I can feel them now in many sentences I write. It is a mixed feeling. I state is simply, but it wasn't simple at all. I tried for a whole semester to write a paper using the word "language" as he used it in talking about how the language "worked" in "Upon Appleton House." It took me a whole semester to use the word in a sentence that actually made sense to me, in a sentence I felt I could control. I felt that I had gained access to a profession by exercises like these. At the time it didn't feel like surrender. It was inspiring to feel that I could use his language and mimic, as I could, his way of reading and writing.

And I remember very well how shocked I was when one of my other professors, after admiring a paper I had written, commented in passing to me in the hall, "Don't you ever get tired of that Poirier routine?" It was not then, nor could it ever be for me now, simply a "routine," largely because what Poirier taught and how he taught and how he wrote were and remain central to my own beliefs and my professional identity. I felt ashamed, however, and began in my dissertation to try to write myself free from his influence, to find a project and a way of talking that I could claim for my own. This was a difficult and unsettling thing to attempt. I felt that I had found a place for myself, a way of thinking and talking that located me in the world of professionals, and now I had to push against it, misread it, in Bloom's terms. This is not a battle that a student wins, but for me it marked a stage in my education.

This is why I have little patience for Stanley Fish and the apparent pleasure he takes in revealing the gamesmanship of the classroom. In *Is There a Text in This Class?* he tells the following story:

> Thus, while there is no core of agreement *in* the text, there is a core of agreement (although one subject to change) concerning ways of *producing* the text. Nowhere is this set of acceptable ways written down, but it is a part of everyone's knowledge of what it means to be operating within the literary institution as it is now constituted. A student of mine recently demonstrated this knowledge when, with an air of giving away a trade secret, she confided that she could go into any classroom, no matter what the subject of the course, and win approval for running one of a number of well-defined interpretive routines: she could view the assigned text as the instance of the tension between nature and culture; she could look in the text for evidence of large mythological oppositions; she could argue that the true subject of the text was its own composition, or that in the guise of fashioning a narrative the speaker was fragmenting and displacing his own anxieties and fears.[16]

I find myself arguing both with and against Fish. I'd like to call his student's bluff, give her a copy of (say) *Hunger of Memory* and ask her to write an essay. If she could do what she says she can do, and if she could do it well, write a paper that is not mechanical and deadly, then she could not speak of what she has learned in such a flip way, for she would have learned the power as well as the emptiness of those routines, she would have felt the achievement as well as the betrayal. If these routines do not grant wisdom, they grant position, an enabling power, not just title; they grant not only a teacher's approval, but a place within a discourse that makes intellectual work possible.

I would agree, however, that what we must finally concern ourselves with is not what is in the text but in ways of producing the text. And for this reason, a reading course is necessarily a writing course and a writing course must be a course in reading.

Notes

[1] My work on this paper was supported by the Learning Research and Development Center at the University of Pittsburgh. LRDC, in turn, is supported by grants from NIE. I'm grateful. I'm grateful also to Steve Carr who helped me gather papers on the *Phaedrus*, who taught me how to read it, and who showed me how a fine and serious teacher might go about teaching such an elusive and difficult book. Portions of this essay are drawn from other pieces of mine: "Inventing the University" in *When a Writer Can't Write*, ed. Mike Rose (New York: Guilford Press, 1985); "Facts, Artifacts and Counterfacts" (with Anthony R. Petrosky) in *Facts, Artifacts and Counterfacts*, eds. Bartholomae and Petrosky (Upper Montclair, NJ: Boynton/Cook, forthcoming). and "Against the Grain" in *Writers on Writing*, ed. Thomas Waldrep (New York: Random House, 1985).

[2] Hans-Georg Gadamer, *Philosophical Hermeneutics*, ed. and trans. David E. Linge (Berkeley: University of California Press, 1977), 57. This quotation and the passages that follow all come from the chapter "On The Problem of Self-Understanding." Mariolina Salvatori introduced me to Gadamer in her essay, "The Dialogical Nature of Reading and Writing," in *Facts, Artifacts and Counterfacts*. I owe a debt also to Salvatori's essays "Reading and Writing a Text," *College English* 459L983) 657–67; and "*If on a Winter's Night a Traveler:* Writer's Authority, Reader's Autonomy" in *Modern Literature*, forthcoming.

[3] George Steiner, *After Babel* (New York: Oxford University Press, 1975) 473.

[4] Jonathan Culler, *On Deconstruction: Theory and Criticism After Structuralism* (Ithaca, NY: Cornell University Press, 1982) 67.

[5] This paper is not meant to be in defense of any particular curriculum. I've got one to defend, however, and I would be willing to send a sequence of assignments to anyone who writes. See also Bartholomae and Petrosky, *Facts, Artifacts and Counterfacts*.

[6] Jonathan Culler, *Structuralist Poetics* (Ithaca, NY: Cornell University Press, 1975), 28. Cited in Fish, *Is There a Text in This Class?* (see below).

[7] Stanley Fish, *Is There a Text in This Class? The Authority of Interpretive Communities* (Cambridge, MA: Harvard University Press, 1980) 335.

[8] Frank Kermode, *The Genesis of Secrecy: On the Interpretation of Narrative* (Cambridge, MA: Harvard University Press, 1979) 45.

[9] Culler, *On Deconstruction* 67.

[10] Fish, 334.

[11] Edward Said, *Beginnings: Intention and Method* (Baltimore: Johns Hopkins University Press, 1975) 8.

[12] Said 8.

[13] Harold Bloom, *A Map of Misreading* (New York: Oxford University Press, 1975) 3.

[14] Bloom 32.

[15] Bloom 19.

[16] Fish 343.

5

"Reading the World... Reading the Word": Paulo Freire's Pedagogy of Knowing

ANN E. BERTHOFF

University of Massachusetts at Boston

Paulo Freire warns against sloganeering, in which words substitute for critical thinking; but mottoes and maxims by which we may formulate critical attitudes are something else. Freire is himself a superb aphorist, like I. A. Richards whom he curiously resembles—curiously, because though they come from markedly different backgrounds and do not in the least sound like one another, they nevertheless see eye to eye about the nature of language and learning; about the urgency of comprehending the significance of illiteracy the world around; about the character of the pedagogy which will be required if the political challenge posed by illiteracy is to be met. When Freire juxtaposes *reading the world* and *reading the word*, he identifies, it seems to me, the only foundation upon which literacy can be firmly established, and that is interpretation, seen as the act of making meaning. *Reading the world* and *reading the word* brought thus into analogous conjunction become models for one another and they can do so because they belong to that family of radical metaphors, the chief of which is seeing as a way of knowing and knowing as both insight and the power of envisagement. Knowledge, Coleridge said, is "vision nascent."

The springs of Paulo Freire's wisdom are in nineteenth century political thought and the New Testament; that's why his ideas can sound familiar to us, though his guides might not be our own. Occasionally he deploys the language of Marxism, but not in a doctrinaire fashion, for he has his own versions of what is entailed in *praxis, dialectic, oppression, revolution,* and *struggle* so that the words themselves serve new purposes, thereby taking on new meanings. The same holds for his deployment of the lexicon of Christianity. My colleague

Richard Horsley, professor of religion at the University of Massachu-
setts/Boston, has remarked that after hearing Paulo Freire at the Harvard Divinity School in the early seventies, he began reading the New
Testament in a completely new way. Of course to read Scripture dialectically is nothing new; typology is nothing if not dialectical. Freire
is one of the mentors of liberation theology the world over because
his pedagogy of knowing provides a method by which such powers of
interpretation are made accessible to all who can learn. He is a profoundly traditional man, but no one should think that reading Freire
is an exercise in surveying received ideas. He transforms whatever he
uses; every idea gains in significance as he develops contexts and draws
out implications. Paulo Freire is not only a superb theoretician: he is
one of the great teachers of the century. We can learn from him because his conception of education as a pedagogy of knowing helps us
teach reading and writing as interpretive acts and thus helps us comprehend our comprehensions of literacy more comprehensively.

Forming the concept of literacy, which is to say, thinking about
what we mean when we define the relationship of reading and writing
to each other and to language, considered biologically and philosophically as a species-specific power, is not the same thing as formulating
an unambiguous definition. "What IS literacy?" would not be an advantageous point of departure, and yet we must ask over and over
again what we mean when we consider the relationship of reading and
writing to each other and of each to the private and public uses of
language, to the functions of language so often forgotten by rhetoricians and linguists, viz., expression and representation. I want to begin
by claiming that when literacy is reduced to meaning manipulation of
the graphic code, the consequences can be hazardous. Consider these
cases.

The dean of a college which has developed a competency-based
program was recently very reluctant to expand support for a skills
center. "Why should our students have to write at all?" he asked.
"They are very good talkers. Let them use tape recorders." An ignorant remark—one might almost say an illiterate remark—but it expresses a view which is not at all uncommon and is certainly not limited to the left-over radicals of American education. In Kenya, for
instance, the universities have been closed. Daniel arap Moi, the
virtually illiterate successor of Jomo Kenyatta, has decided that higher
education is not a priority for Kenya; indeed, education at all levels
has been neglected—but that is too mild a term: education has been
virtually forgotten. In the schools there is no chalk, no paper or pens.
(The fifty shilling note nevertheless depicts a multiracial group of
youngsters sitting on the ground reading to one another.) Instruction
is generally by drill, with blows on the knuckles for errors—a parody

of the worst educational practice of former colonial masters. In some instances, teachers stress the oral tradition. They urge their students, when they return to their shambas on the weekends, to have their grannies tell them stories. But the grannies don't know any stories; the oral tradition is no more alive in Nairobi and its environs than it is in those institutes on orality where English teachers huddle by the ski lodge fire, trying to tell stories to one another. Kenyans are caught between two cultures, one powerless to be borne as long as those in power turn all inadequacies and insufficiencies to their ideological purpose. I believe the same sort of judgment could be made of the students victimized by the aforementioned dean.

Ideologues for whom it is important to discount the value of literacy could find support for their views in the research of Michael Cole and Sylvia Scribner. In an attempt to isolate literacy from schooling and to identify and differentiate the effects of each, they studied a tribe in Western Africa which has had a syllabic script for a hundred and fifty years, a form of writing employed only by certain males and limited to commercial purposes, chiefly accounting, as in the case of Sumerian clay tablets, and to the composition of letters which are as conventionalized as a Berlitz phrase book. It is entirely expectable, then, that Cole and Scribner should conclude as follows:

> We did not find literacy in the Vai script associated with generalized competence that might be characterized as abstraction or verbal reasoning or metalinguistic skills. The situation with regard to reading and writing is not dissimilar from that of other skilled practices such as weaving and pottery-making.[1]

I am amused at the echo here of Cardinal Newman's judgment that since music has no intellectual or moral value it should be relegated to the class of harmless but worthless activities, along with the stuffing of birds.

These conceptions of literacy are certainly impoverished: one identifies writing with the graphic means of representing sound, which is then easily dismissed as less efficient than a tape recorder and less authentic than speech; the other assumes that literacy can be represented by communicative functions which are absolutely minimal. Reading and writing are thus demeaned when the underlying view of language is restrictive. Those who consider reading and writing as "technologies" generally consider language itself as, simply, a communication medium and knowledge, a matter of information processing, or in its soft form, *"human* information processing."

These reductive views of literacy are, however, scarcely more harmful than the stretching that is done in the case of "cultural literacy." The test of any idea should be what it can do for us, and the

notion of "cultural literacy," as far as I can see, has led to no new
thinking about the relationship of reading and writing; it fosters no
new ideas about how to read a book, much less about how to read a
page: "cultural literacy" has nothing whatsoever to do with pedagogy.
It is helping to persuade people that something can be done about illiteracy in America if only we can get high school students to read
Fifty Good Books in their summer vacations so that they'll be ready
for One Hundred Great Books in college.

Both reducing and stretching what we mean by *literacy* yields
pseudo-concepts, in Vygotsky's sense. The only way we can protect
ourselves from the ill effects of such misrepresentations is to be good
pragmatists: how we use an idea, how it invites us to put it into practice, will tell us best what the significance of the idea is. English
teachers will come into their own when they realize that it is pedagogy, and not psycholinguistics and cognitive psychology, which provides the authentic means of discovering "what we are trying to do
and thereby how to do it."[2]

For Paulo Freire, as for I. A. Richards, Maria Montessori, William
James and other great teachers, theory and practice are mutually supportive, generating one another, each offering the means of critical revision of the other. Freire's *method* thus brings theory and practice
together and keeps them in conjunction. I want to turn now to considering how his pedagogy—his method—is informed by a philosophically
sound view of language and is inspirited by that unsentimental respect
for human beings which only a sound philosophy of mind can assure.

Freire's pedagogy is the antithesis of that spoonfeeding of letters
and attitudes which Sartre scornfully called "alimentary education."
("Here! Swallow this! It'll be good for you!") The digestive theory of
education is inescapably authoritarian: the teacher knows what's good
for you; it requires passive subjects who are in no sense creators of
knowledge. A pedagogy of knowing converts learners to agents who
are actively aware of what they are doing. Peasants and teacher are engaged in dialogic action, an active exchange from which meanings
emerge and *are seen to emerge.* It is central to Freire's pedagogy that
learners are empowered by the *knowledge that* they are learners.[3] This
conscientization or "critical consciousness,"—this awareness of oneself
as a knower, as meaning-maker—is brought into being in the course of
dialogue, which is, Freire has written, "the encounter between men to
name the world." The learners are engaged continually in thinking
about thinking, in those reflective acts of interpreting interpretations
which language makes possible. We are sometimes so used to thinking
of language as a "communication medium" that it can be a surprise to
discover, or to be reminded, that language is the means of making
those meanings which we communicate. Freire's pedagogy is founded

on a philosophical understanding of this generative power of language. When we speak, the discursive power of language—its tendency toward syntax—brings thought along with it. We don't think our thoughts and then put them into words: we say and mean at the same time; utterance and meaning-making are simultaneous and correlative.[4]

The principles of conscientization and dialogic action are given substance and authenticity by the philosophy of language which undergirds them. The pedagogy of knowing is empowered by the principle that naming the world entails identifying and classifying and that by those acts of mind learners are engaged in making meanings. The act of naming, of speaking the word, entails the naming of the world: "Human beings," Freire said at U Mass/Boston, "did not start by calling A! F! N! They first freed the hand and grasped the world." (Freire would know what Emerson meant in speaking of "the hand of the mind.") This understanding of the etiology of naming is biologically and philosophically grounded in a conception of man as the language animal, the *animal symbolicum*. And, indeed, to turn from a study of Freire's pedagogy of knowing to a study of Cassirer's *Essay on Man*, setting forth his philosophy of symbolic form, or to Susanne K. Langer's *Mind: An Essay on Human Feeling* is like hearing variations on a theme.

In a recent talk to a conference on reading in Brazil, Freire has recounted how in writing his text—the text of his remarks—he had "recreated and lived," as he says, "the experience I lived at a time when I did not yet read words." Here is the passage in which Freire tells of reading that early world:

> I see myself then in the average Recife house where I was born, encircled by trees. Some of the trees were like persons to me, such was the intimacy between us. In their shadow I played, and in the branches accessible to my height I experienced the small risks which prepared me for greater risks and adventures. The old house, its bedrooms, hall, attic, terrace—the setting for my mother's ferns—the back yard where the terrace was located, all this was my first world. In this world I crawled, gurgled, first stood up, took my first steps, said my first words. Truly, that special world presented itself to me as the arena of my perceptual activity, and therefore as the world of my first reading. The *texts*, the *words*, the *letters* of that context were incarnated in a series of things, objects, signs. In perceiving these, I experienced myself, and the more I experienced myself, the more my perceptual capacity increased. I learned to understand things, objects, signs through using them in relationship to my older brothers and sisters and my parents.

The *texts, words, letters* of that context were incarnated in the song of the birds—tanager, flycatcher, thrush; in the dance of boughs blown by the strong winds announcing storms; thunder and lightning; rain waters playing with geography: creating lakes, islands, rivers, streams. The *texts, words, letters* of that context were incarnated as well in the whistle of the wind, the clouds of the sky, the sky's color, its movement; in the color of foliage, the shape of leaves, the fragrance of flowers—roses, jasmine; in tree trunks; in fruit rinds: the varying color tones of the same fruit at different times—the green of a mango when the fruit is first forming, the green of a mango fully formed, the greenish yellow of the same mango ripening, the black spots of an overripe mango—the relationship among these colors, the developing fruit, its resistance to our manipulation, and its taste. It was possibly at this time, by doing it myself and seeing others do it, that I learned the meaning of the word *squashing.*

Animals were equally part of that context—the way the family cats rubbed themselves coyly against our legs, their mewing of entreaty or anger; the ill-humor of Joli, my father's old black dog, when one of the cats carelessly approached too near to where he was eating what was his. In such instances, Joli's mood was completely different from when he rather sportively chased, caught, and killed one of the many opossums responsible for the disappearance of my grandmother's fat chickens.

Part of the context of my immediate world was also the language universe of my elders, expressing their beliefs, tastes, fears, values, and which linked my world to wider contexts whose existence I could not even suspect.[5]

Paulo Freire's pedagogy of knowing is based on the principle that all human beings read the world; we all make sense of our experience, construing and constructing and representing it by means of language. His pedagogy takes advantage of the fact that imagination is "the prime agent of all human perception," that the forming power of mind is God-given and species-specific.

Paulo Freire's real work as a teacher began when he faced the fact that beginning with vowel sounds—*ba, be, bi, bo, bu*—was not the way to proceed with the people he was trying to reach, the peasants of Brazil. Many people note the fact, but few ever face it—I mean the fact that the elements into which a process can be analyzed do not themselves constitute the process nor do they, lined up, offer a model for the way in which a process can best be learned. Tolstoy recognized the fact, faced it, and set it down this way: "To the teacher the simplest and most general appears easiest—pigs, pots, a table—whereas for the pupil, only the complex and living appears easy." Freire's genius has been to begin with pigs and pots in such a way that they become significant, the bearers of import, representative and emblematic. Tolstoy's method—discovered by chance—was to give his pupils a proverb for which they then imagined the agents and action, the setting and events, thus creating the incarnation of its meaning.[6] Freire, too, begins with narrative which is not merely psychological, merely personal. His method is to "problematize the existential situation," to lead the would-be learners to transform the scenes and events, the dull routines of their lives, so that unexamined answers become provocative questions. As the peasants who have joined the culture circles look and look again at the actuality of their lives, recognizing the meanings represented by a picture of a squalid kitchen or a bowl of dirty water, they come to questions—not to problem-solving but to problem-posing.

One measure of the success of this method of literacy training is that Freire was exiled: the step from a personal narrative, recounting orally a childhood experience of carrying water from a stream a mile distant, to descriptions of dirty water from the local pump led to further questions about the taxes paid for the use of that pump. At the heart of Paulo Freire's pedagogy of knowing is the idea that naming the world become a model for changing the world. (Indeed, Freire seems to be playing with the terms of Marx's famous slogan, that the aim should no longer be to explain but to change.) Education does not substitute for political action, but it is indispensable to it because of the role it plays in the development of critical consciousness. That, in turn, is dependent on the transforming power of language.

In naming the world, the peasants of the culture circles are asked to survey their farms and villages and to collect the names of tools, places, and activities which are of central importance in their lives. The collections differ from village to village, but in every list of generative words, Freire includes the word for *vote* and the word for *atom bomb*. (Does this help explain why the CIA cooperated when the police burned his primers and broke his slide projectors?) These "generative words" are then organized in "discovery cards," a kind of vowel grid, a do-it-yourself lexicon generator. Some of the words it produces are nonsense; others are recognizable when sounded. The crucial point is that sound and letter shape are matched with one another and with meaning or the possibility of meaning. Instead of reducing literacy to a matter of manipulating the graphic code or beginning with the process of learning the relation of letter to sound—*ba, be, bi, bo, bu*—Freire's pedagogy of knowing insures that this decoding is always carried out simultaneously with the making of meaning: *reading the word* and *reading the world*. He differentiates *decoding*— matching sound and letter shape—from *decodification*, which is inter-

pretation, *in order to insure that they not be pedagogically separated.*
This careful distinction between the signal which is decoded and the
message which is decodified is precisely the opposite of what happens
when we conflate *information* in the purely technical sense—absence
of noise in the channel—with *information* in the sense of what can be
communicated. Correlation is not the same thing as muddling. As a
good dialectician, Freire divides in order to unite, an act which can remind us that the inventor of the pedagogy of knowing was a literacy expert living in ancient Greece.

Attempting to translate Freire's pedagogy, to adapt it to our classroom, is difficult because, for one thing, we have so much to unteach
and because, for another, our students are often cut off from those experiences of the natural world which provide the best models of learning—or so I believe. Deeply-rooted and purposeful sensory knowing
has not generally been a dimension of their educational development.
Our students find generalization difficult—and generalization is not the
same thing as abstraction—because nobody every taught them how to
go about it, and in the modern world such teaching is absolutely necessary. Our students are uninstructed in looking and looking again at
what they read and write; in noting likes and differents; in attending
to what varies with what. They can *decode* their world, recognizing
different brands of sneakers at forty paces, specifying the drawbacks
of five varieties of car radios, and they can *decodify*: they know what
these differences mean. But how many teachers have learned how to
teach reading and writing on this model, to encourage them in reading
the word as they read the world? How many of us have learned how
to make writing serve this enterprise?

Our first task, it seems to me, is to offer our students assisted in-
vitations[7] to discover the naming and articulating powers of language,
to see how language provides the means of making meaning. Generally
speaking, our students have not had such experiences and the difficulty
of collecting generative words suggests as much. That is a matter illumi-
nated by Sylvia Ashton-Warner's account in *Spearpoint* of her American
experience, of how it was impossible to proceed in Colorado as she had
in New Zealand. Her work with Maori children features what she calls
the "Key Vocabulary," "the captions of the dynamic life itself," her
own fascinating version of generative words. She describes the frustration she felt when she was unable, in her Rocky Mountain infant room,
to identify any key words at all. She was deeply shocked when the
children stood on the guitar or refused to volunteer as chalk monitors,
but when she could find no words, beyond *Mama* and the names of
their pets, which generated or represented complex and living meanings, she was terrified.

But our classrooms are not infant rooms and collecting a list of generative words might not be quite the point. We do not need to teach decoding, as the elementary teacher must, but that does not mean that we needn't teach our students to look and look again—not at bunny rabbits perhaps, but at natural forms and designs, at texts and the topography of their own lives. I believe that we must begin with our students as makers of meaning, trusting to the mediation provided by perception and dialogue: as they learn to problematize the existential situation, our students will be discovering the generative powers of language. It isn't easy; indeed, I think it's probably harder to engage the attention of American undergraduates and to encourage their critical thinking than it is to bring peasants along from the point of believing that hailstones are the souls of aggrieved ancestors. But I think we must remember Freire's problematic bowl of dirty water and his significant pigs and pots. If we ask our students to name their world and we get *digital clocks* and *designer jeans*, that is one place to begin; that is a point of departure for conscientization and dialogic action. It's a lot harder than running those rap sessions which used to pass for the pedagogy of the oppressed. I can remember the shock I had in discovering that at U Mass in the early seventies, young radical teachers— and some not so young—whose only pedagogy was to sit on the floor with their students, were claiming to be putting Freire into practice by asking their students "Did you know you're oppressed?" And I've heard accounts of how dismayed Freire was to find Harvard and Radcliffe students making banners with slogans meant to awaken the oppressed of Harvard Square.

If we begin with our students as meaning-makers, what happens is that objects of their field of vision become, slowly, emblems of their lives; trivial personal narratives of, for instance, the hassles experienced in getting to school by subway become "representative anecdotes," as Kenneth Burke puts it. And as this happens, our students are becoming critically conscious: they are learning to ask themselves not "What can I say to fulfill the requirements of this assignment—or to give the teacher what he wants?" but "What do I think about all this?" And they are learning to return to what they think about all that, to think about their thinking and to interpret their interpretations. These newfound powers of critical consciousness can then be exercised in the interest of initiating and sustaining the dialectic of *what is said* and *what is meant* as we read what others and what we ourselves have written. If we are to keep interpretation central, our best hope is to encourage our students to read the word as they read the world. *If we can make writing represent the processes of perception and dialogue, we will find ways of teaching composition as the kind of non-linear process it is.* I believe that writing becomes an authentic mode of learning and way of

knowing when it serves to enable students to record dialogic action
and to represent the inner dialogue which is thought. If students learn
to keep what I have elsewhere described as a dialectical notebook, the
facing pages in dialogue with one another so that they learn to take
notes on their notes, they will be learning to return to the meanings
they have made, to reflect on them, discovering thereby how meanings
provide the means of making further meaning.[8] Writing dialectically
encourages, as it *requires*, conscientization, the critical consciousness
of oneself as meaning-maker.

As we liberate ourselves from a pedagogy of exhortation, we will
be free to discover our own special powers as composition teachers.
Josephine Miles cheers us by remarking those powers. In one of her
crisp and instructive essays in *Working Out Ideas: Predication and
Other Uses of Language*, she first speculates about the reasons for the
failure of her students to take "a responsible point of view," reminding
us that

> sentence-making is predication, and to predicate is to assert an
> idea, selecting and treating facts from a point of view. Paragraph-
> making is the development of such ideas and the relationship be-
> tween them. Composition involves an individual responsibility of
> thought.

She then notes that students seem not to realize that chronology—their
only mode of organization—is an order or to understand "to what purpose they [are] putting it. And of the other logical orders, like implication, alternation, exemplification, they seem unaware." She then concludes as follows:

> It may be that we are so unaware ourselves of how to choose,
> how to co-ordinate and subordinate, how to generalize and ex-
> emplify, above all how to compose, that we cannot teach a
> younger generation. We may be, as the scientists have suggested
> to us, the victims of sheer uninterpreted data, as meaningless as
> can be. If we have no attitudes for our facts, we shall have no
> predicates for our subjects, no themes for our essays, no points
> for our remarks, no responsibilities for our actions.
>
> But I think the teachers of composition are the very ones who
> need not be so lost. They know that the subject is what the pred-
> icate makes it. They know that the human mind can take a con-
> sistent responsibility for what it has to say. They know that the
> selection and arrangement of materials to a purpose, a purpose
> weighed and evaluated, is as serious a task as can be conceived of.[9]

Josephine Miles here summons us—we composition teachers need not
be so lost—to a new prospect, a new sense of our powers and purposes,

which should surely include forming the concept of literacy. She is herself one of our most trustworthy guides in the enterprise of learning to teach writing as a means of making meaning, as a way of coming to know, of working out ideas. But to let writing thus serve a pedagogy of knowing requires that we liberate ourselves from the positivist support system which is the chief cause of all our woe: I mean the assignment of packaged topics and the dependence on pre-fabricated study questions and courses of study; I mean the use of linear models which do not and cannot represent the dialectical character of composing; I mean a trivialized conception of heuristics as problem solving which ignores both the role of problem posing and the heuristic power of language; I mean the dependence on a defunct rhetoric of categories arranged in dichotomous pairs like narrative-exposition and description-definition; I mean a conception of empirical research in which what can be measured becomes by default what it is important to teach. But it is exhilarating to remember that the pedagogy of knowing not only requires such liberation: it brings it about.

Paulo Freire's ideas are accessible and adaptable: if we can reconstitute our professional meetings as culture circles and our journals as authentic forums, we can begin to hear from one another about all attempts to develop a pedagogy of knowing. We will surely be engaged in forming the concept of literacy and thereby we will eventually change the state of affairs.

Let me close with one of Freire's characteristically optimistic contemplations from his talk at U Mass/Boston:

For me, philosophically, existentially, the fundamental task of human beings should be reading the world, writing the world; reading the words, writing the words. If we did that consciously, with a critical consciousness, of course we would be active, willing, choosing subjects of history. Then we could speak freely about our presence in the world.

Notes

[1] "Literacy Without Schooling: Testing for Intellectual Effects," *Harvard Educational Review*, 48 (November 1978), 448–461.

[2] I. A. Richards, *Design for Escape* (New York: Harcourt, 1968), p. 111. The dialectic of aims and means is central to Richards's conception of language and learning.

[3] The complex relationship of knowing *how* and knowing *that* is analogous, of course, to the relationship of practice and theory. Freire's argument is based on a thorough understanding of man as a historical being. It is set forth most substantially in Chapter Three of *Pedagogy of the Oppressed* (New York: Herder and Herder, 1970).

[4] The phrase is Owen Barfield's. Teachers interested in the relationship of the philosophy of rhetoric and theories of literary meaning will find useful discussions in Barfield's *The Rediscovery of Meaning* (Middletown, CT: Wesleyan University Press, 1977).

[5] "The Importance of the Act of Reading," *Boston University Journal of Education,* 155 (Winter 1983), 5–11.

[6] I have discussed some of the implications for composition pedagogy in "Tolstoy, Vygotsky, and the Making of Meaning," in *The Making of Meaning: Metaphors, Models and Maxims for Writing Teachers* (Upper Montclair, NJ: Boynton/Cook, 1981), 85–93.

[7] I have borrowed this phrase from I. A. Richards for the exercises in my textbook, *Forming/Thinking/Writing* (Rochelle Park, NJ: Hayden, 1978).

[8] See "A Curious Triangle and the Double-Entry Notebook; or, How Theory Can Help Us Teach Reading and Writing," in *The Making of Meaning.*

[9] *Working Out Ideas: Predication and Other Uses of Language* (Berkeley: Bay Area Writing Project, 1979), 8–9.

6

The Dialogic Imagination: More Than We've Been Taught

JUDITH GOLEMAN

Boston University

Language—like the living concrete environment in which the conscious-ness of the verbal artist lives—is never unitary. It is unitary only as an abstract grammatical system of normative forms, taken in isolation from the concrete, ideological conceptualizations that fill it, and in isolation from the uninterrupted process of historical becoming that is characteristic of all living language.

Mikhail Bakhtin

In *The Dialogic Imagination*, Mikhail Bakhtin reconstitutes our notion of language to languages in a way that can inform our work in reading and writing, both our research and our pedagogy. The dialogic philosophy of Bakhtin, however, presents a writer who tries to use it with a particular challenge—the challenge of not interring this preemi-nently lively theory through stilling references to a body of knowledge. If one is to represent accurately the philosophy of Bakhtin, the writing itself must evince the uninterrupted play that Bakhtin speaks of be-tween the centripetal and centrifugal forces of language, between the processes of centralization and decentralization, unification and disuni-fication (272). In the spirit of these processes, I will present a variety of professional and student texts with the intention of developing what Bakhtin might call an orchestration of themes and languages and not a transposition of multiple languages onto the piano keyboard of his sin-gle instrument or text (263).

Bakhtin's philosophy of language is founded on the principles of heteroglossia and dialogism: " . . . at any given moment in its historical existence, language is heteroglot from top to bottom," stratified by different classes, races, genders, ages, professions, families, locales and more. Furthermore, the interactions among these languages are constantly constructing new socially typifying languages (291). These languages do have one thing in common, Bakhtin stresses: they are all "specific points of view on the world, forms for conceptualizing the world in words" (291–292). And because language is always a "concrete heteroglot conception of the world" (293), one's language, one's individual consciousness is always already saturated by the otherness of living language, the language as it "exists in other people's mouths, in other people's contexts, serving other people's intentions: it is from there that one must take the word, and make it one's own" (294).

For Bakhtin, in other words, all our discourse is already social through and through, already in dialogue. "Only the mythical Adam," whose word and whose world were verbally unqualified was free of the internal dialogism of the word (279); the rest of us, structured by historical human discourse, continue to structure what we know and how we know it within this polyglot language environment.

How then, we must ask along with Bakhtin, can one create a language of "one's own" given the social nature of language? The answer, it would seem, lies not in some effort to carve out for oneself an autonomous realm of language free from sociality, but rather to become a more knowing participant in the social dialogue which constitutes all discourse, with ourselves and others. No person or group can ever really be free of the social chorus within; however, whole groups of people may live as if they are. For such groups, multi-voicedness is lived as predetermined shifts, not as thought processes. Under such circumstances, dialogic interorientation is automatic: "There is no attempt," Bakhtin writes, "to look at one of these languages through the eyes of another language" (295). Like Paulo Freire after him, Bakhtin links the ability to look at one's movement among languages with the possibility for political awareness and action; both link literacy to social freedom through the creative process by which a person comes into dialogical consciousness of conflicting languages for conceptualizing the world. Speaking of the illiterate Russian peasantry in the early twentieth century, Bakhtin wrote that only when a "critical interanimation of languages" began to occur, only as it became clear that the ideological systems of these languages were in contradiction and could not coexist peacefully—only then the "predetermined quality of these languages came to an end, and the necessity of actively choosing one's orientation among them began" (296).

In other words, consciousness of heterglossia is a prerequisite for choosing one's own language orientation, and so imagination in a heteroglot world is always dialogical, always aware of multiple, conflicting meanings for the same things.

It is precisely this belief in dialogism which links the philosophy of Bakhtin with the ethnographic research and pedagogy of Shirley Brice Heath. Specifically, it has been Heath's goal to bring dialogical consciousness to non-mainstream school children traditionally bound to failure in school by a passive, unconscious relationship to language. Her method has made it possible for children of non-mainstream communities to become translators of "the social reality of the familiar community domain into the unfamiliar school domain" (322). Her method, in short, has made it possible for school children to begin the process of looking at one language through the eyes of another language.

To begin my presentation of Heath's work, I have reproduced below part of a student conversation among four fifth graders in a science class in 1974 which Heath transcribes in her book, *Ways with Words: Language, life and work in communities and classrooms.* In this book, Heath reports her research as an ethnographer of communication and as a teacher trainer focusing on child language in the Piedmont Carolinas during desegregation in the South from the late sixties to the late seventies. On the basis of this research, Heath argues two points: 1) that teachers should learn to become ethnographers of their students' language use, researching the ways in which language acquisition constitutes socially specific patterns of talking, knowing and being; 2) that once teachers understand the specific ways children have learned to use language at home and in their communities, they should lead these children, themselves, to become ethnographers of their own and others' language use. Heath argues, in other words, that teachers can help students to build bridges between their communities' ways of knowing and the ways of knowing practiced in the schools.

Heath presents a model for such a bridging process through her description of a science project in one fifth grade class she observed. In this project, students became ethnographers on plant life, translating the local ways of talking about growing into scientific ways. As translators, these students engaged in a "two-way manipulation of knowledge from community to school," thereby increasing their awareness of both domains (321).

In the excerpt of student discussion about this project we come in on a group of black youngsters who were in the lowest track science class in their grade, having been tested as reading at a second grade level or below. The science project that they were working on required them to imagine that they were scouts for an outside group planning to set up an agricultural resource center in the community. Their task was to learn as much as possible about the growing methods of the local farmers and to study the "ways in which the local farmers' folk concepts about growing were like or different from 'scientific'

approaches" (317). Their task, in other words, was to do an ethnographic study of the neighborhood ways of talking about growing
methods and to translate these expressed methods into scientific concepts taken from textbooks, films and commercial material on plant
life (319–320). Working together, one group sounded like this:

> *Terry:* What'd you get?
> *Tony:* Wait 'til you hear ol' Mr. Feld.
> *Paul:* We gonna do the old informant or the new one first?
> *Tony:* The old — I talk to him a long time 'fore he tol' me 'bout
> gardenin'. Then he start 'memberin' 'bout how to cut the potato
> eyes, how to hill 'em up.
> *Terry:* You get drawings?
> *Tony:* Yea, [pulls pencil sketches out of folder and passes them
> around] 'n he checked 'em.
> *Terry:* Did he say when he planted, why the sprout come from
> the eye?
> *Tony:* Yea, wanna hear the tape?
> *Mike:* But we gotta hear Mr. Purcey tape too. Ol' Mr. Feld'll be
> different from somebody young as Mr. Purcey.
> *Tony:* All that's gotta go on the informant chart. (315)

Heath reports that the boys went on and listened to the tapes of
Mr. Feld, an eighty-six year old retired farmer and Mr. Purcey, a thirty-
five year old farmer, both from their community, stopping the tapes
frequently to ask questions, making scratch lists of terms and methods
used by informants, and debating the different emphases the farmers
placed on the growing processes: Mr. Feld believed in planting by the
moon; Mr. Purcey emphasized buying seed potatoes at the feed store
instead of using potatoes from the grocery store, as Mr. Feld did,
which sprouted under his kitchen sink. By the end of class, the boys
had decided to interview Mr. Purcey again because they needed more
information to complete a comparison chart with Mr. Feld. For instance, they needed to know if he too planted by the moon. They also
decided to interview the feedstore owner to find out how his potatoes
were different from the grocery store's (316).

In her transcription of this student dialogue, Heath allows us to
hear how these school children actually sound as they teach themselves
to bridge the gaps between their ways of using language at home, in the
community and at school. The methods of questioning, compiling and
sorting which they are learning to apply to their object of study are
evident here in their four-way conversation with each other. Through
question and answer, the conversation builds to a point where their
compiling process would seem to threaten a data overload and possibly
group dissension when Mike says, "But we gotta hear Mr. Purcey tape

too. Ol' Mr. Feld'll be different from somebody young as Mr. Purcey."
Tony, however, has a language for dealing with the growing complexity of their material and he uses it reflexively and transitively, in dialogue with himself *and* another to confirm Mike's point and to perpetuate the coherency of his group's work: "All that's gotta go on the informant chart," he says, using the school discourse which accommodates difference to mediate a moment of difference between himself and a classmate as well.

Using the language of transcription and report, Heath engages in a dialogical method herself which gives us a glimpse at how rich and dense this bi-directional movement between languages and the conceptual worlds they frame is. The language of student dialogue allows us to hear one way: "You get drawings?" "Yea, 'n he checked 'em"; the language of report allows us to hear another way:

> Learners in this science classroom had become ethnographers of a sort; in doing so, they had improved their knowledge of science. In addition, they had learned to talk about ways of obtaining and verifying information; terms such as *sources, check out* (in the sense of *verify*), *summarize,* and *translate* had become part of their vocabulary. They had come to recognize, use, and produce knowledge about the skills of inquiring, compiling, sorting, and refining information. . . . Their world of science uses had expanded far beyond the classroom. . . . Many had, for the first time in their lives, carried on conversations with feed store owners, nurserymen, and local agricultural agents. They had been forced into situations in which they had to formulate specific questions to obtain particular bits of information. . . . Traditionally these boys and their families . . . preferred giving a story in narrative form in answer to a generalized query: they had noticed this trait in their informants and came to laugh about the fact that they "couldn't get ol' Mr. Feld to answer a question directly." They had come to pay attention to the kinds of questions people in different situations in life asked and answered directly. . . . [W]ith guidance by the teacher on ways in which vocabulary, styles of language use, and features of discourse differ across situations, the students had . . . through the structure of the unit, begun to articulate these differences. (320–321)

Fifth grade students who are coming to know that discourse differs across situations and who are developing a means by which they are able to move among these languages are developing dialogical awareness and creativity. Dialogical awareness of languages differences, of course, precedes the possibility of choice among these languages. It ends the predetermined experience of a language and the conceptual world it frames and begins the process by which one actively chooses one's orientation among languages and the conceptual words they frame. In their "two way manipulation of knowledge about plant life from community to school and from school to community," these students learned how to translate knowledge from one domain into another (321). They "moved between the personalized, contextualized, orally expressed knowledge of home to the depersonalized, decontextualized, primarily written knowledge of the classroom" (321).

This bi-directional translation process between the two knowledge domains of home and school is comparable, I would suspect, to the process that Bakhtin imagines when he describes dialogical awareness as an interanimating process between two languages. We have seen that what Bakhtin argues will result from the interanimation of languages is not merely an identification of equivalencies, but a recognition of multiple, sometimes conflicting meanings for things. He writes: "All languages of heteroglossia . . . are forms for conceptualizing the world in words. . . . As such, they may all be juxtaposed to one another, mutually supplement one another, contradict one another and be interrelated dialogically" (291–292). This crucial recognition of multiple relations is not lost on Heath, who reports that by trying to translate folk concepts about plant life into scientific concepts, these students discovered that there were "definite relations" between the two systems—relations of "equivalence, contradiction, complementation and generalization" (324).

Learning how to orient themselves in the different worlds of home, community and school, these fifth graders are beginning to use one language interactively and critically to think about another, struggling between these languages, juxtaposing them and discovering the limits of any one language for themselves. In short, these students are having a rare experience where the dialogical struggle among languages has become the school's project and process, where the student as ethnographer can become a student of his *own* language so as to become a student of others' ways with words, as well.

In my work as a teacher of Freshman English at an urban, public university, the University of Massachusetts at Boston, I tried to find a method of teaching dialogical awareness to students of widely different backgrounds, both mainstream and non-mainstream. A university teacher cannot research a local community for the social roots of thought and language usage among her diverse students in the manner that Heath was able to research discrete communities in the Piedmont. Neither can a university teacher make the assumption that the students themselves have direct access to their original home and community language environments in the way Heath's young students had access. The college level development of dialogical awareness through ethnographic study must therefore be indirect for both the teacher as a researcher of her students' language use and for the student as a student of his or her own language use.

A substitute for this direct access to home and community can be found in the adult student's ability to recollect and to represent his or her own history in language. For in a student's language about home and community can be found the operative ways of knowing which the student, helped by the teacher, can learn from and begin to translate into other ways of knowing, specifically those ways practiced in the schools. In other words, a student's writing can become both the object of dialogical consciousness and the means by which such consciousness is developed.

I have found John Berger's book, *A Fortunate Man*, to be a useful, even unique, text for such a writing course because it provides a socially specific, fully contextualized model of one dialogical thinker in process. In the compelling figure of a country doctor, students can follow the history of John Sassall, a young medical professional coming to reflect on his ways of knowing as these ways of knowing constitute limits on his ability to understand and to help his impoverished rural patients.

Through a series of sequenced assignments,[1] my students move back and forth between articulations of the doctor's changing method and narratives of their own experiences. Writing about the doctor's cases, students must imaginately become Sassall as he acquires his new method of dialogical thinking, as he listens to his patients' language about themselves, observes them over time, in short, as he imaginatively tries to know his patients in the way they know themselves. As the doctor learns to listen, he develops new categories for his conceptualization and treatment of his patients' problems, categories that go beyond strictly medical knowledge, categories which help him to take in "all the possibly relevant facts—emotional, historical, environmental as well as physical" (73). And as the doctor enlarges his categories, so too, the students enlarge their own categories for conceptualizing the doctor's new thinking process. For the doctor, every diagnosis is the result of dialogical inquiry with his patients, by which he tests and revises his own ways of knowing and his own ways of treating. "He never stops speculating, testing, comparing," Berger writes. "The more open the question the more it interests him" (103).

For the students writing about the doctor's dialogical method of inquiry, every new case they read about must be explained in the light of his prior cases as they have written *about* these prior cases. For example, when the students write about the doctor's first case, they unequivocally praise his horn-honking, gate-crashing heroism as he rushes to save a woodman pinned under a tree; however, these actions come under scrutiny and are reassessed when the students must consider the second case of an emotionally unstable asthmatic. In this case, the doctor tries to cure a sick woman by crashing the "cage of her illness" (21) with a shocking question. He fails. Consequently, students must reexamine their prior assumptions about heroism, spontaneity and individualism. At other times, students use what they learn in a later case to explain a detail that did not seem important or was not clear in an earlier case. For example, as one student wrote about the case of an impoverished, heartsick woman, he began to understand why the doctor considered conversation in a patient's home a form of treatment. This reminded him of an earlier paper about the case of a dying woman where he had not been able to understand why Berger had included the detail of the doctor curbing his impulse to leave after a treatment and instead staying for tea with the family. Connecting the two cases with the phrase "sit-down compassion," the writer was able to fill a gap in his understanding of a prior case. In this way, the students, writing about the doctor's dialogical process, are themselves engaged in their *own* dialogical process, as well, by which they are constantly testing, comparing, and revising their own ways of making meaning[2] about the doctor at work.

As they compose experiences from their own lives, students begin to use categories from the doctor's new method to expand their means of conceptualizing their own experiences, interanimating the language they bring from their prior schooling, their homes, and communities with the new language of the text. Through an incremental and repetitive looping movement from the doctor and his cases to themselves and their own social relations, these writers become engaged in an ongoing dialogical activity by which they are constantly looking at their own language as a way of knowing through interanimation with the language of Berger's text as a way of knowing. Slowly, this intertextual and reflexive activity which is so awkward at first becomes a new intellectual motion whose value is conveyed not only by the way it serves the doctor in reading and composing the meaning of his cases, but in the way it serves the students in their own reading and composing practice.

In this way, the student writing, which is always read aloud and shared,[3] becomes itself a new source of reference for the class, a valued and comparable text about dialogical thinking in process, a record of their own expanding means of making meaning. And while no single student paper can or should be used to epitomize such a process, I believe it is possible to see in a single student essay the specific effects of dialogic thinking on the mind and the voice of one writer. To this end, a student paper is reproduced below. It was written in response to the sixth of fifteen assignments in the course, an assignment which asked the students to think about a particular passage in Berger's book. In it Berger describes the doctor's surprise that his patient, a dying woman who is suffering massive chest pain, should flinch at the pin-prick from an injection he is giving her. In this assignment, the students are asked to think about the significance of this passage by writing about a time when their own common-sense notions were surprised; that is, when, in reference to a statement by Sassall, "the obvious, the easiest, the most readily available" way of knowing something failed them (62). One student, Mary Ellen, responded as follows:

Her mother was a woman of denial and born again faith. She believed in a heart trained to accept the ways of her newly found religion. Her fourteen year old daughter was still a child and, until this point, accepted the dogma her mother handed her. One occasion, though, forced the daughter to begin to understand her mother's behavior and need for answers that come from beyond common sense.

The girl had developed a terrible case of exzema that had spread all over her hands. She was a shy girl. She was not too pretty, and though well dressed, did not appear to be because she was acutely self-conscious. She seemed to herself, taller than the girls her age and because of a combination of these realities, did not have a healthy self-esteem. The exzema was embarassing enough, but she learned to live with this day to day. It was painful. As a result of this plague, all ten of her fingers needed to be bandaged to prevent her incessant scratching. Things like writing in school proved to be difficult. The mother was ironically, a registered nurse who taught in a nearby college. She taught the principles of medicine but she did not succumb to its practicality. She did tend to the most immediate needs of her daughter's hands. She soaked the red parched hands and bandaged them in sterile, white guaze. This did not seem to be enough to the girl. Because of her mother's consuming faith, she prayed to her God and did not take the girl to a doctor for more immediate relief. Instead, on Sunday after church services, she brought the girl to the altar and with the minister and several other clergy, laid hands on the girl to pray for her immediate recovery, shouting at heavan didn't work. There was no miracle. After a week and a half the exzema continued to spread and become almost unbearable to the already sensitive girl. It was only at this point that the mother permitted her to see a doctor. He prescribed a strong ointment and soak that brought the plague under control.

It seemed to the girl that after this ordeal, the most practically accessible way to her recovery was unjustifiably witheld from her.

On the other hand, her mother's life was ruled by a need for
something that she couldn't define to the daughter's satisfaction.

In John Berger's *A Fortunate Man*, the doctor, in the case of
the dying woman, sees beyond what he does in his previous cases.
He tries, in this case, to look beyond common sense. He notices
the effect the pin-prick had on his patient and in doing do, looks
beyond the obvious. He becomes more sensitive to the things that
are going on around him.

Only looking back on this incident in my life, can I understand
my mother's need to look beyond the easiest answer. She needed
something more than she taught. Unfortunately, I was the one to
feel the painful effects and become angry. Sometimes the common sense approach is the most effective, as in the case of the
woodman or for a suffering child. When dealing with death and
the dying woman, and the asthmatic's emotional problems,
though, the least obvious is sometimes most effective. The doctor now finds himself becoming more sensitive to the details of
his case. Now I have become more sensitive to the deatals in my
own case history. Just as the pain of an injection made the doctor more aware of her other pains and the inevitability of death,
the laying on of hands makes me realize the need in others to
grasp for an alternitive to common sense.

In this paper, the writer juxtaposes her own story about her
mother's hurtful avoidance of common sense with Berger's story about
the doctor's self-conscious determination always to avoid common
sense. What she knows from her painful home and community experience appears to contradict what she reads in the school text. For a
student faced with such an apparent contradiction between the language of home and the language of the school text, "things like writing
in school" could certainly "prove to be difficult." However, this student is not trapped by a passive relationship to language; she is not
language bound to choose *between* her experience with common sense
and the doctor's because she now has a method which, like the doctor,
frees her to go beyond common sense choices herself toward a type of
understanding which is sensitive to the details of each case and the possibility of multiple, conflicting and supplementing relations between
cases.

In this paper, the writer is able to interact critically with the conceptual language of Berger's text because she sees it *as* a language in
specific relations of contradiction and complementation to her own
personal history. Berger's presentation of the concept common sense
does not include an example of the doctor failing because he avoided
the most readily available way of knowing. By telling her own story,

the writer juxtaposes one language about common sense with another; that is, she dialogically interacts with the language of the text and revises it. By virtue of this dialogical interaction, she has bridged the gap between home and school. She has established a complementary, bidirectional relationship with Berger's text about the doctor whose dialogical method is mirrored in her own. Going beyond the obvious herself in her recognition of her mother's own imagination, she has applied the dialogical method of knowing provided in her school text to her home life and it has given her a new language by which to bridge the gap between herself and her mother, and between home and school.

Like the country doctor, Sassall, and Heath's fifth graders, Mary Ellen is on new epistemological ground where meaning is made by the composing of relations among the languages of home, community and school, and not by the substitution of one bounded language for another. She is now a more knowing participant in the social dialogue which constructs our discourse with ourselves and others. By discovering the dialogical structure of relations among multiple and conflicting languages in her mother, Mary Ellen has begun to understand the multiple and conflicting languages which structure her own dialogic imagination.

In her final self-evaluation for the course, Mary Ellen described the discovery of her dialogic imagination this way: "The paper that pleased me the most was my personal experience paper in Assignment #6 . . . it taught me to look at a painful situation outside my usual reactions and discover imagination. By discovering imagination in my mother, I also discovered imagination in myself."

Notes

[1] I would like to acknowledge my debt to William E. Coles, Jr. for the concept of sequenced assignments.

[2] I would like to acknowledge the influence of Ann E. Berthoff's dialectical theory of the composing process as a meaning making process.

[3] I would like to acknowledge the influence that the work of Rosemary Deen and Marie Ponsot has had on my use of student writing in the classroom.

References

Bakhtin, M. (1981). *The dialogic imagination* (C. Emerson & M. Helquist, Trans.). Austin: University of Texas Press.

Berger, J. & Mohr, J. (1967). *A fortunate man, the story of a country doctor.* New York: Pantheon.

Berthoff, A. E. (1978). *Forming/thinking/writing.* Rochelle Park, NJ: Hayden.

_____. (1981). *The making of meaning.* Montclair, NJ: Boynton/ Cook.

Coles, W. E., Jr. (1974). *Teaching composing.* Rochelle Park, NJ: Hayden.

_____. (1978). *The plural I.* New York: Holt, Rinehart and Winston.

Deen, R. & Ponsot, M. (1982). *Beat not the poor desk.* Montclair, NJ: Boynton/Cook.

Freire, P. (1968). *Pedagogy of the oppressed* (M. Bergman Ramos, Trans.). New York: Seabury Press.

_____. (1973). *Education for critical consciousness* (M. Bergman Ramos, Trans.). New York: Seabury Press.

Heath, S. B. (1983). *Ways with words: Language, life and work in communities and classrooms.* Cambridge: Cambridge University Press.

7

Coming to Words: Writing as Process and the Reading of Literature

GARY LINDBERG

University of New Hampshire

I am a teacher of literature who came rather late to the field of composition research. My motive was simple. I wanted to know more about teaching writing. But it's hard to keep one's teaching interests separated. As I discovered how much of the writing process had been newly described in the last few decades and how radically this research is affecting the classroom, I caught the contagion and began to think about what we actually do when we read literature and when we teach it. This paper is an attempt to form a concept of reading that reflects what we have learned about the process of writing.

Reading and writing may seem like counterparts of each other, but their bond is at once closer and more tenuous than that. Words and experience are not the same. When we write, we attempt to map experience onto a relatively stable system of language. When we read, we try to make words on the page reach back into our own experience. In both gestures we come to words. But it is easy to forget how changeable and approximate this process is. Something about the finality of the printed page tempts even experienced readers to regard the words as inevitable—they state what the writer wanted to say, and our job is simply to find the meaning. Coming to words, however, is not like discovering a key or having a dove descend in a beam of light. The writer faces a blank page and has somehow to work things out. The reader in turn has to recognize the printed words as the tracks of that human effort. To follow them is not a matter of decoding. We have to imagine the human activity that produced them, letting the needs and puzzlements of the writer come to life again in us as we also attempt to work out what the words are trying to say. Instead of thinking of the pearl as a well wrought object of beauty, we need to remember that it's the oyster's way of saying, Ouch!

What makes imaginative literature different from other kinds of writing is that it forces us to recognize that human gesture of coming to words. Stories and poems show us people trying to make sense of their experiences—to name them, to fit them into orderly sequences, to find language fresh and exact enough to catch what is too personal for the stock phrases. We watch both authors and characters making meanings out of what has happened to them, attributing motives to explain the odd conduct of others, and finding patterns within which their feelings count. In other words, the characters in stories and poems are busy doing exactly what we do as their readers. We are all interpreters. And these imaginary people help us reflect on our own acts of interpretation. We see how their meanings are affected by their own temperaments and circumstances, how those meanings change, what consequences they produce. We come to recognize that meanings are constructed by people who need to make them, and for good specific reasons.

This is why people write and read in the first place. Someone needs to say something and someone else needs to hear. Both need to make sense of things. Despite the elaborate systems of analysis that characterize academic reading, literary works are not repositories of hidden meanings but human gestures. They record someone's attempt to come to words. And to read them is not to be given an interpretation of experience but to witness one in the making.

What I'm talking about is the very core of literacy. To be literate is more than a matter of cracking codes or applying formulas. Literacy is the capacity to relate words on the page to personal experience. It is a mysterious filling in. When we read about a mountain, we go beyond dictionary definitions to flesh out the word with our own experience, whether from our senses, our imaginations, or what we have already heard and read. And we read between the lines in the same way, filling in the unstated motive, linking cause with effect. We use our imaginations. How we do that filling in varies, of course, with our experience. *Huckleberry Finn* is a radically different book to a fourteen-year-old reader and to a twenty-six-year-old reader. It is also very different to black and white readers. Imagining an ideal reader may be an interesting exercise, but it isn't related to literacy or to what happens when we teach literature. What matters is the actual meeting between the text and the reader's experience.

That meeting is not inevitable. Even those who read a great deal may not be literate. The problem arises in how we are conditioned to deal with language. In our time it completely surrounds us. Think how many signs or slogans we inadvertently read for every one that has any real impact. Or how much talk on radio or television we simply tune out. Even when we listen attentively, there is too rarely a real connection. We know how important are such matters as economic trends, balances of nuclear weaponry, or sources of acid rain. But when we read or hear about them, we are confronted with events so big and so distant from us that we cannot personally affect them. Even joining a concerned group diffuses and blurs our own influence. Up against the world presented to us by the media, we usually feel powerless. In time we learn how to process words without having to do anything about them. Imaginative literature can help us unlearn this habit. There we witness people making such meanings as they have to and then living with those meanings. It is a world of consequences. What people say about their lives matters. Literacy, in this sense, is discovering the consequences of words. To make that kind of experience possible for our students—to help them relate written words to their lives—seems to me of far more urgency than to present them with the ideal readings of a set of great books.

If words on the page have consequences, then they make a difference. We change as we read. That seems like a commonplace observation. But if we really grasped its implications, it would transform the study of literature. For our concerns with such matters as literary artifacts, structures, authoritative readings, codes, and systems of interpretation make it almost impossible to attend properly to our changes. After all, they're embarrassing. If we read one way early in a text and another way later, isn't the first way wrong, perhaps even stupid? What's more, the changes are potentially endless. If today's reading is better than yesterday's, how do we know that tomorrow's won't be better yet? So we lie about our reading experience and teach our students to lie about theirs. We pretend that the text is a fixed object in space instead of a fluid development in time. And we pretend that its "meaning" is another text that we produce by decoding the given one.

Maybe if we had another way of thinking about meaning, it would be easier to attend to our changes as readers. Doris Lessing provides a good one in her recent speculative fictions. The meaning of a phenomenon is not a deeper truth about it but the change it produces, the difference it makes. Meaning is related to consequences. It is an occurrence, not an assertion. So the meaning of a literary work depends on the changes it brings about in readers. From that perspective we can be more precise about what happens when we read. Things change in the text, and things change in the reader. If readers attend to their own changes as natural and appropriate, they can in turn look back at the text to see what caused their change. And such scrutiny not only forces more exact reading. Its primary effect is to reveal a specific connection between printed words and personal experience.

What kinds of changes actually take place in readers of imaginative literature? Our impulse on hearing this question is to think of large changes in response to an entire book. When I taught Lessing's *Shikasta* last year, one student decided to join the anti-nuclear movement and another applied for the Peace Corps. Dramatic and public changes like that do occur, but they mislead us about the essential kind of change. They encourage us to fall into vague lessons—I learned to be more tolerant, I understood better why women are angry—and these suggest that meaning is the "moral" of the text. The core of literary experience, however, is on a much smaller scale. Smaller, more exact, more demanding. Imaginative literature draws us to the immediacies of experience, where the larger lessons are first tentatively formulated and as often undone. What I want to describe, then, are the small changes, the well marked moments of surprise or revision, that make up the most intimate bond between reader and text.

As one reads, something clicks. It seems as if one's mind has leaped from one level to another: one suddenly sees the pattern or finds the name for that dim awareness hovering at the edge of one's mind. Let me illustrate by reference to a well-known sequence in *Huckleberry Finn* where Huck gets separated from Jim and the raft in the fog and then pretends he has been asleep on the raft all along, so that Jim will believe the fog was only a dream. While Jim has been heartbroken over the possibility that Huck had drowned, Huck is ready to make a game of it, gloating over Jim's puzzlement when he sees the trash on the raft and knows he has been fooled. Jim properly scolds Huck for playing with his feelings. Faced with Jim's anger, Huck works the matter over for fifteen minutes and finally apologizes: "I didn't do him no more mean tricks, and I wouldn't done that one if I'd a knowed it would make him feel that way." One's first reaction to this development—like Huck's—is to be ashamed at his trick and then moved by his growth of awareness. He has learned a lesson about Jim's feelings and about personal loyalty.

But then most readers jump to another level of understanding. They recognize a form behind the immediate incident. One form is that of playing tricks: *Huckleberry Finn* is filled with shenanigans in which someone completely disregards the feelings of others, as Huck and Tom are still doing at the end of the novel with Aunt Sally, Uncle Silas, and Jim. Another form is that of racism: Huck is particularly ready to play this kind of trick on Jim because he doesn't quite believe that black people are human and have feelings. If one thinks about the incident from that perspective, Huck's insight about Jim's feelings seems even more impressive because it emerges despite a deeply conditioned prejudice.

This kind of discovery of pattern is the most familiar change in a reader. One goes from recognitions about the immediate action to a larger context. One perceives and names the form behind the action. One generalizes, deals with the experience more abstractly. Piaget bases one of the most important of his developmental transitions on this kind of leap, as older children move from "concrete operations" to "formal operations." Huck himself, of course, is still in the stage of concrete operations. He does not recognize the pattern in what has just happened. *Jim* has feelings, but that doesn't change his estimate of other blacks or of slavery. Later on he will even forget Jim's feelings again.

When we turn from the concrete occurrence to the form of it or the abstract essence, we move to a higher logical type. We transcend and escape our bondage to the immediate. It is tempting, then, to think that the kinds of changes we should cultivate in readers would involve higher and higher levels of awareness. This is exactly the pattern that unites many well-known theorists of cognitive and moral development—Piaget, Kohlberg, Perry, Erikson. But to a person who loves reading imaginative literature, there is something disquieting about a consistent preference for the form over the substance or for the moral generality over the emphatic concern for particular circumstances. The higher logical type is not always better. And that moment in a reader's mind when something clicks does not always involve a leap to a more abstract plane. Let's return to Huck's apology to Jim and try to describe the reader's change more precisely. Huck doesn't in fact say that he apologized to Jim. What he says is, "It was fifteen minutes before I could work myself up to go and humble myself to a nigger—but I done it, and I warn't ever sorry for it afterwards, neither." Huck does perceive a form underlying his conduct. At the very moment of his greatest moral growth in this episode, he formulates it in the most stratified racial prejudice. What are we to make of that? Is Huck overcoming his racist training or reconfirming it?

This question also applies to our experience as readers. To say that we keep jumping to higher levels of understanding implies an irreversible development, whereas in instances like the present it seems as if we may equally well descend again. When something clicks in our minds as we read, it may be more accurate to describe the change as a sudden shifting of contexts. To recognize a higher logical type is only one example of the pattern, not the pattern itself. We change by seeing the immediate gesture in a new context. Such changes are reversible. In fact in some of the moments of reading that move us most, we never do settle on an ultimate context. That is why we can repeatedly return to them and find something new, talk about them with other readers and deepen our pleasure. And that is why some interpretive arguments never end. From one perspective Huck's discovery about Jim's feelings becomes more admirable when we note the self-conscious racism it has to break through. From another perspective that continuing explicit prejudice undermines the whole development, tainting Huck's apology with an ineradicable smugness.

What is it about imaginative literature that makes readers self-consciously jump from one context to another? What in the text *means* this kind of change in a reader's experience? An obvious answer to this question is that poets and storytellers deliberately play contexts off against each other. But there is another feature of their works that draws even more on the reader's capacity to re-imagine. When we see a detail or a gesture in a context, that context furnishes a basis for interpretation. We perceive the detail as part of a certain pattern, a set of relationships. The emergence of such a pattern makes the mind click with a new discovery. But what if we have found a satisfactory interpretive scheme and suddenly a detail appears that simply doesn't fit? Just before they get lost in the fog, Huck tells Jim that French people talk differently than Americans. Jim won't believe it. So Huck sets about convincing him that it makes sense for people to speak different languages. He points out that cats and cows talk differently from each other and from us, and he gets Jim to agree that this is natural and right.

"Well, then, why ain't it natural and right for a *Frenchman* to talk different from us? You answer me that."

"Is a cat a man, Huck?"

"No."

"Well, den, dey ain't no sense in a cat talkin' like a man. Is a cow a man? — er is a cow a cat?"

"No, she ain't either of them."

"Well, den, she ain't got no business to talk like either one er the yuther of 'em. Is a Frenchman a man?"

"Yes."

"*Well*, den! Dad blame it, why doan' he *talk* like a man? You answer me *dat*!"

I see it warn't no use wasting words — you can't learn a nigger to argue. So I quit.

What does it mean for readers to follow this sequence? We see the pattern behind Huck's persuasion: he gradually leads Jim toward understanding by a simple analogy. We can see where he is headed and we thus fill in the sense. When Jim imitates the form, however, it's not so evident where he is going because we don't share his perspective in which there is only one human language. His conclusion is every bit as logical as Huck's, but it jars with our perception of pattern. We feel both a comic satisfaction in the completion of the logical movement and an intellectual dissonance. And Huck's final racist summary disrupts the pattern completely. We don't take easily to such disruptions. We try to find another pattern. In this case Jim succeeds because Huck's analogy is not as sound as it seemed. Cats and people belong to different species, whereas Frenchmen and Americans belong merely to different races or nations. But how do we fit in Huck's conclusion? The same kind of racist thought that flawed his analogy lets him off the hook: "you can't learn a nigger to argue." Jim's argument in this context is a plea for recognition of common humanity despite differences in speech or race.

The jump from a comic play on logic to that kind of insight is characteristic of how literature can make us change. It is natural for us to perceive in patterns, to make sense of particularities by finding a structural essence or a sequence of causes that threads them together. But again and again as we read stories and poems, a detail appears that disrupts the order, forcing us to imagine yet another context, another system of relations. Back and forth we go from order to dissonance, from the familiar to the strange. All intellectual growth, in fact, follows that kind of dialectical development, from jarring details to new adaptations of the system. But when we study other kinds of writing—history, sociology, biology, economics—we are primarily concerned with the systems that people have constructed to help us make sense of our experience. Each one can be elaborated into a whole discipline. Imaginative literature, in contrast, deliberately explores the disruptions of those schemes. It has a bias toward moments of uncertainty, details that don't fit, and it repeatedly shows characters having to grope for new explanations. It thus renews our appreciation for the very act of making meaning. It is imaginative not only because of the nature of the writer's work but because readers as well constantly have to use their imaginations to invent new contexts and thus rise to new levels of thought and feeling. Imaginative literature threatens the system. It makes us slow down, go back, pause, look again.

Let me summarize this view of the reader's experience by an illustration from a student's essay. She is writing about manners in the scene I've been discussing.

> Huck's actions reveal a lot about the attitude of whites toward blacks. When he reached the raft, Huck could have awakened Jim and told him everything was okay. He might have even asked Jim if he was all right. Instead Huck plays a trick so simple that it should have been an insult to anyone's intelligence. Yet Huck knew it would fool Jim. He doesn't credit Jim with the brains to see through his ruse. Nor does Huck expect Jim to be worried; indeed, he seems surprised to find that Jim had feelings or was

capable of forming human attachments. And most importantly, Huck knew his trick would work because he knew that Jim would have to believe anything Huck told him because Huck was white.

Jim is taken in, just as Huck expected, but he shames Huck in the end. When Jim finds out that he's been fooled, he doesn't give Huck a dressing down, nor does he take him over his knee. Both justifiable responses to Huck's behavior. Instead he calmly tells Huck what he thinks and slowly retreats to the wigwam.

Jim's behavior indicates how imprisoned he still is by the manners of the 1800's. He is an adult, but he is not in charge. He must defer to Huck, because Huck is white. Jim can't punish Huck's thoughtlessness. He is so dominated by white folks, that he even doubts his own experiences because Huck's story contradicts his recollections.

Whatever we mean by higher order thinking in literary interpretation, this seems to me a good sample of it. The writer's mind moves back and forth between constructing patterns and recognizing the problematic details. It is constant discovery.

But the passage is also interesting in relation to another context, that of the introductory American Lit survey in which it was written. I had assigned a series of specific interpretive options from which students could choose in writing short papers. The one on manners in a particular scene included the instruction: "For each character involved describe what the character *could* say or *could* do in the scene but chooses *not* to. Explain as clearly as you can why the characters behave as they do. Do you see any unspoken rules or habits or patterns that are guiding them?" When I made up that assignment, I had in mind the importance of imagining alternatives as a way of seeing what actually happened and what needs explaining. But I don't always read that way myself. Nor do I think of *Huckleberry Finn* as a novel of manners. Imagine my surprise, then, in getting a paper on manners in this novel. If she were going to write on manners, why not choose an author like Henry James or Mary Wilkins Freeman? And the particular scene she chose was one that I knew all about already from repeated reading and teaching. It illustrates Huck's callousness about Jim's feelings and indirectly his racism. That is what it means. I had stopped attending to the details because I knew how to interpret them.

But what's this? Huck *could have* wakened Jim immediately and asked if he was all right. Of course he could have, but in my fifteen or twenty readings of this scene I'd never thought of that. Why? This scene turns out to be more interesting than I thought. And Huck's trick is so simple as to insult one's intelligence. That's true, too, but I had reread the scene so often knowing the "point" of it in advance, that I never thought of that angle on it. Nor of the problem it raises of *why* Jim fell for it. So what this paper did for me was turn a familiar scene strange again and show me how much more complicated and extensive the racism in it actually is than I had assumed. It had even affected my own reading. I would not in fact be using so overly familiar a text as *Huckleberry Finn* for my illustrations here had it not been brought back to life for me by this essay. Now this student's paper doesn't offer a ground-breaking interpretation of the novel. It is not a publishable article but a short exercise in an American Lit survey. But it did its job. It seems to me a perfect illustration of why we read literature in the first place. The discoveries the writer made herself and those she drove me to as her reader are so intrinsically satisfying that once students start making them we don't have to worry about their continuing motivation as readers.

I emphasize this classroom example because it shows that literary reading involves more than the single reader poised over the text. My experience as a teacher was changed by my student's paper in a way formally similar to her experience of change with the novel itself. Class discussion involves further play of alternative contexts, so that the same clicks of discovery occur there as occur when the reader faces the text. Class discussion, in fact, *is* reading; it isn't simply a report on an earlier experience. And students writing papers on literary texts are reading. They construct patterns out of their immediate discoveries, find moments of dissonance, return to the text, discover still larger or more complicated patterns. In other words, the same kinds of personal changes characterize all parts of a literature class. But only if we teach our students to respect their own moments of change, to account for them, share them, and make something of them.

If we think of composition and of the reading of literature as human gestures of coming to words, one of the things we have to accept, then, is the centrality of change. Changing issues, changing contexts, changing perspectives, changing selves. Reading is messier than we like to believe. There is another even more disturbing consequence of this view of reading. We never do come to words. It is always an approximation. Flaubert, who could spend an afternoon searching for *le mot juste*, said, "human speech is like a cracked kettle on which we tap crude rhythms for bears to dance to, while we long to make music that will melt the stars." Of course, he wrote pretty well, nonetheless. Practically, the approximation is good enough when it serves its purpose in a particular context. Readers and writers have other things to do, so at a certain point they stop going back. That will do, they think, that's what I wanted to say, or that's what the passage means. But we misconceive both processes if we regard that stopping as the attainment of accuracy.

Coming to words is not like shooting at a target—hit or miss. When words connect with our experience, it is not that the one duplicates or reproduces the other. There is no copy. The connection is itself a process, an interchange. If the meaning of a text is the difference it makes for a reader, then the meaning occurs as the reader actively approximates the text, veering from one perspective to another. This process will vary from reader to reader because each will come to the words of the text from a different world of experience. And the writer's personal feeling also undergoes a certain displacement in coming to words. There is no perfect phrase, no perfect reading.

What makes this view of reading hard to accept is the weight of our critical traditions. Stephen Dedalus's famous analysis of esthetic experience is still in the background of a great deal of teaching. He argues that the esthetic emotion is static. "The mind is arrested and raised above desire and loathing." What evokes that emotion has a harmonious relation of parts. It isn't a human gesture but purely an object: "the esthetic image is first luminously apprehended as selfbounded and selfcontained upon the immeasurable background of space and time." It is the perfect artifact which the New Criticism showed us how to analyze and how to teach. But the aspiration is much older. To defeat time, change, and mortality by carving one's words or images in stone seems itself a timeless yearning. "Not marble nor the gilded monuments/Of princes shall outlive this pow'rful rhyme." If speech involves an inevitable give and take, writing, on which one spends time and effort, should stand on its own outside the particular occasion. Art against nature.

But the artifact doesn't stand alone. To comprehend what is written requires the same kind of trial-and-error process that produced the writing in the first place. Both writing and the reading of literature have much more in common with natural biological processes than the model of the timeless artifact suggests. Such processes, like learning to walk or adjusting one's perception of a distant object, require that one be allowed the experience of error and the feedback that accompanies it. The same kind of thing happens in reading and writing. Both Mina Shaughnessy in *Errors and Expectations* and Frank Smith in *Reading Without Nonsense* show specifically how important it is to experience error and adjustment as one learns to write or to read. But we tend to play down the value of error for more sophisticated readers. Smith describes effective reading as a lively use of context and expectation to narrow the range of alternative meanings that one considers. Since only that information which is organized and interrelated enters one's long-term memory, one reads with greater comprehension by using the whole sentence as a way of grasping the individual word, and the whole paragraph as a way of construing the sentence. Necessarily this means reading rather quickly and comprehensively.

But does this description—which works so well for informational reading—also apply to our experience with imaginative literature? Let's consider a poem composed in regular meter. As soon as we get the feel of the meter, we carry on the convention more quickly, and at the point of metrical variation we might read right over the phrasal rhythm in order to preserve the metrical regularity. But that jars with our sense of the sentence itself or the pronunciation of the word, so we return and reread, thereby giving extra attention to the jarring phrase and perhaps discovering that something in the idea or feeling behind the phrase is also jarring. Misreading, in other words, helps us understand. Unlike informational writing, imaginative literature is filled with impediments. We have to slow down, look back, study the isolated phrase or detail that breaks up the order within which things were making sense. Our natural use of prediction and organization to follow what someone says is turned back on itself by odd particularities. We constantly correct ourselves by new attention to phrase and gesture or new construings of form. Reading literature thus depends on feedback just as natural processes do. We pass from misreading through self-consciousness to discovery.

The idea of personal feedback will help to clarify how this misreading differs from the "objective" misreading so endlessly argued about by literary critics ranging from I. A. Richards to Harold Bloom. I am not referring to the belief in an absolute measure of erroneous reading, nor am I alluding to the currently more fashionable idea that if there is no one right reading, *all* readings must be misreadings. Both approaches assume that our interest lies in some impersonal ultimate truth about texts, and the second makes the very concept of misreading meaningless. But our interest—being interest—is personal by its very nature, and it is in our personal experience of reading that the term "misreading" has real force. What I'm referring to is that step in our own reading when we look back and say, "Hey! I misread that." It may be motivated by our own rereading or by someone else's variant reading, but it is our own judgment. It is a moment of correction just as when one moves a hand to maintain one's balance. The new reading may later appear to us as another misreading, *but not at the time.* Misreading refers to our present perception of a reading after we have corrected it, and it is important to us because of our very desire to read well. It gives us the occasion to ask ourselves why we misread and thus to find out something about ourselves and about the text.

Instead of teaching students to avoid misreading, we should help them see how essential it is to the process of reading literature. Unfortunately, such phrases as error, correction, and misreading all seem to imply the existence of an accurate or ideal reading, and that I do not wish to suggest. The problem is that we think about these concepts technologically. Such things as mechanisms and artifacts can have templates. A builder corrects the construction by reference to the template. Small errors can be tolerated; larger ones mar the artifact or make it dysfunctional. Correction in the biological world isn't like that. It involves continuous adjustment and interaction. Both physical structure and functional patterns emerge in that ongoing process of adaptation. By the experience of trial and error, one performs certain gestures more gracefully and efficiently, but there is no ideal. Literary misreading should be understood through the biological model. As we reread or compare readings, we do not so much become more accurate as we become more complicated and comprehensive. We take account of more, see more, name more of what we see, and name it more precisely. But the process does not end in an exact inward representation of what we have read; it enriches our understanding of the text and of ourselves. Gregory Bateson, in his brilliant studies of mind and natural process, argues that the interaction between parts of a mind is triggered by a difference. Some difference in the perceptible world, a change in experience, begins mental activity. From this perspective misreading is a vital step in our approximation of the text. By allowing us to recognize change or difference, it initiates thought, discovery, and self-awareness. Without it we would have a mere photograph.

What happens to our teaching if we work from this conception of literary reading? The popular view of our profession is that we have something to convey to students. It is from this perspective that our governor recently suggested a way to make our work more efficient— why not videotape all our lectures and have done with it? Once we acknowledge reading and writing as approximate gestures, clearly we need a different view of teaching. The teacher provides the occasion for students to *do* something and to make discoveries in the process. Instead of leading them to right readings of books or proper historical and critical placement of them, the teacher helps students get into new relations with words on the page. We don't give them truth; we give them power. Or more precisely, we help them seize on their own authority as interpreters.

This changes the very meaning of our own expertise. Instead of using it directly to interpret texts, we apply it at one remove to design interpretive experiences for our students. These designs will of course vary with the literary period, the nature of the text, and the level of the students. Furthermore, if we agree it is more important that we help our students come to words than that we convey to them certain truths about the great books, we have to give up our conception of the fixed text and the accurate reading. The real connections between printed words and personal experience are formed through the very processes of approximation, misreading, and change. Only when we honor these processes, give them a place in our courses, use them in building interpretations, will we allow our students to be honest with themselves and with each other about their reading experience.

This shift of conception also suggests something about the scale of our assignments. If we want to help our students be good readers who continue to make discoveries about books and about themselves by shifting contexts, and if the essential changes for readers of literature occur at immediate points of dissonance in the text, it would seem that many brief exercises would accomplish more than one or two grand semester projects. On the one hand, such exercises would encourage precise recognitions of personal changes and their textual sources. On the other hand, these exercises would not put students in the false position of saying something big, vague, and by implication, final. An alternative approach is to use reading journals in which students record their own experiences of change, puzzlement, or misreading. These can be especially effective if students then go back over their changes, reflect on them and connect with them, and then share their discoveries with other students or with the teacher in conference.

Our role involves more, of course, than the design of experiences for individual students. There is also the classroom. From the perspective I have been developing, the essential quality of classroom discussion is that it is a continuation of the very process of reading. Other students are like more characters in the text, each bringing a unique perspective to bear on the situation. It isn't a contest to see whose reading is right but an opportunity to make even more discoveries than each single reader already made with the text itself. Contrasts in readers' perspectives serve the same purpose in discussion as dissonant details do in the text—they provide a fresh start for thought, the difference that makes a difference. Your reading not only opens up for me something new in the text, another context for its details; it also lets me see again the nature of my own reading and what I have invested in it.

Such an attitude toward discussion, however, does not come naturally. Teachers need to introduce and reinforce it, not rewarding the best interpretation but forcing into the open those contradictions that produce thought in the first place. Some students enter class discussion as if it were a military encounter—win or lose. Others hesitate to voice an opinion once someone else has occupied a position. Both types of student have to learn by experience that when people respect each other and expect to learn from each other, it is their differences that make growth possible. Teachers can help by naming the disagreements, by making readers look carefully at their own readings as they differ from others. Many discoveries spring from exactly that self-consciousness, the quickened awareness of one self in contrast to others.

All of these suggestions about the teacher's role involve a return of authority to students as readers and interpreters. When they recognize themselves as the authors of the concepts through which they understand what they read, they will also see others' readings for what they are. Coming to words is finally an act of collaboration, first between writer and reader and then between reader and reader. As readers compare their readings, they approximate the text by finding the ground they share. But they also use their divergences to explore both perspectives and thus to see even more in the text itself and in the situations of those who read it. They do not, however, arrive at something final in the process. There is perhaps something to be said for those truths about texts that supposedly hold their shape independent of the biases of particular readers. They satisfy our wish for something stable, authoritative, and pure. But they are also dead. By their very nature they are irrelevant to the human needs of readers. There is much more to be said for those messier truths that we formulate, undo, and remake again and again in the human gesture of coming to words. Such truths never last. They are too tentative to connect in elaborate systems of meaning. But they renew our acquaintance with the things of the world, they loosen our bondage to a fixed perspective, and they open us to the endless surprise of dialogue with someone else. Such, to me, are the pleasures of reading literature.

Note

The concept of reading developed in this essay shares with reader-response criticism an essential principle—that meaning is a property not of the text but of the reader's interaction with the text. It was not the theorists of reader-response, however, who provided the ground for my analysis of reading. That came indirectly from studies of the writing process by James Britton, Peter Elbow, Janet Emig, Ken Macrorie, James Moffett, Donald Murray, Richard Ohmann, and Mina Shaughnessy. It came more directly from accounts of the making of meaning by Lev Vygotsky, Paulo Freire, and Ann Berthoff. And in spirit my thinking was impelled by the apparently unrelated work of Gregory Bateson on mind and nature. The value of these thinkers for me lay in their good cheer about the possibilities of individual learning, their grasp of practical methods closely related to the natural development of the mind, and their acceptance of reality as an ongoing process of give and take. And it is those qualities that I find thwarted by the rise of critical theory to its current eminence in literary study. Thus the primary aim of reader-response criticism is not to help actual readers but to establish theoretically the status of reader and text, to examine the grounds of readability or the systems of signs or communities of interpreters that make reading significant. In the context of issues like these, my approach implies what Stanley Fish calls a "naive epistemology." But then so does most reading experience. I don't find my own reading of literature enabled or enriched by thinking of a reader inscribed in the text, or of a virtual text between the words and the reader, or of a self that is merely a structure of signs. Concepts like these make suspect the personal experience of words that is the very core of literacy. Part of what I say in this essay may sound like Wolfgang Iser describing the reader's building of gestalts and then breaking them down because of textual discrepancies. Another part may sound like Stanley Fish arguing that meaning is an experience the reader has and that it includes the reader's mistakes. But our aims are so different that our occasionally similar phrases do not describe the same process at all. I will happily remain naive about the theoretical status of readers if I can help actual readers increase their capacity to change, to recognize their changes, and to make something of the text by using their imaginations and their experience.

8

Enigma Variations: Reading and Writing Through Metaphor

LOUISE Z. SMITH

University of Massachusetts at Boston

In "Coming to Words," Gary Lindberg tells us that

All writing is a gesture of interpretation; what makes imaginative literature distinct is its forcing the reader to ponder those acts of interpretation and to see them in the particularities of circumstance and motivation that make them human, complex, and provisional.

Pondering gestures of interpretation is surely central to the study of literature, and metaphor is a particularly ponderable gesture. But pondering metaphor is also central to the study of what is called "nonliterature," e.g. historiography and hermeneutics, and to the study of composition. Because of its too-seldom recognized *triadic* structure, metaphor particularly rewards readers and writers for pondering the "particularities of circumstance and motivation." To make public and accessible the process of pondering, I have experimented with a two-part process of brief in-class writings. The members of an "interpretive community" within the classroom first write individual responses to a metaphor and then write ethnographically about their collective responses, about what was "said" and the grounds upon which it was "said." This two-stage dialogue, first with the metaphor and later with the contexts its interpreters perceive helps us recognize that metaphor in *any* context (literary or not) expresses, again in Professor Lindberg's words, "not a perception of truth but a continued dialogue with the knotty particularities of experience." Like ethnographic inscriptions, these in-class writings encourage us to "read" both the text and the interpretive community, to read each meditatively in search of a rich multiplicity of meanings. And they encourage us to use language precisely, both writing and listening carefully to find implicit (not just explicit) contexts.

A moment ago, I said that metaphor is not a two-part invention, "tenor" and "vehicle," but a triad. I'd like to claim that the triadicity of metaphor is not strained, that it droppeth as the gentle rain from theory upon the classroom beneath. But I learned it the hard way. By telling how, I hope to show not only *that* it is true, but also that its truth reunifies the teaching of reading and writing. Here is my story:

Once upon a time, a "basic" writing class wrote about three stories: Lois Gould's being held hostage in her apartment; Vladimir Bukovsky's surviving incarceration in Soviet prisons; and Maya Angelou's recalling how Momma prevailed over the racism of the only dentist in Stamps, Arkansas. As usual on the day papers were due, all the students read aloud in class and got some reactions. For eleven weeks, they had practiced avoiding vague, judgmental responses ("That's good" or "That's boring") and giving content-specific responses ("I'd like to know more about that," or "I never realized until now that Gould and Bukovsky were talking about the same thing"). Toward the end of class, Kristen Berg read her paper, making a thoughtful connection: Gould's and Bukovsky's physical confinement had made their preservation of mental and spiritual freedom quite simple, while Angelou's apparent physical freedom made fighting confinement by racist attitudes much more difficult. Kristin wrote, "Blacks were criminals imprisoned by racism." Her metaphor evoked vociferous denial from over half the class: "I don't like what she said. I'm Black and I'm not a criminal." After a few minutes (which I felt I was spending underwater), Lynda Ramsey came to the rescue: "No, you don't get it! That's only a metaphor! She's not saying literally that Blacks *are* criminals. She's just saying Blacks were being treated *like* criminals. See?" The dust settled, the class ended, and I started wondering if I knew anything about metaphor or about teaching.

How could this have happened? How could mature students, most in their mid-twenties, nearly all veterans of Boston school desegregation over the past decade, who already had freely discussed racial issues with tact and sensitivity, suddenly stumble into such an argument? How could they think that Kristin really meant Blacks were criminals? On the other hand, as welcome as Lynda's explanation had been at the moment, was it exactly true? Her paraphrase was a simile, "Blacks were being treated *like* criminals," which weakened the metaphor "Blacks *were* criminals." Did her "See?" mean simply "Do you get it?" or further propose envisioning "particularities of circumstance and motivation" that made Angelou's act of interpretation and Kristin's pondering of it "human, complex, and provisional"?

Finding answers has taken a long time. My first hypothesis was that "literary incompetence" had caused the metaphor to be misunderstood. People hadn't recognized the metaphor, but as soon as Lynda explained that "Blacks were criminals" was *only* a metaphor, everything was OK. But this wasn't true. Anyone who sings "Deep River, I want to cross over into campground" or says "That cat may be a cool dude, but he really fries my grits" obviously *does* know metaphor! In fact, narratives by adolescent BEV speakers reveal their ability to use hints, quotations, ascriptions of the "moral" to what another speaker said to them, all elaborate devices to ward off the listener's question "so what?" (Labov, 1972). Lack of literary terminology has little to do with literary competence (though we may use "literary incompetence" to cover a multitude of pedagogical incompetences).

When condescension failed, I found my second hypothesis in amateur sociology: they knew it was metaphor, but they *chose* to take it literally. They were fed up—with busing, rock-throwing, cafeteria-rumbling, and disruption of learning. Now three women had kindergartners starting the same thing all over again. This particular metaphor, "Blacks are criminals," fried *their* grits. For the moment, they *wanted* to take it literally because they had a lot of frustration to express. Their ready acceptance of Lynda's explanation showed that they *knew* their misunderstanding had been deliberate. Having had their say, they willingly admitted that Kristin hadn't actually said what they had heard. This hypothesis was even worse than the first. The whole class had gotten along just fine for eleven weeks. So why would the atmosphere suddenly turn so mean? Sure, they had a right to feel frustrated. But they were too mature, too basically *nice*, too honest to insist that Kristin had said what they knew she hadn't said. This hypothesis produced only a fresh awareness of how the "said" can be negotiated.

The third hypothesis produced more. For centuries, metaphor has been held suspect because, as a proposition, its truth value is in question. Our contretemps recalled classical objections to metaphor as an "abuse of language" on the grounds that by definition it states a proposition more false than true. Hobbes and Locke, for instance, would say that "Blacks were criminals" was a false proposition, hence an abuse. Lynda's explanation that "Blacks were being treated *like* criminals" had *tamed* the metaphor by making it into a simile. Clearly, a simile is always a true proposition: somehow or other, anything can be *like* something else. But paraphrasing robs metaphor of its power. Its resonant ponderability must come from beyond the "true or false." Perhaps that is why metaphor has been placed under preventive detention in the custody of imaginative literature.

Metaphor is also weakened by being seen as merely a decorative substitution, a "garment" of thought that has already been arrived at. As J. Hillis Miller (1983) found, our handbooks treat metaphor as decoration. My own informal survey reveals that "critical reading" texts appearing in 1983 and 1984 treat metaphors superficially if at all, a curious fact since metaphors are especially amenable to critical reading. To my knowledge the only college texts that help student writers recognize and employ the power of metaphor to generate—not just decorate—ideas are Ann Berthoff's (1978), Susan Horton's (1982), and Marie Ponsot and Rosemary Deen's (1982). Clearly, our texts have a long way to go in overcoming the classical attitudes toward metaphor as an "abuse" of language that may be tolerated only so long as it is "decoration" and not to be taken seriously.

Of course, metaphor *does* generate ideas in non-literature. Just look at recent computer books—*MicroMillenium, The New Alchemists, Soul of a New Machine, Fire in the Valley*—all using metaphors not simply to make "vivid" but to imagine, explore, and name the coming computer age. Just look at politics—The New Frontier, Camelot, and "Where's the beef?"—all metaphors used to imagine, explore, and weigh American dreams. Just look at some metaphors of historiography: the historian as novelist seeking appropriate tropes (Collingwood, 1946; White, 1973) or as archaeologist (Foucault, 1972). Just look at some metaphors of hermeneutics: Mill and Comte applying the laws of physics to society or Gadamer seeking "fusion of horizons." Clearly, the computer folks, the pols and pundits, the historiographers and the hermeneuticists all know what Aristotle and Cicero knew (and what Hobbes, too, must have known when he thought up his Leviathan): metaphor is—as Ann Berthoff shows in her essay on Freire's metaphors of reading—*heuristic.*

What about the supposed distinction, then, between literature and non-literature? It commonly goes like this: literature emphasizes imagination, values, tropes, circular forms, and enigmas, while non-literature emphasizes reason, facts, plain style, linear forms, and resolutions. Nowadays, research about "discourse communities" enshrines these supposed distinctions. But many modern theorists emphasize the continuities. For instance, Susanne K. Langer (1957, pp. 163-70 sees art and logic as complementary:

> Both in art and in logic . . . 'abstraction' is the recognition of a
> relevant structure, or form, apart from the specific thing (or
> event, fact, image, etc.) in which it is exemplified.

In her view, imagination does not oppose reason but is "the common source of dream, reason, religion, and all true general observation." Paul de Man (1979, pp. 11-28) too rejects distinctions between aesthetic and epistemological categories, arguing instead that all philosophy must depend to some extent on the figurative, and all literature must be to some extent philosophical. Since variations in presentational and discursive form, not the use or non-use of metaphor, distinguish literature from non-literature, knowing the ways of metaphor becomes all the more important. It underlies the humanistic consensus upon which reunification of literature teaching and composition teaching—especially across the curriculum—depends.

Admittedly, the humanistic consensus was pretty hard to detect the last time we saw Kristin, Lynda, and the other "basic" students of metaphor including me. Even so, the third hypothesis revealed some important characteristics of metaphor. First, it should not be understood as an "abuse of language" just because it always answers "false" to true/false questions. We should ask it other questions. Second, it should not be weakened through paraphrase into simile or trivialized as a "garment of thought"; it is a powerful heuristic. Third, it should not be confined to literature, since its heuristic power functions well in non-literature, so well in fact that metaphor overcomes some distinctions between the two forms. So far, so good. But what do we tell Kristin, Lynda, and Louise?

My current hypothesis says that we misunderstood "Blacks were criminals" because our questions forced metaphor to be substitutive, a 1:1 equivalency between signifier and signified. When "Blacks" didn't match "criminals," the argument ensued. This same argument— whether metaphor is a *substitution* (as Saussure and Chomsky believe) or an *interaction* (as I. A. Richards and Max Black believe)—occupied philosophers in the 1970s (Sacks, 1979). The interactionist view holds that the hidden power of metaphor lies not in its 1:1 clarity but in its enigma. For example, Paul Ricoeur (1979) thinks that metaphor works in two stages: the maker states an enigma (i.e. a literal deviance but figurative likeness), and then the hearer suspends the ordinary language in which the sense of deviance predominates in order to let imagination and feeling (i.e. intuition, intentionality) find the new congruence. These interactionist terms—*enigma, hidden power, imagination and feeling*—indicate a much broader and subtler approach to metaphor than the substitutionist view affords.

Admitting imagination and feeling, as well as cognition, as ways of responding to metaphor provides a philosophical basis for welcoming the reading of literature and "non-literature" back into the writing class. In *S/Z* (1970) Barthes distinguishes "readable" texts, which make the reader an "inert consumer" of the author's ideologies, from "writable" texts, which involve the reader in creating a world *now*, together with the author, as they go along, open to the "play" of codes (Hawkes, 1977, pp. 106–122). Barthes's theory of "writability" prepares the way for Eco's theory of reading (1979), welcoming readers to participate in constructing meanings:

> every reception of a work of art is both an *interpretation* and a *performance* of it, because in every reception the work takes on a fresh perspective for itself.

Eco's two-part theory of reception—interpretation and performance— is a major rationale for my experiments with the two-part in-class writings. A piece of music or a metaphor, each "fixed" by writing on paper, is always in some senses "the same." But just as performance brings life to music, so each reader's response at each reading brings life to metaphor. David Bartholomae's essay "Wanderings" demonstrates how this is so.

In my two-part in-class writings, the first stage might be called the reader's "performance" of the metaphor; the second stage of analyzing the initial response might be considered the "interpretation." When our class stumbled over the metaphor "Blacks were criminals," we had cut short our performance. We had seized on the most immediate 1:1 substitution instead of patiently performing our reading all the way through in as many variations as we could and only then arriving at some interpretation. We didn't give the metaphor's "writability" a chance.

But no traditional figure is more "writable" than metaphor. By now it is obvious that "writable" does not mean "concrete" or "specific" or "easy to read or write." It does mean that all metaphors (yes, all!—"dead" metaphors are not metaphors any more) invite the reader to participate in exploring their enigmas and constructing their intelligibilities. Accepting their invitation helps us cultivate judiciously imaginative minds, the goal of a liberal education. Robert Frost ("Education by Poetry: A Meditative Monologue," 1930) knew why: "all thinking is metaphorical" and liberal education means knowing your way around metaphor:

> What I am pointing out is that unless you are at home in the metaphor, unless you have had your proper poetical education in the metaphor, you are not safe anywhere. Because you are not at ease with figurative values: you don't know the metaphor in its strength and its weakness. You don't know how far you may expect to ride it and when it may break down with you. You are not safe in science; you are not safe in history.

On the surface Frost is urging us to recognize the heuristic role of metaphors in the non-literary writing of science and history. Like Eco, he does not advocate reading literature *as something else.* He does not want us to read *I Know Why the Caged Bird Sings* as a document of social history, but as the story of how Marguerite, Bailey, Uncle Willie, and Momma lived in Stamps, Arkansas. Furthermore, Frost wants us not to be taken in by metaphors. We are not to believe that the identity they assert between A and B fits as a perfect garment fits the body, but instead to look them over carefully and to notice the holes and gaps, since "All metaphor breaks down somewhere." But Frost does more than promote skepticism; unlike Hobbes and Locke, he doesn't condemn metaphor for breaking down. In fact, the substitutionists' view that metaphor lacks cognitive value would have amused him. Instead of fretting about that, Frost cheerfully admits

> All metaphor breaks down somewhere. That is the *beauty* [emphasis mine] of it. It is touch and go with the metaphor, and until you have lived with it long enough you don't know when it is going. You don't know how much you can get out of it and when it will cease to yield. It is a very living thing. It is life itself.

Frost's recognition precedes that of contemporary interactionists like Ricoeur: metaphor's breakdown is its beauty; its gaps, mistakes, and enigmas are its living "writability."

But how can I stand up with a straight face in front of Kristin, Lynda, and their friends and tell them that Frost says beauty appears through the "holes" in metaphor? that a metaphor's "mistakes" are pleasant? Knowing their fondness for the literal, I expect they would say: "Holes and mistakes are beautiful! Does that mean in *our* papers, too? Best news we've had all day!" My challenge is to show that enigma invites us to generate meaning—not just cognitively, but also imaginatively and with the sense of "felt life," of taking in and "owning" an idea. Alas, my own education in metaphor has underemphasized its enigma. Just about all of us, suckled on Thrall, Hibbard, and Holman's *Handbook of Literature*, think metaphor consists of two parts, I. A. Richards's "tenor" or idea and "vehicle" or image (1936, pp. 94–95). One of my colleagues always imagines Richards' "vehicle" as a great big bus with the "tenor" passenger riding around in it; my private image has Lauritz Melchior as Lohengrin arriving onstage aboard the swan. Clearly, we both have been thinking of metaphor as a two-part figure. That is because "tenor" and "vehicle" is not Richards' whole story: metaphor is a "transaction between contexts." His series of *three*-part images explains the transaction:

> Our theory [of metaphor], as it has its roots in practice, must also have its fruit in improved skill. "I am the child," says the Sufi mystic, "whose father is his son, and the wine whose vine is its jar."

Richards explains the relation of practice, theory, and skill by identifying them with three three-wheeled "vehicles":

roots / [trunk (implied)] / fruit

father /   child   / child's son

vine /   wine   / jar

Yet if we draw non-mystical 1:1 equivalencies between, say, "theory" and "wine," we soon find more deviance than correspondence. That is obvious, for metaphor by definition identifies two things that are more different than they are similar. In short, we experience metaphor as an *interaction*, as a form of language that Richards says "cannot be paraphrased without remainder." The "remainder" is what interactionists call the "enigma" and what Frost calls the "holes," the places where metaphor breaks down *and* becomes beautiful. Like all metaphor, Richards' metaphor is "writable," inviting us to find ways in which "theory" obviously fits "wine"—their careful aging, their redolence of former days, their preciousness, their fragility, and so on— and rewarding us with pleasure when we do. But the "mistakes," the ways in which the fit between "theory" and "wine" breaks down, are even more "writable" and reward us with more than pleasure.

Let us accept the invitation of "writability" to play with one of the apparent "mistakes" in Richards' metaphor: *consumption*. Wine can be consumed, but theory cannot. Once wine is consumed its taste becomes only a fading memory, but since theory is not consumed, it can always be uncorked again and tasted afresh. Having found this "mistake," we could dismiss the metaphor as an abuse of language. But what if we think about the "mistake" more positively as an enigma with a potential for further revelation? Theory is not consumed— maybe. Have you considered the Phlogiston Theory lately? When did you last debate natural selection or Social Darwinism? In 2084—or maybe sooner, given our accelerating rates of theory consumption— who will be reading Thomas Kuhn and wondering, "Is research on the *processes* of composing indicative of a 'paradigm shift'?" So perhaps, after all, theory is consumed *with regard to the public's intoxication* with it. "With regard to" opens a new context. Accepting the invitation of "writability," we become willing to see "mistakes" as "enigmas," and then we find more than pleasure: we find what Barthes calls *jouissance*, the bliss of glimpsing within the apparent disintegration of a "mistake" the beauty of a new wisdom.

In accepting the invitation to play with the enigmas, as Professor Lindberg's student did in re-imagining manners in *Huckleberry Finn*, we discover new senses in which the metaphor has meaning—partly cognitive, partly imaginative, partly intentional. The enigma makes us interactionists, seeking a "third" element by means of which the other two are mediated into truth. This "third" element has many names, besides "holes," "mistakes," and "remainder." Susanne Langer (1957, pp. 170–71) finds that opposite words grow from a "root-metaphor" that expresses their shared "feeling tones"; thus "black" and "blanc" come from the Norwegian root "blakk" meaning "bleak," and "high' and "deep" meet in the common feeling-quality of "shallowness." As Berthoff (1984, pp. 167–172) explains, C. S. Peirce's semiotics rejects Saussurean equivalence between signifier and signified. Peirce proposes a three-part sign, consisting of the object, the representamen, and the interpretant (i.e., the purpose or intention—not the interpreter). By mediating between the first two, the interpretant brings meaning to the sign. In their individual ways, Richards, Langer, and Peirce all find a "third" element inherent in metaphor.

My favorite explanation of the "third" element is Walker Percy's (1958). He says beauty comes not from the resolution of an ambiguity, as the New Criticism held, but from the *obscure term* of the ambiguity, the logically "wrong" but possibly analogous symbol. (Donald Murray recognizes this kind of beauty when he hopes that we may be "blessed with a problem we can never 'solve.'") The metaphor's "mistake" is itself a means of knowing, "an error only if we do not recognize its intentional quality":

> There must be a space between name and thing, for otherwise the private apprehension is straitened and oppressed. What is required is that the thing be both sanctioned and yet allowed freedom to be what it is. . . . The essence of metaphorical truth and the almost impossible task of the poet is, it seems to me, to name unmistakably and yet to name by such a gentle analogy that the thing beheld . . . may be truly formulated for what it is.

Percy playfully concludes his essay with a "mistaken" metaphor: men "must know one thing through the mirror of another." The mirror metaphor seems so odd because it suggests a neat 1:1 equivalency between thing and its representation. However, if we follow Percy's advice, viewing a "mistake" as an enigma and speculating on what else the mirror metaphor might mean, we notice the word "through" and remember the medieval paintings and poems in which mirrors were both shiny reflective surfaces and windows through which to view the world. Maybe the author "intended" us to remember that, and maybe not. What is important is that the "third"—or mistake, hole, gap, remainder—kept us searching for other contexts to partake in the metaphoric transaction; the "third" gives metaphor its "writability."

My two-stage in-class writings put this recognition to work. In the first stage, the readers write for five to ten minutes about the metaphor. Since the freedom of "writability" is quite new, they take a while to get over trying to give the "right" answer they think the teacher expects. Their earliest responses usually list 1:1 substitutions (reflecting their experience with "hidden meaning" known only to the teacher); these resemble the displacement that Professor Bartholomae describes. After a little experience, the "third" element appears; their responses take the form "A is B *with respect to* C." Eventually, emboldened by "writability," they write responses of the form, "Even though A at first seems very different from B, when you think about it *in terms of* C or D or E, they are actually the same." Using this more complex form, the writers explore apparent "mistakes" and speculate on what meanings various contexts or "thirds" might reveal. The whole process resembles Piaget's theory of developing from literal to more complex mental operators, of which Gary Lindberg's essay reminds us.

While samples of student writing cannot by themselves capture the broad, speculative give-and-take of classroom writing, reading aloud, and discussion among sixteen participants, the following may sketch how the process works. In "Letter from Birmingham Jail," Martin Luther King gives a new twist to a familiar metaphor:

> when you see the vast majority of your twenty million Negro brothers smothering in an airtight cage of poverty in the midst of an affluent society; . . . .

Most of the sixteen readers found "cage of poverty" conventionally clear. However, "smothering in an airtight cage" was an apparent mistake. "Cages are not airtight," they said. "Air circulates through the bars, keeping captives alive indefinitely instead of smothering them in minutes." Several first-stage responses made sense of the contradiction between "airtight" and "cage" by thinking of it with respect to invisible barriers. For instance,

1. When I think about "airtight cage," I imagine a sealed box, like a coffin. But a cage has openings. Maybe King means that poverty *looks* like a cage you could live in. But its openings are really sealed with something invisible, so it's actually airtight, a death-trap, but you can't tell by just looking at it.

   Hey!! That's it—some of the oppression is *visible* (like rules about where blacks can sit on the bus) but a lot is invisible (like when the city council denied King a parade permit because of "law and order"). There, "law and order" was just concealing injustice, making it invisible. And it's the invisible or hidden oppression that actually kills. So when you think of "airtight" and "cage" with respect to how civil laws can make injustice invisible, it makes sense.

This writer practically shouts "Eureka!" when she sees how perfectly the "mistake" conveys King's point: mere law and order can make a society *seem* open and just, can make injustice hard to see. A similar response expresses the "mistake" in terms of *where* laws may be observed:

2. This phrase could mean that the visible, physical enclosure of poverty can kill you by depriving you of visible, material things (like housing, or a lawyer to argue your case). But it can kill you even faster by depriving you of invisible, spiritual rights (like dignity and real justice).

Both of these writers make sense of the "mistake" by seeing it in terms of King's philosophical distinction between just and unjust laws.

Other first-stage writings illumine some of the "stories of reading" being told by theorists today. Readers attempt to fill what Percy calls the vital "space" between "name" and "thing," a "filling" process recognized by contemporary reading theorists such as Roman Ingarden, Wolfgang Iser, and Umberto Eco. Their "fillers" consist partly of personal, psychological responses like those described by Norman Holland (1975) and David Bleich (1975). For instance,

3. Maybe this is far-fetched, but "airtight cage" reminds me of that poem on the Statue of Liberty, about masses "yearning to breathe free." My grandparents were just as "caged" by oppression in ghettos in Lodz and Warsaw as the blacks were in Alabama. By "breathe free" is meant voting, living where you want, being your own boss. If you can't do any of those things, the cage might as well be "airtight" and you might as well be dead!

Both history and intertextuality provide contexts for this reader's understanding of the "mistake." The "fillers" also draw upon whichever ideologies the individual finds significant. A student who had been active in the prisoners' rights movement wrote, for example,

4. I think "smothering in an airtight cage" refers to the terrible conditions in the jails where civil rights protesters were kept. The dampness, the crowding, the lack of fresh air all made the jails seem "airtight" and inescapable. Russia isn't the only country that keeps political prisoners (like Vladimir Bukovsky).

And several students provided feminism as a context of interpretation, illustrating Judith Fetterley's observations (1978) of ways in which some women readers resist the paternal power of the male Author:

5. What about the *sisters* who were smothering? I don't see how King can ignore the fact that black women were even more exploited than black men. He doesn't even tell the name of the woman who started the Montgomery bus boycott: Rosa Parks! He's got her in an "airtight cage" of "nobodiness"—his sexism!

Other responses illustrate reading as an experience of intertextuality, as the writer of response # 3 did. A metaphor might remind the student writer of a proverb which Michael Riffaterre (1979) calls a "hypogram":

6. "Airtight cage" reminds me of "Iron bars do not a prison make." It isn't the bars—the racist rules and attitudes—that smother a person, but the "airtightness," which means the impossibility of escape. King is saying if he can write this "Letter from Birmingham Jail" from his jail cell, he can break the "airtight" seal and make other people extremists for non-violence and justice. But if he can't, then he as a person, along with the civil rights movement, will be smothered, killed.

I have not observed students engaging in the intricate heuristic and hermeneutic quest through a series of re-readings on three levels (text, matrix, and model) Riffaterre describes, perhaps because the time is too short, but more probably because these readers lack the sophistication he assumes. However, many students use other passages in the "Letter" as "third" contexts:

7. How can you smother in an "airtight cage"? I think King means that if you don't speak up for yourself, you LET the cage be airtight. At the end of his letter, he talks about having a lot of time in jail to "write long letters, think long thoughts and pray long prayers." As long as you keep preaching (through his letter) and praying, your soul can breathe. But if you let the bars on the cage silence you, you'll let your soul be smothered.

8. The word "smothering" reminds me that King also says the contemporary church speaks with "a weak, ineffectual voice with an uncertain sound." The Negroes inside the cage are being smothered by poverty. But it also seems as if the church's voice is being smothered by too much respect for "law and order." King criticizes the smug white church for excluding the members who say it should speak out. The jail smothers the jailer too.

9. This phrase reminds me of how King described organized religion as the "paralyzing chains of conformity." He said that real Christians had to break loose from them and do what they knew was God's will, not just what the Church and the City Council said was legal. Too much respect for "law and order" paralyzed them, just as it smothered the Negro brothers before King taught them about civil disobedience and non-violent protest.

And sometimes readers find "thirds" in their own word-play:

10. "Airtight cage" sounds like "airtight case," and I think King might mean that white society had made up an "airtight case" against civil rights—"airtight"meaning that there would be no escape, no gaps in their arguments. If he kept quiet, he'd be op-

pressed; if he spoke up, he'd be arrested as a criminal and an "extremist" and he'd be excluded by the nice, law-abiding clergymen (white and black) and community leaders.

11. I'm thinking about "of." It could mean that the cage IS poverty. But it could also mean that the cage is a CREATION OF poverty or BELONGS TO poverty in some way—maybe poverty in the spiritual sense. Maybe the cage was created by the spiritual poverty of white society, particularly the white liberals and churchmen.

For the sake of this essay's brevity, I have been categorizing the responses—philosophical, psychological, historical, ideological, intertextual and textual. However, in the classroom these responses are simply read aloud and acknowledged with a "thank you." The naming process forms the basis for the second phase of in-class writing.

After students take turns reading aloud their first responses, each person "inscribes" as precisely as possible what was "said" and names the patterns in the "said." These second-stage responses build from close observation of the first individual responses a more abstract sense of how the community of readers understood the metaphor. It entails establishing rapport among "participant observers," the members of the class. It cultivates intimacy among participants, as they note the personal and cultural contexts each individual used to mediate and bring meaning to the metaphor.

A sampling from the sixteen second-stage responses reveals what the first-stage writings "said." The writer of response #3, finding that others saw "airtight cage" in various historical contexts, decided that her response was not so far-fetched after all:

Some other people's responses agreed with mine that history was one way to understand "airtight cage." They mentioned quite a few different historical situations—prison conditions here and in Russia [4], the history of the white church in Alabama [8,9], and the contributions of black women [5].

Other students (from Hispanic and Southeast Asian backgrounds) found that immigration clarified "airtight cage" and helped them understand the kinds of oppression King experienced. Several felt this response was no more "far-fetched" than King's constant historical references. Thus, one "said" was that historical contexts made sense of the metaphor. Another cluster of responses noted the usefulness of intratextual references. For example, the writer of #11 wrote:

I heard a lot of people referring to King's language, comparing "smothering" with "paralyzing" [9], saying that his letters and prayers kept him from being smothered [7], and that the church's "weak" voice was smothered [8]. It seems one thing our responses "said" was that King's own language gives clues for understanding what seems like a mistake.

The importance of writing down these accounts of the "said" cannot be overemphasized: inscription *fixes* a passing event or observation which can be reconsulted, rescuing the "gist" of each response from the flow of discourse (as Lynda rescued Kristin's "said" from the discussion it evoked.) Metaphor not only rewards close attention to the text, but also assumes an intimate community between its maker and its appreciators: as Ted Cohen (1979) says,

> a figurative use can be inaccessible to all but those who share information about one another's knowledge, beliefs, intentions and attitudes.

We name the correspondences and differences among our readings not in order to make them coherent, but to listen to their harmonies.

However, this process does not permit crackpot egalitarianism or rejoicing in the "death of the Author." Each class's mutually persuasive dialogue finds the aleatory "rules" which they actually practice in eliminating meanings that seem unsubstantiated by the text. This class ruled out responses #5, 6, and 10 for reasons such as these:

> Maybe King was a male chauvinist [5]. OK, he should have told Rosa Parks's name. But that doesn't explain "airtight case." It isn't fair to apply today's standards to the 1960's. So what if he didn't fight sexism? He had his hands full fighting racism!

> The proverb "Iron bars do not a prison make" [6] fits King's situation—and about a hundred others. It's too general. "Iron bars" doesn't explain "airtight" or "smothering."

> CASE? Sure, it sounds like "cage" [10], but I doubt that King heard it that way. Besides, I don't think he would make a joke or pun in the middle of his serious message.

While the "said" affirms this class's acceptance of historical and textual references, it questions using contexts of 1980s feminism, of overly general proverbs, and of word-play. Persuasive dialogue asks how many different and complementary contexts can mediate and bring forth meaning from "airtight cage" or from the phrase we began with: "Blacks were criminals" *with respect to* "a civil law that defied divine justice" and "their isolation from the rest of society" and "their willingness to commit civil disobedience" and "their deprivation of ordinary humane treatment" and so on—as far as persuasion, or in Professor Lindberg's words "the continued dialogue with the knotty particularities of experience," allows.

If Saussurean substitution has been the villain of this piece, I must now acknowledge that Saussure's distinction between *parole* (each individual's speech) and *langue* (the intersection of all the *paroles*) may be just the metaphor I want to use for this dialogic process of persuasion: each triad of thing / name / "space" is one *parole* of the metaphor, and all the complementary triads taken together are the metaphor's *langue*. The dialogue of response and persuasion is a negotiated, dialectical making of meaning, a "web of significance."

Of course my two-stage model has many uses besides interpreting metaphor. Whenever students pause in the midst of a discussion or lecture to write down how they are responding at the moment—what they think the text and the lecturer "said" and how the two are related, what the next question should be, and so forth—they are practicing close reading *and listening* and are becoming active interpreters (not just accurate note-takers). By reading aloud and inscribing the "said," they *negotiate* a consensus of what was "said" or "implied" and appreciate the roles of varied cultural contexts in interpretation. The ensuing dialogue of interpretation is a way of giving back to readers the enthusiasm and the power that some "experts" have taken. The dialogue of persuasion gives back belief in the value of one's own reading and in the aesthetic, as well as the informative, value of what is read. But of course Frost says this better. From living with poetry, he knows more about belief in himself, in love, in society: the last belief he writes about is the belief in

> every work of art, not of cunning and craft, mind you, but of real art; that believing the thing into existence, saying as you go more than you even hoped you were going to be able to say, and coming with surprise to an end that you foreknew only with some sort of emotion.

References

Berthoff, A. (1978). *Forming/thinking/writing.* Rochelle Park, NJ: Hayden.

_____. (1984). *Reclaiming the imagination.* Upper Montclair, NJ: Boynton/Cook.

Bleich, D. (1975). *Readings and feelings: An introduction to subjective criticism.* Urbana, IL: National Council of Teachers of English.

Cohen, T. (1979). Metaphor and the cultivation of intimacy. In S. Sacks (Ed.), *On metaphor.* Chicago: University of Chicago Press, p. 7.

Collingwood, R. G. (1946). *The idea of history.* Oxford: Oxford University Press.

de Man, P. (1979). *Allegories of reading: Figural language in Rousseau, Nietzsche, Rilke, and Proust.* New Haven: Yale University Press.

Eco, U. (1979). *The role of the reader.* Bloomington: Indiana University Press.

Fetterly, J. (1978). *The resisting reader.* Bloomington: Indiana University Press.

Foucault, M. (1972). *The archaeology of knowledge.* New York: Harper and Row.

Hawkes, T. (1977). *Structuralism & semiotics.* Berkeley: University of California Press.

Holland, N. (1975). *5 readers reading.* New Haven: Yale University Press.

Horton, S. R. (1982). *Thinking through writing.* Baltimore: The Johns Hopkins University Press.

Howard, R. (1982). *Three faces of hermeneutics: An introduction to current theories of understanding.* Berkeley: University of California Press.

Iser, W. (1978). *The act of reading: A theory of aesthetic response.* Baltimore: The Johns Hopkins University Press.

Labov, W. (1972). *Language in the inner city.* Philadelphia: University of Pennsylvania Press, pp. 360–366.

Langer, S. K. (1957). *Problems of art.* New York: Charles Scribner's Sons.

Miller, J. H. (1979). Composition and decomposition: Deconstruction and the teaching of writing. In W. Horner (Ed.), *Composition and literature: Bridging the gap.* Chicago: University of Chicago Press, pp. 38–56.

Percy, W. (1984). Metaphor as mistake. In A. Berthoff (Ed.), *Reclaiming the imagination.* Upper Montclair, NJ: Boynton/Cook, pp. 132–144.

Pettit, P. (1977). *The concept of structuralism: A critical analysis* Berkeley: University of California Press.

Ponsot, M. & Deen, R. (1982). *Beat not the poor desk.* Montclair, NJ: Boynton/Cook.

Richards, I. A. (1936). *The philosophy of rhetoric.* London: Oxford University Press.

Ricoeur, P. (1979). The metaphorical process as cognition, imagination, and feeling. In S. Sacks (Ed.), *On metaphor.* Chicago: University of Chicago Press, pp. 141–57.

Riffaterre, M. (1979). *The semiotics of poetry.* Bloomington: Indiana University Press.

Sacks, S. (Ed.). (1979). *On metaphor.* Chicago: University of Chicago Press.

White, H. (1973). *Metahistory: the historical imagination in nineteenth-century Europe.* Baltimore: The Johns Hopkins University Press.

9

An Interplay of Powers: Writing About Literature

ROSEMARY DEEN

Queens College

All writers can originate literature and read it with pleasure; they can write to know literature and write to take possession of their knowledge. These acts are primary and best put into play directly, without being analyzed or predicted for writers. They can be learned and taught inductively; structure is latent in experience.

These are the elemental ideas of the workshop whose experience and structure I'm going to lay out. In planning the workshop I wanted to reverse the usual proportion of talk and writing in a writing conference as in a writing classroom: to spend 75 minutes listening to well-tempered and equal discourse from all workshop members, discourses which I would simply evoke.

That writing is the main voice of this paper. I present the session as it was enacted, so that you readers can sit in the writers' seats, even write if you like, and see the inductive design for yourselves. Of course, a teacher presenting her material inductively is deriving it from a deductive framework in her mind.

The Work

We worked for 60 minutes; I saved 15 minutes after that for reflection: writing about what we had done and reading that aloud to each other. The hour session is a concentration of a week or week and a half of class work. I knew I could count on my colleagues' zest and confidence to make them quick studies. Often students write tamely until they realize they have permission to be witty and metaphoric. Teachers are confident that a very simple sentence weighs as much as a ponderous one. In other words, teachers give themselves more permissions more easily. I didn't need to count on any greater teacherly intelligence or familiarity with literature. Any set of readers has the same range of intelligence and imaginative power.

The Fable

In an actual class we begin by writing the fable, but here I didn't have time for that or for reading a round of fables. In a class, I'd ask writers to recall one fable and have its author read it again. In our workshop I began at this point, by reading a fable written in one of my basic writing courses by Debbie Dunn. Here it is:

Wolf and Pig

Wolf: What are you doing alone wallowing in that mud?
Pig: I'm cooling off until the others get back. Say, why don't you come over here and try it. I'm sure it would do the same for you.
Wolf: Well, if you're sure there's nobody here. That does look awfully inviting.

The wolf anxiously leaped into the mud and cracked a smile at the pig.
Pig: Many wolves have been in this mud before.
Wolf: Really? Well, I will be the first to have taken such an easy meal, won't I?

The moral of this fable is:

1. What's good for a pig can be good for a wolf.
2. Kindness can become a liability.
3. A tender heart can be devoured.

Writing and Reading New Aphorisms

I read the fable twice; then we wrote three new morals for it. I said, "It's easier to write three than one because with only one chance at it, we have more trouble deciding what to say. Just write nonstop for three or four minutes. You can't do it wrong." We all wrote and read these morals, listening appreciatively with no interruption. Here's a sample:

— A pig and his mud are soon parted.
— Beware of wolves in mud clothing.
— Some pleasures are better left solitary.
— Don't invite strangers to dinner.
— Judge each wolf by the gleam in his eye.

— Aggression is best concealed by feigning doubt.
— Dirty is as dirty does.
— Wolves deserve their reputation.
— Hospitality is over-rated.
— Beware of strangers who are too polite.
— True pigs don't share in the first place.
— We always invite our own destruction.

We recalled two of the morals we'd heard and copied them down: "True pigs don't share in the first place," and "Some pleasures are better left solitary."

Observations

I said, "Choose one of these morals and reread it. Write a list of what you notice about how the sentence is written. Begin with the obvious. For example, in the first sentence I notice that the verb is negative. Write your list nonstop." If I see anyone looking stricken or paralyzed, I say, "Just write. You can't do it wrong." We read these observations aloud, listening appreciatively and without interruption. Sample observations for "True pigs":

- Sentence follows the pattern of "true men don't eat quiche"— that is, it qualifies the subject with an adjective that really doesn't say anything specifically but grabs us because of its quality and, now, familiarity. The prepositional phrase at the end: why at the end? Is it because truth (true pigs) has to come first? Is it because we like the *when* part of the sentence to follow the *who* and *what* parts?

- The negative verb is a reaction to the pig's silliness. The hearer of the fable has been saying no! no! all along, and sure enough, the pig has been trapped by his own hubris: "Other pigs are caught by wolves, but this is a modern fable, and I am going to be a new sort of pig. All this stuff about the pig needing to keep his guard up needs to be stopped." The sentence gains by containing a 3-word slogan. "Pigs don't share" could appear on a billboard.

- I don't know what to say about this sentence. It contains 8 monosyllabic words, the most important of which seems to be *true*, at first—seemed to be *true*—but it's really "true pigs" isn't it? *True pigs* can be finished in lots of ways. True pigs never clean their rooms. True pigs never stop eating. This pig gets eaten. True pigs smoke cigars. . . .

Here are some observations on "Some pleasures."

- *Some* starts out carefully—with implied distinctions. There's one abstract word: *pleasures*—and one adjective for a characteristic quality: *solitary*. It's a periodic sentence: the last word, the key. The verb is hardly there, just a joining. That sends all the force over to *better*, so the sentence tips that way. *Left* is not emphatic, a minimum thing to say as it is a minimum thing to do. But left keeps getting stronger as I reread the sentence: the focus of irony, of all the writer refrains from saying.

• The subject is limited—also the verb is limited by the *better*. It's not a law but a warning about how to live with your skin intact. It's slightly awkward—the "left solitary." We expect "left alone."

The Poem

I put this Frost poem on the board, we read it aloud, and I asked people to copy it:

The Span of Life

The old dog barks backward without getting up.
I can remember when he was a pup.

I said, "As you did before, write a list of what you notice about how the sentences of the poem are written. Begin with the obvious. For instance, I notice that the subject of the second sentence shifts to 'I.' Write your list nonstop; you can't do it wrong." After three or four minutes, we read our observations aloud, still listening with pleasure, still without interruption.

• Starts with strong visual image given to reader & ends with an implied image which the reader imagines simply from the word *pup*. The title abstracts the situation. Starts with *dog* and ends with *pup*—life going backwards, "backward" is a key word for the image, the title, & the last word. *Pup* is a silly sounding word. The dog, the poet, the reader have a past & therefore have age. Not only is the dog the echo . . . . All three are getting older; we were once all pups.

• *Old dog* at the beginning of the sentence and *pup* at the end contrast the two ages. The most powerful phrase for me is the alliterative *barks backward* with its implied meanings. The dog feels intimidated, endangered, or disturbed from behind. His bark shows his irritation, his anger at a disturbance. The span of life has been hard, and he is in a nasty, a bitter mood. He is worn out—the word *without* heightens the sense that the dog lacks the stamina of earlier life. *I can remember* brings poet and reader into the reflection—we too, can remember pups but we too can remember *old dogs* and the lesson to be learned. *Remember* drives home the point of something lost—the mobility of the pup. *Pup* holds the two connotations of happiness and vitality, as contrasted with *old dog* who is worn out.

- It's a rhymed couplet beginning with *old* and ending with *pup*. The second line has only the action of "I" remembering, no images of how the pup looked—only the remembering of the pup. Alliteration and 6 monosyllabic words. It's difficult for the dog to get up because he's so old. The first line is in the present tense; the second in the present and past.

- The first line has a symmetry that hinges on the middle word— "backward"—the line builds to "backward"—modifiers, a subject, and a verb—straightforward sentence order—which gets blocked, stopped at "backward"—monosyllabic words and then *backward*. The heaviness begun there continues in "without getting" and lightens in "up"—We're stuck there as the dog is. But the *up* is an extra syllable which pushes to the next line rhyme which is coming—and bring the . . . .

- It begins with a sentence apparently written in the third person and ends with a sentence where the speaker is obvious. Thus it moves from a kind of objectivity (or apparent objectivity) to subjectivity (a recollection from memory), a movement from outside to inside. *Barks backward* is alliterative and central to the short poem. How does a dog do this? It must be because he is so old, so unable to move, to look ahead that he must recline and alliterate . . . until he becomes activated. The speaker connects himself to the dog by remembering *when* . . . remembering when he & the dog were young.

- The force of the word backward: set off by caesura; substantively the word is directional, mirroring the movement of the couplet from "now" to "then." The alliterative "b" reinforces the strength of that word, existing as it does in a constellation of other hard consonants, but this plays off against the abstract behavior of persona in second line: he "remembers," while the dog "barks." Further, the image of the dog barking backward (turning its head around to bark, rather than moving its entire body) becomes iconic, physically apt, intellectually resonant. The persona *can*, the dog *can't*, but what the dog cannot do is physical, while what the persona can do is only mental, recollective.

- old/pup—time going backwards like memory. "I" is older now too than when "I" was a pup. *Barks backward* suggests physical movement that dog makes when he barks lying down: with each bark he rises a little bit & seems to move very slightly backward, probably because he's tensing his paws and legs a little as he barks.

[The writer bracketed these first three observations and commented, "These are too interpretive—not our assignment."] *without getting up*—he's just grumbling, not seriously warning/excited, etc. *backward* is the key puzzle/word, puzzle written thought. The um' papa rhythm makes this seem light & silly, and suggests that aging is no big deal, not sad, just there. *backward* parallels *remember*. Rhythm quickens as you go from *old* toward *pup*.

The Turning Point, the Attractive Center

If this were a class, I would ask students to write nonstop for 10 minutes in answer to a question. But time in the 60-minute segment of the workshop was almost up. I said, "Write for 3 minutes nonstop to answer this question, "What is the turning point of the poem, and why do you think so?" If students ask what I mean by "turning point," I say that in every piece of literature something turns or changes between the beginning and the end. The "turning point" is what we sense as that change. Or think of it as a center—the attractive center of the work.

After students had written, I'd send them home with all their writings to write more observations, and to write for 40 minutes nonstop to complete their answer to the question. If anyone said, "But suppose I have the wrong turning point or the wrong center?" I'd say, "You can't do it wrong. There's no one right answer to the question. In any unified writing the center is everywhere. So the right answer is the one you support with your observations."

Here are some sample three-minute essays from the workshop:

- The turning point comes with the word *remember* in the second line. Remember pulls us back to the puppyhood of the dog and also, somehow emphasizes the new focus on the *I* of the persona so that we begin to suspect that the speaker is remembering himself as well as the dog.

- The turning point is the change from the first to second sentence —from physical action of old dog to mental action of human "I" —from sensory, harsh, concrete to mental, intangible, less controlled—from animal response (to whatever it was) to human response to dog, that encompasses dog & human—

- I want to say "I" is the turning point because it introduces the speaker and his memory. But I really don't think so. The speaker is there from the beginning, and it *is* the word "backward" which places the speaker there—in the observation and in the movement to reflection on the connections between his own aging and the dog's which the realization of the backward sag of the dog's bark —the backward look he . . . .

- There are two points—the word "backward" . . . because it is literally and figuratively that moment when direction alters—the dog turns backwards, the verbally established present tense turns to the past. But the other possibility would be "I" as the persona introduces himself subjectively, the recognizably Frostean alteration from folksy to something resonating with metaphysical meaning. The tone changes, rhythm changes. And thus the dog barks backward to the "I," who "catches" the bark, transforms this stimulus into recollective trigger.

- The turning point is *backward*. After it, the / ⌣ rhythm begins, putting the ponderous /// / ⌵ opening in a lighter-sounding key. *Backward* is the puzzle—could be seen in many contexts:
  1. physiologically (see Wheeler's idea that he swallows his bar; Louise's that he hops backward),
  2. linguistically (new idiom to old),
  3. intellectually (backwardly—barking and canine thoughts),
  4. memory
  and the puzzle is "solved" by the palindrome "pup."

This is an essay written in a full five minutes:

- One turning point is after the title which creates great expectations of deep meaning. The turning point is the gap between this abstraction and a particular small pair of observations—small because it's a dog's life the poet refers to, not a man's, and he spans it in two lines. The poem deflates the title and interprets it. Life is short span, for dog and man; man's life is a dog's life—his remembrance is a bark backwards. Further: the span is not only a movement forward into age; it is a two-way bridge; dog and man look backward. We see the span best in hindsight. Title and poem are to each other: abstract and concrete, question and answer, philosophy and fiction, large and small. We go from a grander voice, a big phrase, to the colloquial "pup." The title is to the couplet as the moral to a fable. But by coming first it raises a question rather than wrap everything up. The question is *The Question:* What and why is the span of life? For an answer, Frost advises, look to your dog.

Reflections

Finally I asked writers to jot down in three or four minutes what they noticed about what we had done. We read these aloud, which took the place of a question and answer period and economically completed our 75 minutes. Sample noticings:

- The exercise asks the reader to slow down his reading. The writing allows for scrutiny and reflection on the importance of words (especially connotation), sentence structure, meter (the poem) and the ways such devices are used to shape and convey meaning. Students need to know the importance of scrutiny and reflection.

- Starting with common experience—the fable, the Frost poem— permutated into multiple reactions—that through the reading aloud came together again into thinking and rethinkings. Through fable and two-line poem—both attention to language & form. Totally non-threatening atmosphere of question & response. Hard not to interpret.

- Relief at being allowed to write & read our own thinking instead of continuing listening as we've been doing for two days. Increasing ability to trust in the value of our own thinking as we stopped apologizing for it as we heard the:
  Variety of response & felt the value of *each* idea,
  New perceptions springing from each other's ideas.

- "You can't do it wrong" was tested and proven true. Everyone took part, many critical-interpretive contexts, all useful. Many wanted to outrun the assignment, wanted to interpret before or instead of observing—peer pressure to look learned, clever, subtle?? Humor, lots of reinforcement from class & RD. This got stronger as the session went on; we grew impatient to produce a product of interpretation. The "turning point" essay satisfied this urgency. What a wonderful array of responses—thoughts & feelings & images—this technique evokes in so short a space without "mystifying" apparatus.

- We started with the obvious and moved to the less obvious. "Obvious" was the type of sounds, words, sentences. These sounds & sentences led us to meanings or interpretations. The interpretations could only be gotten by closely looking at the obvious. Behind the obvious is meaning. We read our observations out loud to each other. This led us to different insights and might have changed our own thinking. We wrote down our observations first. We paused to think in order to be able to write them down. Something written gave us something to start with.

Notes on the Design of the Work

A class time is like a moving design—a kind of dance or "game" in Huizinga's sense. A class conceived as a design or unfolding purpose takes its students through certain moves. Repeated and integrated, acted on and enacted by individuals, these moves flow in a dance, an enlivened habit of purpose and expression in which every moment counts, not as time spent but as the rhythm of the dance, the enabling rhythm of class working.

Fable

I begin with the writing of the fable (though short time made me omit that step in the workshop). All writing is literary creation between two poles: poetry and the discursive essay. At one pole, literature is unmediated, source-literature, "fiction" in the form of poem, drama, story. At the other pole, literature is analytical, *about* source-material—literature or other data. At one pole it is primarily experience, and at the other, it's analysis of experience. I want the class to see that unmediated, source-writing comes first, and that they can write it.

Writing and Reading New Aphorisms

Again writers begin by writing source-literature. (By *writer* I mean simply a person who writes. When you write, even if only for a semester, for that semester you are a writer.) In source-literature it's unmistakable that the author generates, originates writing. The author's authority is evident. You can see this in the list of wonderful morals. Some writers revel in slapstick: "A pig and his mud are soon parted." Others are elegant as La Rochefoucauld: "We always invite our own destruction."

Aphorisms represent a form of literature you can always get your students to write, directly and prolifically: "Sentences," *sententiae.* "Sentences" are also sentences, and the dynamism of syntax with its built-in capacity for unpacking thought, endlessly renewable. When a teacher gets students used to writing and rewriting sets of three or four sentences (nonstop, error-free), there's nothing else in composition she can't teach. A sentence is the nucleus for all larger structures; two sentences is the nucleus of discourse. "The *consequent* and *harmonious* fitting of parts in a sentence," says Jonson, "hath almost the fastening and force of knitting and connection; as in stones well squared, which will rise strong a great way without mortar."

All writing was read aloud in our session; listeners recalled what they heard. Writers read, which is their right and glory, and listeners learn to listen and pay attention. Listening is more entertaining and less critical than reading. Listening hears the possibilities of writing; watery or confused spots can't be retained. Seeing that helps inexperienced writers realize that the writings they first complete are drafts. Most criticism (teacher- or peer-) interferes with or takes over writing at the stages of its generation.

In the long run listening and paying attention is the easiest thing the teacher can teach by example—constant, effortless example. The teacher is trained to pay attention; in her attention is present the consensus of all those who have taught her. The teacher also loves and recognizes literature. Finding that in his students' writing sustains and nourishes his attention. As students recognize and name literature they hear, they listen better and longer. Paying attention is the first sign of the awakened intelligence.

Observations

I note that we always wrote observations, never spun them off the top of the head. Written speech differs from impulsive speech. Writing can be read; no student passes with, "I couldn't think of anything."

We wrote lists, lots of things, renewed acts of attention, holding off writing continuous prose which develops a first impression into an investment. "What you notice about how the sentence is written" directs the first moves to language and language structures because they're concrete and easy to recognize. And, of course, literature is made out of language.

The obvious: it gives an easy start; it can't be wrong. The obvious is the attractive center; we keep teaching students to go to the center. Some students think that "original" means "different." Writing about literature, such students go against the current of the work, writing hard, progressing little. "Begin with the obvious" points to genuine originality, to originating what we write by exercising our perceptions. I always give an example. Writing down my observation gives anyone who wants it a few seconds to oil the works.

The Poem

The move to the poem is a big one, but it comes in the form of a repetition. At this point everything is in place. Repetition is the structural principle of teaching as of any art. The poem is two sentences; its brevity relates it to the aphorism.

About observations I note two things. First nomenclature. Students usually originate more of their own terms than teachers do. (A student defined ballad structure as "advancing repetition," a more discriminating term, I thought, than "incremental repetition.") For some teachers, special terms are the chief way of teaching literature to students. They wouldn't say so, but they do so. And their special terms are passports to conversation about literature with other cultivated people. There are deep feelings here: feelings of the sacred (where the normative is higher than the descriptive) and feelings for magic (where

word and being are one). I don't underestimate the strength of such
feelings, but I note that the canon of terms changes a little in 10 years
and a lot in a generation. I'm a nominalist in such matters and will
doubtless go to the nominalist's hell (carrying Ockham's razor and
muttering, "Entities must not be multiplied unnecessarily"). I hold
with the man who said, "I know only that there ought to be enough
words to think with" (Frye, 1970, p. 100).

I note too that the observations don't disagree and are infinitely
varied. I relish their differences and their accuracy. They are perceptions, prior to inferences; and public, our gifts to each other. Their
communality helps create the community of the class. The *logos*,
Heraclitus said, is *koinon*, a common thing.

Turning Point or Center: the Organizing Idea

The turning point or centering question is a way of organizing
observations into an idea, a way of interpreting them. The question is
elemental to any literature: anything that begins and ends, changes the
beginning into the end. Answers to elemental questions aren't going to
sort out into right and wrong. The "right" answer is the idea the writer
develops and supports. I noticed that as these experienced writers in
the workshop interpreted their observations, they began to speak the
language of the poem.

Reflections

One of the workshop members, Don Roemer, promised to send
me a "legible" copy of his writing and did. He added this remarkable
postscript:

> You might be interested in something I tried in one of my classes
> as a consequence of attending your session. This is a junior-senior
> honors class. I had planned to begin *Beowulf* last Tuesday, intro-
> ducing the work with the usual comments on background neces-
> sary to make the poem accessible to these kids. Driving back from
> the conference I rethought my strategy, and developed what I
> ultimately did that Tuesday. I handed out the books, told the
> class only that the poem was a translation from an eighth-century
> Old English epic, warned them away from the introduction and
> afterward that brackets our edition of the text, and then had
> them follow along in the text as I read the Prologue out loud.
> Next they wrote down whatever responses they had to this read-
> ing, from the most obvious to the most subtle, which responses
> we shared with each other. Next each student wrote a response
> to what had been read, which secondary responses were also
> shared. And finally I had them write down and then read aloud

what expectations were raised for them by this prologue. Surely not a startling or innovative strategy, appropriated as it had been from your presentation. But what was startling were the results.

Either declaratively or interrogatively these high school students, for whom "Old English" means saying "hot" instead of "cool," managed to discern the value systems of the Danish-Geat world, anticipate the epic structure and context of the poem to follow, question the role to be played by Fate, and, perhaps most remarkable for me, inquire into the theological basis for the poem —pagan or Christian.

Had I delivered that originally scheduled lecture, I probably would have covered all those points, but I would also have effectively foreclosed their transaction with the text. Now, however, they have ownership of those concerns, and as they proceed through the poem, reading *and* writing the text, what would most probably have been a univocal experience will now be richly polysemous as each student makes his own meaning and then the interpretive community of the classroom will negotiate the space between the many readers and the text.

Prolific and *purposeful* are often divided in writing classes. Students need to generate writing with structure, to write prolifically with a purpose. The structure the student writes is the expository essay, the essay that supports the idea it asserts. The structure of class work is the essay in large, enacted in a design of four steps: Concrete Center, Abstraction, Organization, Return.

To begin with the center means that the teacher presents the work or the selection as a center, as Don Roemer did with the Prologue to *Beowulf*, evoking its elements from the students' reading in three stages of writing. The last stage, which asked students to ratify those elements as they continue to read the poem, made it clear that the prologue is also a center.

Abstracting or pulling the idea out of the data or observations gives us our first expressible definition or interpretation of the data. It's our hypothesis; it goes up front as a beginning of the essay. Abstraction is not abstruse or heroic, but ordinary: the insights or intuitions of our daily perceptions of the structure latent in experience. "Thus the mind perceives," says Locke, "that white is not black, that a circle is not a triangle, that three are more than two; and equal to one and two" (Langer, 1957). By abstraction we "recognize distinctions and identities, contradictions and entailments . . . " (Langer, p. 65). We perceive relations, forms, significance, and examples—all, as Susanne Langer says, "either logical or semantical" (Langer, p. 66). *Because* these forms of insight are all logical or semantical, they can be expressed in the writing of sets of sentences. Rewriting sentences brings them to definition, brings the structure to consciousness.

Then we use our hypothesis to organize the material as the center of an essay. We work through the material yet once more on behalf of our idea. The material the idea organizes becomes the support of the idea. The students' extended writing at home to answer the question is a first draft of an essay.

The return is rewriting. To complete the first draft of the essay, the writer returns to the hypothesis together with its organized evidence and redefines them as her thesis, her conclusion: the well-examined, well-imagined idea. The return movement to complete the essay continues through a rewriting of the entire essay, beginning with the ending.

All experience is concrete structure. Perception is empirical and inductive, and therefore class work can be so. Writing and rewriting hold experience, renew it, let us work through it till we bring its structures to consciousness. In a class we begin with naive and source-experience, the students' powers; and with consciousness of structure, the teacher's powers. The teacher begins by making a gift of structure to the students, not by putting information into them, but by putting work into them, freeing and exercising their powers till they come to mastery and their ideas to consciousness.

The spider's silk hypotheses unfold
Tenacious, tenable.

(Miles, 1974, p. 36)

References

Frye, N. (1970). *The stubborn structure.* Ithaca: Cornell University Press.

Langer, S. M. (1957). *Problems of art.* New York: Charles Scribner's Sons.

Miles, J. (1974). *To all appearances.* Urbana: University of Illinois Press.

10

Closeness to Text: A Delineation of Reading Processes as They Affect Composing

LYNN QUITMAN TROYKA

City University of New York

Teachers, at root, seek to help students to *become*—to gain power over their lives, have options, be fulfilled. Most people find it easier *to do* or *to be* than *to become* in our society.[1] A person can *do* something, such as design a computer program; a person can *be* something, such as a computer programer; but for a person *to become*—to grow and evolve over a lifetime—that person must tolerate well uncertainty, change, and ambiguity.

Perhaps more than any other teachers, teachers of writing and of reading can help people *become.* Teachers of reading and of writing deal with language, with making meaning,[2] with helping people make sense of their lives and the world.

To our shame, however, we who teach English have put a stumbling block in our students' way. We have condoned, by omission more than by commission, the curricular separation of reading and writing. Writing and reading are reciprocal meaning-making activities; one is diminished without orientation toward the other. Yet, most American colleges separate reading and writing courses, almost always at the developmental level and usually at the freshman level when reading for composition means looking at essays as models or for discussion of ideas. Many college teachers of writing and of literature consider reading *qua* reading an alien subject.

At the developmental level in college, the unfortunate separation between reading and writing instruction had its genesis in the fact that "remedial-reading specialists" began to join college faculty when many underprepared students had to be served. By training, usually in colleges of education rather than of liberal arts, these remedial specialists

were seen as the experts in helping students catch up. Composition
teachers were the novices. Thus, instead of looking for similarities in
the substance of our subjects, we focused on differences in our subjects and ourselves. I am reminded of H. L. Mencken's line: "For every
human problem there is a solution that is simple, neat, and wrong."

Such a perspective got me into some trouble about ten years ago
when as a teacher of basic writing, I was accused of teaching reading.
I was reminded that the developmental reading course was different
from the developmental writing course. I was told that I had no formal
training in reading, that I was going to confuse students who were en-
rolled in reading courses. My explanation was accepted after a while,
and it still holds: I don't know anymore how to teach students about
writing without teaching them about reading.

I need the rest of this paper to explain. For if there is any hope
to lighten the weight of mass illiteracy that is crushing our nation, or
to stop the perpetuation of illiteracy, we have to change our ways. In-
tegrating reading and writing will help. Depending on how literacy is
defined, America has 30 million illiterate adults (unable to read or
write) or 60 million illiterate adults (including those who cannot read
third-grade level materials). Too many people are closed off from
becoming.

My discussion begins with college basic writers, though my point
applies to writing at all levels. Next, to set a context for specific inte-
grations of reading and writing instruction, I summarize psycholinguistic theories of reading and a related research project I undertook to
observe readers of Braille. Finally, using my notion of "closeness to
text," I describe some ways to integrate the teaching of reading and
writing. I end where I began, with *becoming.*

I

Basic writers are often also very basic readers. Many read haltingly
aloud. Silently, they often subvocalize, not to hear rhythm but to
sound out the words laboriously. Comprehension often eludes these
students because they have to concentrate on looking at each word
rather than on looking through the words to make meaning.

When Phyllis (name changed) was in my basic writing class a few
years ago, she was 26 years old. Like many two-year college students,
she had decided to start college almost a decade after having graduated
from high school. Phyllis always came to class, even in the worst of our
New York winter, but she always chose a seat as far in the back of the
room as possible, and she spoke up only in conference with me or in an
all-female group. She was gracefully pretty, but she ignored the men
who clearly noticed her.

At the beginning of the semester, when faced with written prose of any complexity, Phyllis read word by word, phrase by phrase. She often subvocalized, moving her lips to try to decipher words. When she did not know how to read a word, she would ask one of the female students or me how to call it. (Students from strongly oral traditions[3] "call" words just as all of us "call" things. For example, a word that reads "serendipity" is called "serendipity," just as something to type on is called a typewriter or a word processor.) Although Phyllis comprehended little on a first pass at new academic material, she pushed on, and she reread with determination.

Look with me at two pieces of Phyllis's writing, produced eight weeks apart. As always when I publish student samples, I present Phyllis' work with her written permission. Here is Phyllis' first in-class writing, with errors as shown, composed the first day of the semester.

The New York City Subway System can be very unreliable at times and at other times they run on schedule. This happens in other city transportations also so therefore commutors will have to compromise.

The $0.75c is very difficult for some people while for others its alright. Considering if you do not have the correct money one cannot purchase the token and without this, entering the subway is impossible.

On the other hand paying 75c for poor services is unfair to commutors who can hardly find the daily fare.

Where to begin? Teach Phyllis how to write seventy-five cents correctly? Show how to spell *commuter*? Go into an explanation of how pronoun-antecedent agreement works? No. After writing a brief comment in which I agree with her last sentence, I simply put the paper aside. Then I take my cue from the way Phyllis reads, and I begin by teaching about reading.

Here is another of Phyllis's in-class writings, written just after the middle of the semester, about eight weeks after the piece above.

Rules are very important to many people. As a child, there are many rules that one had to abide by. Growing into adulthood was one way to get away from harsh rules.

My childhood days were not the best times of my life. The regulations were very harsh. Considering that I was the youngest child of my parents, one would think that I had the best of everything. Yes, I did in their eyes, but to me it was not. After reaching the age of twelve, the trouble began. My parents were so strict that I was afraid to become friends with other children. The rules were that I should put everything aside until I became a woman. "When will that be? I asked myself." During that time, my only friends were going to school. church, and home. For

some people reaching the age of eighteen would be adulthood.
But for me it was still abiding by the rules and regulations of
my parents. The rules in my classrooms were not harsh to me
because I was so afraid, I always try to do the right things at the
right time. At the age of twenty yrs old I broke the rules by
having a child. My parents were very upset but then it was all
their fault.

After my daughter was born I though this would be freedom
for me but it was not. I find myself still abiding by these rules. I
am still afraid to stay out late. There are so many things that "I"
am presently doing at the age of 26 yrs, which I can recalled I
use to do 10 years ago. I am a very scared person who is trying
to find happiness and the will to become a real adult.

Discipline must be maintained through out life. But, from my
experience too many harsh rules can scar an individual through
out life.

Accomplished writing? Not yet. But we find no cryptic sentences or
vague, rambling generalizations. We see a smaller percentage of errors;
a clear beginning, middle, and end; and sufficient details to raise the
hair on the back of our necks.

Phyllis has become conscious of how readers read, and she has
written to that consciousness. Awareness of how people read—the
process they go through to make meaning—does not refer here to the
notion of audience in its narrow sense of "who is the person out there
reading this?" A broader key question must occupy the writer:
*"Exactly how does my reader read, and, therefore, what must I do to
help my reader function?"*

II

The answer, I have come to see, can be found in psycholinguistic
theories of the reading process, from the work of Frank Smith, David
Pearson, Kenneth and Yetta Goodman, Judith Langer, and others.[4]
For the purposes of this discussion, I will unify the various models
around four common elements; I do so recognizing fully that the models differ in their details and that lively debates rage within reading
circles about the contrastive merits of each model.

A. Reading is a text-processing activity. It is a complex interaction
of page, eye, and brain. Meaning is made during reading by the association of ideas represented on the page to ideas already known to the
reader. This making of meaning is central to comprehension and to
learning.

B. Prior knowledge in the reader's brain permits new information to
be learned. New information is hooked into the old; the context in

place is hospitable to expansion. But if a reader has little prior knowledge about a given subject, he or she can assimilate only a limited amount of new information at any one time. For example, were I to be asked to learn from a text on astrophysics, I would have trouble. I would be a very basic, slow reader. I know almost nothing about the field in general, about the technical jargon, or even about the conventional sentence structures used by most writers on the subject; my prior knowledge is scant. On the other hand, many basic writers I know could easily learn from an issue of *Popular Mechanics*, a magazine I find almost as difficult to comprehend as an astrophysics textbook. These readers have considerable prior knowledge of the subjects covered as well as the jargon, prose structures, and visuals.

C. A reader uses prior knowledge to make predictions about what will come next in a text. A reader predicts everything from words ("Once upon a _____") to concepts ("The arguments for giving up cigarettes are many. For example, _____). Without a preconscious anticipating and estimating of what to expect next, reading would proceed at an excruciatingly slowly pace. The brain fills in as it goes along. If each new word were a total surprise, the brain would be unable to make connections and would not, therefore, comprehend. I cannot read astrophysics well because I have no idea what to expect next—in words or concepts.

D. Precision in predicting is not needed. Indeed, it is often undesirable. When predicting, a reader does not have to forecast the precise words that come next. Semantic and structural equivalents work just as well. Approximations are entirely acceptable for the making of meaning. For example, should someone read "John's car was blue" for "John's auto was blue," no injury to the meaning would take place. This so-called "miscue" aids meaning; good readers miscue well. (At first, some of us who teach English are offended by the notion that relative imprecision is acceptable, but the overriding priority for essential comprehension is not aesthetics but efficient substitution. Distractions at the making-meaning level of comprehension have to be minimal.)

Almost ten years ago, my search for evidence of these unseen associative activities led me to study readers of Braille. Does the theory hold up when people must perceive through their fingers, letter by letter?

Braille, I learned, is taught in stages. First, students are given readiness materials to touch so that they can come to distinguish, for example, a circle from a square, and one grouping of circles from another. Next, the alphabet is described, with each letter and number represented by a different configuration within a cell of only six tiny dots.

Braille Alphabet and Numerals

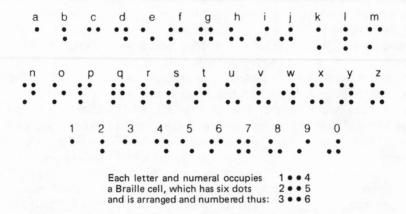

Each letter and numeral occupies a Braille cell, which has six dots and is arranged and numbered thus:

1 • • 4
2 • • 5
3 • • 6

Braille readers must learn minute differences in the feel of each letter and number. Letters are then combined to make words. Finally, after students are minimally familiar with the letters, the concept of Braille contractions is introduced. A Braille contraction is a few letters that represents an entire word: for example, *imm* stands for *immediate*, *afn* stands for *afternoon*, and *onef* stands for *oneself.*[5]

Many Braille teachers tell their students to begin reading text by (1) using the left forefinger as a placeholder for staying at the beginning of each line of text as it is being read, and (2) using the right forefinger to move across the line feeling the letters. At the end of each line, the reader is told to bring the right forefinger quickly back to meet the placeholding left forefinger and then to move both fingers down one line.

Learning to read Braille demands enormous concentration and brute determination. A high threshold for frustration is essential, and a good sense of humor helps.

Brenda (name changed) had all these qualities. I observed her at The Lighthouse in New York City, a respected training and counseling center for the blind. Brenda was 15 years old, bright, outgoing, curious, and outspoken. For example, the first day that I was with her teacher, Brenda wasn't expecting a visitor, but she knew instantly before we could say anything that someone extra was in the room. My procedure had been to wait to be introduced by the teacher, explain why I was there, and ask if I could observe. Brenda didn't give me a chance to be so formal. She fired questions at me: Are you sighted or blind? Are you black or white (I am white, Brenda is black)? Can I look at your face (she called me "four eyes" from then on)? When I told her that I wanted to observe how people learned to read Braille, she told me I need search no further. She had the answer. Motivation. Nothing else mattered. She couldn't learn Braille before because she had not wanted to badly enough, she said. She told me to be sure to write down everything she was saying. I did.

My observations of Brenda, and others, demonstrated for me the validity of psycholinguistic theories. My observations led me, also, to think about what I call "closeness to text," the concept that I'll discuss presently concerning the integration of reading and writing instruction.

Observation 1: Brenda was reading aloud about library research. She came to the words "file cards." She read "index cards." The teacher corrected her. Brenda tossed her hand as if waving the teacher off and said brusquely, "I know, I know. Same thing." She had made a good substitution, she had predicted well, and she did not want her meaning-making activity to be interrupted.

Observation 2: The teacher was called out of the room for a few minutes. The instant the door shut, Brenda said to me "Don't tell," and she began touching the Braille with all fingers (except the thumb) of her right hand. She moved across each line. She read aloud more slowly, but she read well. She explained, "My friends at the center (a live-in facility for blind teenagers) showed me. They don't do it the way you're supposed to. They showed me you gotta move fast, or you don't make it all out." Brenda's friends had discovered that they needed to get beyond each letter in order to look *through*, not *at*, words represented on a page.

Observation 3: When I told Brenda that I was impressed with her system, she suggested that I see one of the vocational teachers. He was blind. He read with all ten fingers. His hands moved rapidly. He read aloud as well as any schooled adult might. When he turned to a new page, he lightly rubbed his hand across the page before he went to the top of the page to start reading—an anticipating activity that sighted people do with a flick of their eyes. When he read, he used his right hand to move ahead—anticipating—and his left hand to "see" the words.

III

To make meaning of texts, Braille readers do all that they can to distance themselves from the letters represented on the page. The closer they are to the text, the more they have to look at each letter, and the worse they read. They must access their prior knowledge to create meaning, so they have to avoid focusing at the letter level.

Braille writers, I should note, have an almost impossible task. Braille typewriters do not exist. (Today, computer printers that type out in Braille have begun to make a difference, although they are very expensive and not widely available.) To write, a blind person has to tap out each letter of each word using a Braille Writer, which resembles a template. To read the written text, a writer must detach the Braille Writer and touch the dots. Erasing is impossible. Revising is difficult labor. Not surprisingly, few blind people want to write. They cannot scrawl. They get bogged down. They have to stay too close to their text to allow meaning to flow from their words.

Braille readers and writers made me realize that what I call "closeness to text" matters very much. When a reader is very close to a text—reading word by word or phrase by phrase—meaning cannot be made and comprehension is impossible. The brain is concentrating on "calling" the words rather than on making associations derived from prior knowledge. *Closeness to text hurts a reader.* To make meaning from the written page, a reader must scan quickly enough to engage actively with the ideas represented on the page. There must be enough pace or speed for the brain to do its work. For comprehension of ideas, the reader must look through, not at, the text.

Many basic writers stay too close to their texts, writing word by word. They need distance. Exhortations to postpone editing until ideas are drafted onto paper don't work. (The many other basic writers who tend to dash off their writing without rereading or revising are, in my opinion, merely being adaptive; they cannot write when they get too close to their texts so they go to the opposite extreme to get something on paper.) Raising basic writers' consciousness about the reading process helps give them distance from their texts so that they can more successfully make meaning with their language.

I offer here a half dozen ways to integrate reading into a writing classroom. Once the underlying principles are in hand, teachers can devise many other ways to suit their particular teaching style.

1. Teaching Writers How Readers Read: Students take easily to the four elements of the reading process I discuss above. I give them an introduction similar to the one I give in seminars for writing teachers who want to learn about reading. I use the same handouts and overhead transparencies, including some diagrams. I tell them about Brenda. I tell them about my sister being a researcher for an ETS study that observed how children learn to read and how beginning readers miscue.

2. Teaching Writers How Writers Read: Although little has been written about the subject, reading one's own prose during composing is a very different process from reading another's prose. When they read their evolving texts, writers must simultaneously read at three different distances, as if they were wearing trifocals. In close, they must look at letters and at words. At an intermediate distance, they must look at matters of style and arrangement. At far range, they must look through the words, not at them, to make meaning. Experienced readers shift deftly among these three degrees of closeness to text. Inexperienced readers, however, need to become conscious of the differences. They need to know that they have options.

Let me be clear: This is not like insisting that students revise for meaning before they edit for correctness. That dictum is unfair, sometimes crippling for some students, because of students' varying learning styles. Some writers chew on a word to propel themselves into pages of drafting; other writers draft many pages in order to find one word. Telling students how writers read gives students the power of information. We can then trust them to use that information for making choices.

3. Demonstrating the Concept of Prior Knowledge: Many basic writers have low self-esteem. When they hear about the concept of prior knowledge, they assume that they have none. They are impressed, therefore, when they can "fill in the blanks" of a cloze application to a simple paragraph. Material on three levels of difficulty yields more dramatic results. Moving from the less to the more difficult, students can see that new knowledge becomes prior knowledge rather quickly. This works best if the reading is done on three different days, with the previous piece(s) reread on day two and day three.

4. Demonstrating the Concept of Prediction: Making the predicting process in reading concrete helps basic writers write better because they understand what a reader needs in order to read well. I use what I call "prediction sessions"[6] with much success; in fact, they can become so popular that they can take over a course and often have to be curtailed after a while. Prediction sessions are a class or group activity in which a group leader reveals the sentences in a writer's (always a volunteer and always anonymous) essay or paragraph, stopping at the end of each sentence so that the other students can predict the gist of the next sentence. The writer, especially at the beginning of the semester, is almost always surprised to find that the readers expect more elaboration of ideas and more cohesion.

Here is the first draft of a paragraph about crime by Roy (name changed). As you read each sentence, imagine what you might predict to be the gist of the next sentence.

New York City is one of the most densely populated cities in the world. It cannot be compared to other cities when it comes to crime. Killings and beatings of our elderly citizens by teenagers in "the big apple" are the most hideous crimes committed. Crime is on the rampage morning, noon, and night in new York City.

Here is Roy's third draft, after two prediction sessions on his work.

Crime is a reality that haunts New York City night and day. Do
you want to take a subway from Manhattan to the Bronx? You'd
better hold on tight to your purse or make sure that your wallet
is not in your back pocket. Muggers and pickpockets will be
happy to relieve you of your money—or even your life. A favorite
target of thieves is our elderly citizens as they ride the subway or
walk the streets. Old people are easy marks for cruel teenagers
who like to beat and kill old people. One reason for so much
theft in New York City is drug abuse. Junkies want their fix, but
first they want our money. The "big apple" has a worm in it.

5. *Training Students to Score Holistically:* Basic writers are not
very good at scanning text. This keeps them too close to their texts
when they write and when they read. Once they learn the technique
of holistic scoring (using a batch of anonymous essays that have been
scored by experts), they become more distanced from their texts,
often with the result that they write more fluently and easily.

6. *Reading Aloud:* Most basic writing students were not read to
as children. Their mind's ear against which they can test the sound and
rhythm of their writing is underdeveloped. Reading aloud every day
helps students learn to listen for meaning. They create meaning as they
listen, a process they can become conscious of. My evidence for the
success of this activity is the frequency with which students ask for a
selection to be reread, or want to read the selection aloud themselves
when they are in groups.

None of this is to suggest a quick fix. But teaching about reading
in writing classrooms helps students learn about learning, about making
meaning, and about constructing their worlds.

Phyllis illustrates this. I wrote her this past summer at the address
I had on file to explain that I had been delayed in publishing her writing because my husband had been very ill, and that I hadn't had the
time to write the article I was planning. I wanted her to know that I
would be using it in this article. She wrote back:

Dear Dr. T.:

I was pleased to receive your letter and to learn that your husband is in excellent health again. I am very happy, and as you can
see from the above address, there is a little change. This is because
I am now living in my own apartment with my daughter. Her
name is Rosemary. Enclosed is a little picture of her.

Yours truly,
Phyllis

Becoming can happen.

Notes

[1] I am indebted to Robert F. Hogan, Executive Director of the National Council of Teachers of English (NCTE) for nineteen years until 1981, for alerting me to the implied distinctions among these verbs.

[2] I am indebted to Ann E. Berthoff for my first contact with the terms "making of meaning" and "meaning-making." I recommend her powerful book *The Making of Meaning: Metaphors, Models, and Maxims for Writing Teachers* (Montclair, NJ: Boynton/Cook, 1981). For example:

> In composing, we make meanings. We find the forms of thought by means of language, and we find the forms of language by talking thought. . . . I believe we can best teach the composing process by conceiving of it as a continuum of making meaning, by seeing writing as analogous to all those processes by which we make sense of the world. (69)

[3] For more information about college students from strongly oral traditions, see Thomas J. Farrell, "Literacy, the Basics and All That Jazz," *College English* 38 (1977): 443–59; and Lynn Quitman Troyka, "Perpsectives on Legacies and Literacy in the 1980's," *College Composition and Communication* 33 (1982): 252–62.

[4] For those unfamiliar with this field, I recommend highly Frank Smith, *Understanding Reading*, 3rd ed. (New York: Holt, 1982).

[5] A good introduction to Braille can be found in Claudell S. Stocker, *Teacher's Manual: Modern Methods of Teaching Braille: Book One and Book Two* (Louisville: American Printing House for the Blind, 1970). 1970.

[6] For a detailed discussion of "prediction sessions," see my paper "The Writer as Conscious Reader." Until it appears in the forthcoming *Sourcebook for Basic Writers*, edited by Theresa Enos, to be published by Random House, it can be found in the ERIC files, Document ED 198 549, July 1981.

11

The Reader in the Writing Class

CAROL BATKER and CHARLES MORAN

University of Massachusetts at Amherst

Since the publication of Janet Emig's *The Composing Processes of Twelfth Graders* (1971), writing classes have focused not only on the writing that students produce, but on the ways in which students go about the process of writing. This shift of focus from the text to the writer has been welcome and productive. But recently a number of us at the University of Massachusetts, driven by our interest in reader-response criticism, have begun to wonder if in our enthusiasm for the student writer and the writing process, we have not rather lost sight of the reader in the composition class.

Student writers are, after all, readers: they read and re-read their own work, they read and subsequently edit and evaluate the work of their peers, and they write to readers—to classmates, to the teacher, and to readers outside the classroom. Through the work of specialists in the fields of reading (Smith, 1973) and of literary criticism (Rosenblatt, 1938, 1978; Bleich, 1975, 1978; Holland, 1975; Mailloux, 1982) we have come to understand that this "reading is a complicated act, a process in which the reader actively participates in the making of meaning. Wolfgang Iser describes the emergence of meaning in this way: "The work is more than the text, for the text only takes on life when it is realized, and furthermore the realization is by no means independent of the individual patterns of the text" (1974, pp. 274–75). A reader composes the text; the text composes a reader. The result of this encounter is "meaning," which, as we now see it, is a property not only of the text but of the reader. Meaning arises in the transaction that takes place between reader and text. Our student writers have been told something like the whole truth about the writing process. Should they not be told something like the whole truth about the reading

198

process, that "transaction" or "response" that takes place when a reader encounters a text?

In our work at the University of Massachusetts/Amherst we have attempted to bring an awareness of the activity of reading into our writing classes. We have tried to help our students toward an understanding that the reader is not simply an abstract and passive "audience" but is an active, highly individual being who collaborates with the text in the making of meaning. Our freshman writing course is rather like a studio art course: during the semester students complete seven "projects" or essays, each proceeding through drafts which are revised on the basis of feedback from peers and teachers. Although the students' writing has been read by clearly identified readers, the responses made by these readers have been cast in text-based language. Teachers and peers have been encouraged to comment upon the essay's structure, its language, its tone—all spoken of as if they were properties of a text. We have replaced much of this text-oriented language with reader-oriented language, particularly in the design of our peer editing instructions, in the language of our teacher-comments, and in the language we use in our one-to-one conferences.

We begin with our peer editing procedures because they are in some ways the least radical. Any peer editing procedure would seem to focus attention on a reader's response, and indeed in the work of Peter Elbow and others it does (Elbow, 1973, 1981; Judy & Judy, 1981). Yet much of the literature in the field suggests that it is the text, and not the reader's response to the text, that should be the focus of attention (Bruffee, 1980, pp. 121–55; Walvoord, 1982, p. 42). If we were to follow what appears to be the main stream, we would direct our peer editors' attention to the text with questions such as these: "What is the main idea in this essay?" "What details or techniques does the writer use to convey this meaning?" "Are there any details, sections, or techniques in this essay that do not help the author convey this meaning?" In our revised peer editing instructions, we direct the peer-readers' attention to the reading of the text with questions like these: "As you read this essay, what meaning did you make?" "What in the reading helped you make this meaning? (Write down specific details, words, phrases.)" According to Iser, as readers read they constantly try, "even if unconsciously, to fit everything together in a consistent pattern" (1974, p. 283). And Norman Holland argues that the reader "will transform the fantasy content, which he has created from the materials of the story his defenses admitted, into some literary point or theme or interpretation"(1975, pp. 121–22). Our reader-response priented peer editing instructions make this active patterning and/or transforming an explicit, legitimate activity, one to be reported and analyzed in the classroom. Once interpretations are brought forward, the question of their validity can be raised and addressed.

In our class work with peer editing, it is clear that personal experience affects the way in which readers make meaning and, therefore, the way in which they evaluate a piece of writing. Holland says flatly that "interpretation is a function of identity" (1975, p. 816), and Iser agrees: "The manner in which the reader experiences the text will reflect his own disposition" (1974, p. 281). In an attempt to get at this aspect of the reading process, we print this question on our peer editing instruction sheets: "What element or detail did you take from your experience as you developed your main idea, your interpretation?" A second question, "When in the course of your reading did you rely most on personal experience to develop your interpretation?" draws the students' attention to the ways in which single words affect particular readers. The word *death*, for example, might trigger one response in Reader A, but in Reader B, recently bereaved, it might trigger an entirely different response.

To give you a sense of our procedures and their results, we give you a sample of this semester's work: the first paragraph of a student's essay, and a partial record of the reader-based peer response.

They staggered single-file into the meeting room like a mob of drunken sailors after a long and eventful night. One by one they collapsed on the floor, knees up, hands behind their heads and staring blankly at the ceiling. A few lucky early birds sat head in hand in the desk chairs facing the blackboard. Coach stood at the board watching the procession with apparently great interest and concern. The blackboard was already splotched with assorted x's and o's. But to a half-conscious band of football players they meant a wearisome review of diagrams and plays previously branded in the depths of their memories.

Chris, the first reader of this essay, found that he had "made" this meaning as he read: "mental preparation." He said that in making this meaning he had drawn on these elements in the text: "the quiet, sober atmosphere" in the locker room, students "in deep thought," and, a phrase from the essay's third paragraph, "a ritual of inner thought." Chris also said that the players were "asking hard questions of themselves" in the locker room, a statement for which there is no explicit evidence in the text. The "sleepiness in the locker-room," Chris said, was irrelevant. When asked to describe the personal experience he brought to the interpretation, Chris wrote as follows:

Before going out to sell books door to door I would spend time by myself praying, thinking, reminiscing. I would get all of my daydreaming out of the way so I wouldn't space out on Mrs.

Jones. It is a ritual of mental preparation to get your attitude right before you jump into the competition. Before a wrestling match I would think to myself—my strong points, weak points, strategy, sum up courage, sum up strength, get your mind right.

Chris brings to this reading some eighteen years of experience; the text causes him to draw upon particular elements of that experience.

Aaron, the second reader of the essay, is a different reader with a different history, constitution, character. When asked to describe the meaning he had made of the essay, Aaron replied, "War." In making his interpretation, he reported, he had drawn on these elements in the text: the military-on-leave metaphor in the first sentence, "like a mob of drunken sailors"; a reference to "veterans" in paragraph three; and the words *stragglers, procession,* and *silence* later in the essay. He reported that he had brought to the reading of the essay his experience of film: "The first paragraph," he wrote, "reminds me of a wharf scene at the beginning of a movie." *"Procession,"* he wrote, "sounds like a funeral, and *stragglers* sounds like wounded."

Peer editing instructions like ours, because they direct students' attention to their responses, may produce distinctly different interpretations, as they have in this case. Chris and Aaron, different readers, have made different meanings as they read the text. What I. A. Richards (1960) took to be a problem, however, we see as an opportunity. After our readers have completed their reading, we put them together with the author in a collaboration session, one similar to those David Bleich describes in the literature classroom (Bleich, 1975, pp. 80–95; 1978, 168–89). In these sessions a dialogue new to our writing classes takes place. The author is confronted with different and initially equally valid interpretations of the text. The author is forced to see how certain words, phrases, or images have been construed—sometimes in ways consistent with authorial intention, sometimes not. The readers, confronted by this same difference, are forced to analyze and evaluate their interpretive strategies. The fact that Aaron's interpretation has been so thoroughly determined by the military-on-leave metaphor of the first sentence is information that is useful to the author—and to Aaron. Aaron needs to consider whether he was giving the text a fair chance; the author needs to consider whether his opening sentences help determine a response not intended. The author of the essay had hoped to make readers feel the deep boredom of the "skull sessions" that preceded football games. Clearly the two readers had not made that meaning as they read. On the basis of this information, the author decided to leave out the reference to "inner thought" which had played so great a part in Chris's interpretation. The author added the words *tired, lagging, boredom,* and *fatigue* to the text in an attempt to narrow the range of meanings a reader might be able to generate. The military-on-leave metaphor of the first sentence was allowed to stand, an implicit criticism by this interpretive community of the way in which Aaron had interpreted the text.

The student is not the only reader in the classroom, however; the teacher as reader is present as well. We have attempted to see this teacher-reader from a reader-response perspective. When we do, we see that this teacher functions in the classroom as a member of that particular interpretive community. The teacher also, however, belongs to another community, one whose interpretive strategies are a function of a profession and/or discipline. The university, when seen from this perspective, is a loose confederation of interpretive communities: there are physicist-readers, economist-readers, art-historian-readers—an interpretive community for each of the fields and disciplines defined and presented in the university catalog. Readers in each of these communities are likely to share some, but not all, interpretive strategies.

In presenting ourselves to our students in Freshman English, we are therefore careful to present ourselves as English teachers, a special kind of reader. We explain that in this role we feel a special responsibility to the language. Moreover, we tell them, we English teachers are most often humanists—not social scientists, or natural scientists, or engineers or marketing experts temporarily, or permanently, on leave from their profession. As humanists, we are deeply concerned with the individual human being—not primarily as data or system but as unique, endowed with mind, imagination, soul. We are almost reflexively drawn to the personal voice, to writing that seems to originate in a deeply personal and unique response to some aspect of the world or self. Our colleagues in the natural sciences will tend to value economy and objectivity; we will tend to value fullness (within limits) and subjectivity. Finally, we, more than most of our colleagues in most other disciplines, are sensitive to the sound, appearance, and history of the language. We are more likely than most to be affected by the appearance of the page presented to us—the typeface, the handwriting, the margins, the visual impact of paragraph length. Our students should know all this, because it affects the way in which we read and evaluate their writing. The advent of writing-across-the-curriculum has made it clear: The academy is a loose confederation of interpretive communities.

But we are more than English teachers; we are individuals. Each of us brings to the words on a page a somewhat different world of experience and belief. From a reader-response perspective, it is our responsibility to present this self, or range of possible selves, to student writers. Teachers do, of course, carry signs of self about them, and students read these signs, "psyching out" the teacher and discovering with some accuracy the kind of reader they are likely to find. And yet student writers may believe that there is one kind of "good writing," a magic prescription which they have, year after year, failed accurately to discover. Or they may not know enough about the teacher/reader to imagine accurately this teacher's range of possible selves, or which of the possible selves the teacher/reader is likely to draw on in a particular reading situation. Students may, in short, need help in discovering the kind of reader their teacher is likely to become.

A good vehicle for communicating this information is the teacher's written response to a piece of student writing. Generally speaking, teacher comments describe and evaluate student writing. Like Agassiz's student and the fish, the process carries with it the assumption that objectivity is possible—that there is a teacher/reader/observer and, in another world entirely, the piece of writing being read. The comment will therefore be text-based and will speak of the text as having certain properties: structure, syntax, tone, manuscript form. There may be words of praise and suggestions for revision, but the focus of the comment will be upon the text, and not upon the reader's response to the text. Even when the comment addresses the topic's *voice* and *audience*, it is likely to do so in terms that carry with them a text-based orientation: "Powerful voice here, but needs a more lucid opening paragraph." This sort of teacher comment must suggest to the writer that the text is an artifact, measured with calipers and string—and not a piece of discourse that has been read and evaluated by a person with specific reading criteria.

One of our students, Lorenzo, had written a draft of an essay titled "Defense in Basketball." He knew his subject—he was a guard on the varsity team—and his draft was written in Edited American English. But we found the draft difficult to read. The problem, we decided, was that his essay had not been conceived as a discourse, but as a paper, due Tuesday, three pages long. Here is our written comment on his draft:

> Lorenzo: you begin with a general essay on "basketball in general" and then you seem to find your focus: an argument that defense is absolutely critical. Suggest you go with the argument. You'll need to imagine a reader. Let me tell you who I am—someone who shot baskets as a kid but never played much or well, someone who knew the Knicks in the Bradley-DeBussher (sp??) era, someone who watches the occasional Celtics game but believes that basketball is only really interesting in the last quarter of a play-off game. I can't watch for defense. What is defense? All I can see is people shooting marvelous baskets. How would I watch for defense? I don't even know what it is.

In this comment we suggest a genre (argument) and then we present
the reader's background, experience, and culture, information that
could not be, or was not, inferred by the writer from acquaintance
and observation. We are giving the author information about how we
will evaluate the essay: professionally, as an undeveloped piece in the
genre *argument*, and personally, as not containing enough information
about the subject, *defense in basketball*, to be useful or even intelligible. This reader reads like an English teacher, and like an English
teacher who has played a little, but not much, basketball. Not all English teachers played basketball as children; not all who did had poor
hand-eye coordination and therefore remained duffers; not all have
subsequently become basketball fans of a particular and limited sort.

As Walker Gibson (1950) and Walter Ong (1975) have told us,
however, the reader is not a fixed entity. One person can become different readers. The range is defined by experience, character, and situation. The text has power, albeit limited, to compose the reader. For
Lorenzo, we have perhaps unwisely simplified the writer-reader transaction and suggested that the reader interprets a text in stable and
characteristic ways. Kandace, our next student writer, gets the whole
truth: the reader is in some degree a creation of the text. The text
directs us to become a certain sort of reader. If the imagined or implied reader is within our range of possible reader-roles, we come along.
If not, we refuse. Kandace had written a rather flat account of a Grateful Dead concert, and we responded in this fashion:

> The difficulty I have as I read this is becoming a reader—compos-
> ing myself, as it were. Who am I as I read this? Who have you
> imagined me to be? Someone, for instance, who is trying to de-
> cide whether or not to go to a GD concert? And if so, an old per-
> son? grumpy/non-grumpy? a young person? male? female? Or do
> you imagine that I am a person who is discussing with you the
> relative uniqueness of different groups? Or am I the inexperienced
> person and you the someone who is telling me, because I want to
> hear and because you want to tell, about the salient features of
> your experience? As you write, and in this case re-write, imagine
> that you are talking to, writing to, a real person—real and alive in
> your imagination.

When we first thought of attempting response-based teacher comment,
we thought it might be too much "truth" for our students, and indeed
we did find some initial resistance to what one student called "shrink-
talk." What we find after the fact, however, is that most students are
pleased that we have given them a relatively full account of the writ-
ing/reading situation.

We have found that reader-based comment also directs the
teacher's attention to the reading process and to the criteria that are

being used in the evaluation that occurs during that process. One of our students, Lisa, wrote a retrospective narrative, "The Big Game," which we found initially to be flat and dull—a clear sign to us now that we have not been able to become the kind of reader the text requires. It seemed to us that we were being asked to assume, and believe, that the events described had significance. We were unable to give these events the significance required, and therefore broke off the reading. Was this our failure, or the writer's, or both? We responded to Lisa's essay in this way:

> Lisa: a quick-moving narrative. My only suggestion, and it's a difficult one, perhaps: I'd like you to imagine a specific listener as you tell this story. Who are you telling this story to, in your imagination, as you write? Your imagined ten-year-old daughter? Or a roommate? or your husband, ten years after your marriage? Or your brother, age fifteen? Or an adult, say 50 or so? I really don't care what the imagined audience is; if the imagination is thorough, I'll be able to become, in my imagination, that reader/listener.

Lisa's reply to our comment was that she had indeed imagined an audience, and a full discourse situation. As she wrote, she had imagined she was speaking to her high-school class at their 20th reunion. So where did the breakdown occur? As we listened to Lisa, and re-read her essay, the fault had been, it seemed, partly ours. The cues were there, certainly—perhaps not enough, or not skillfully placed, but they were there. Perhaps our failure had at its root our appropriately limited tolerance for autobiographical narrative in the freshman writing course. From our perspective, Lisa was writing in the wrong genre, and the interpretive framework we brought to the piece simply didn't work. Lisa deserved, and received, this information. The fault was also, however, partly the writer's. The failure was not one of imagination, but of technique. We needed to be more thoroughly cued into the imagined situation. The writer owed that to her reader.

    The adoption of a reader-response perspective has modified not only our peer editing and our teacher comments; it has taught us new behavior in our student-teacher conferences. In a conference, a teacher may usefully adopt a number of roles. The teacher can become a reflector, asking the occasional question and listening quietly, as Donald Murray describes in his essay, "The Listening Eye" (1979). Or the teacher can become an editor, modeling for the student the act of revision, or a writer, actually producing a paragraph or sentence. Our reader-response perspective suggests another important potential use for this golden time: reading through a student's writing and, as we read, describing as best we can what is happening to us—becoming, in short, a real-life, talking and responding reader. This procedure is not unlike Peter Elbow's "telling" or "giving movies of you mind" (1973,

p. 85 ff.), but it is more closely related to Stanley Fish's procedure of
asking of the text, word by word, line by line, "what does this word,
phrase, sentence, do?" (1970) The reader's response to text is seen to
be linear, as the reader proceeds through the text from beginning to
end, making predictions, testing those predictions against what follows,
and as those predictions are fulfilled, making new predictions and moving on.

Here is an example of a reader-response moment in a one-to-one,
student-teacher conference. Diane had brought to her conference an
essay titled "Transitions from High School to College." The teacher
began to read the essay and, after the first paragraph, felt disengaged
from the text—somewhat angry and unhappy. He was having difficulty
focusing his attention on the words on the page. As the reading continued, the symptoms became worse, and he seemed to be trying to escape altogether from the reading situation. So he told Diane that he
was having difficulty reading the essay and suggested that they both
begin at the beginning and read slowly, seeing if together they could
follow the language along the line and re-create his response. Here are
Diane's opening sentences:

Transitions from High School to College

Upon entering this University, I faced many transitions. Some
were expected and others were not. There were both positive
and negative changes. The first week was complete havoc.

The teacher read Diane's first sentence and asked himself Fish's question, "What does this sentence do?" He then told Diane what he
thought it had done to him, and by extension to other readers—certainly not all, but perhaps a significant percentage of those who might
read this particular passage. The main clause, "I faced many transitions," he told Diane, opens before him the field of "transitions." This
field is as yet un-landscaped; it is pure potential, with as yet no clear
shape or structure. He expects the game, whatever it might be, to be
played on this field. The second sentence, he tells Diane, gives the field
a clear shape: "Some were expected and others were not" divides the
field into two sections, "transitions expected" and "transitions not expected." Sentence three is a bit of a surprise: "There were both positive and negative changes." One of two things happens at this point:
the reader is confused, as one structure seems to replace the other; or
the reader assimilates the two structures into a third structure: a four-
part division of the field into "expected, positive," "expected, negative," "unexpected, positive," and "unexpected, negative." Sentence
four is a rude surprise: "The first week was complete havoc." Here
the writer appears to abandon both the expected/unexpected and the
positive/negative oppositions and gives the cue for retrospective narra-

tive. Somewhere along the way, the teacher tells Diane, his capacity to absorb surprises was exceeded and he stopped reading her text.

Bringing the reader into the writing classroom has, it seems to us, potential benefits for the student writer. There is something to be said, first of all, for telling our students the truth as we see it. And that truth is this: readers make meaning, bringing to bear upon this creative process their unique character and history. The peer reader may be young, old, male, female, black, white—there is great variety in our writing classes, a not-unusual situation. The teacher has a different role in the writing class and is likely to read in that role. Yet the role of teacher can be understood in so many ways that the teacher-reader is hardly more typical than the peer-reader. Both of these readers, peer and teacher, are capable of becoming different readers within a range defined by character, history, and situation. And the student writer, as the maker of the text, can imply a reader that, if all goes well, the peer and/or teacher can become. The more full and honest our description of this system that incorporates reader, text, and writer, the more complicated the system seems. We believe, however, that our college freshmen are more than ready for this complexity.

Beyond this, the consideration of the reader in the composition classroom has other significant potential benefits. By causing the peer readers to see their reading as a creative and personal act, we hope to increase their awareness of the active role they play in the reading process. If students begin to see themselves as active, meaning-making readers, they may be more apt to believe that the reader of *their* writing is a maker of meaning as well. It is generally assumed that audience awareness is one of the writer's most important antennae. When we bring the readers' response into the writing classroom, we create the possibility of audience analysis that is far finer than the broad sorts of audience analysis now current in the field. In addition, student writers will see that the peer and the teacher are different readers, and they will be forced to examine the criteria each reader brings to the text. In this way they will be prepared for the multitude of idiosyncratic readers they will face, both inside and outside the academy. The introduction of a reader response perspective may benefit the writing teacher as well as the writing student. In our work with reader response in the writing classroom, we have ourselves become aware of the ways in which we characteristically read student writing, and these, an inevitable function of our professional situation, are not always useful or good.

We hope, and until further work is done we can only hope, that our students will, as a result of the changes we have made in our pedagogy, less often think of a freshman essay as a "paper," an artifact that is produced on demand and measured by word- or page- count. We hope that our students will more often see their writing as a vehicle for their creation of, and participation in, a particular world of discourse.

References

Bleich, D. (1975). *Readings and feelings: An introduction to subjective criticism.* Urbana, IL: National Council of Teachers of English.

_____. (1978). *Subjective criticism.* Baltimore: Johns Hopkins University Press.

Bruffee, K. A. (1980). *A short course in writing.* Cambridge, MA: Winthrop.

Elbow, P. (1973). *Writing without teachers.* New York: Oxford University Press.

_____. (1981). *Writing with power.* New York: Oxford University Press.

Emig, J. (1971). *The composing processes of twelfth graders.* Urbana, IL: National Council of Teachers of English.

Fish, S. (1970). Literature and the reader: Affective stylistics. *New Literary History 2,* 1970, *1,* 123-62. In J. P. Tompkins, *Reader response criticism.* Baltimore: Johns Hopkins University Press, pp. 70-100.

Gibson, W. (1950). Authors, speakers, readers, and mock readers. *College English, 11* (6), 265-69.

Holland, N. N. (1975). *5 readers reading.* New Haven: Yale University Press.

_____. (1975). Unity identity text self. *PMLA, 90* (5), 813-22.

Iser, W. (1974). *The implied reader: Patterns in communication in prose.* Baltimore: Johns Hopkins University Press.

Judy, S. N. & Judy, S. J. (1981). *An introduction to the teaching of writing.* New York: John Wiley.

Ong, W. J. (1975). The writer's audience is always a fiction. *PMLA 90,* (1), 9-21.

Mailloux, S. (1982). *Interpretive conventions: The reader in the study of American fiction.* Ithaca: Cornell University Press.

Murray, D. M. (1979). The listening eye: Reflections on the writing conference. *College English, 41* (1), 13-19.

Richards, I. A. (1960). *Practical criticism.* New York: Harcourt Brace.

Rosenblatt, L. M. (1938). *Literature as exploration.* New York: D. Appleton Century.

_____. (1978) *The reader, the text, the poem.* Carbondale: Southern Illinois University Press.

Smith, F. (1973). *Psycholinguistics and reading.* New York: Holt, Rinehart and Winston.

Walvoord, B. F. (1982). *Helping students write well.* New York: Modern Language Association.

Fictions

12

Inventing an Elephant:
History as Composition

SARAH W. SHERMAN

University of New Hampshire

I

There's an anecdote in a couple of composition textbooks which has always intrigued and bothered me. It's the one about the sculptor and his visitor. The sculptor is busily working on an enormous statue of an elephant. His visitor, seeing there are no marks on the marble, asks how the sculptor knows where to carve. The sculptor says simply, "I just cut off anything that doesn't look like an elephant." This story usually illustrates the discovery process, whether the students are in the process of discovering their subject through freewriting and reflection, or in the process of refining their essay through revision. I'd like to use it for a somewhat different purpose, to suggest some connections between composition and academic research, particularly historical research.

While I do a good deal of literary criticism, I also consider myself an historian, and I have a practitioner's interest in the philosophy of history. Writing history has taught me the painful necessity of throwing out more information than I keep, as well as the difficulty of focusing my approach. But, as I've said, I have trouble with this story about the sculptor. And the trouble begins with that block of unshaped stone.

First of all, the writer not only invents the elephant, but also the stone. Let's say we have a young woman who sets out, improbable as it may seem, to write a research paper on the elephant. She has to choose and consult her sources, gather her notes, sketch out her ideas; in other words she has to create the material out of which *her* elephant will emerge. But then how does she recognize its figure?

211

Waiting for that figure to emerge, and then recognizing it, is a mysterious process. I like to think of it as Don Murray does in his essay, "Write Before Writing":

Many writers know they are ready to write when they see a pattern in a subject. This pattern is usually quite different from what we think of as an outline which is linear and goes from beginning to end. Usually the writer sees something which might be called a gestalt, which is, in the words of the dictionary, "a unified physical, psychological, or symbolic configuration having properties that can not be derived from its parts." The writer usually in a moment sees the entire piece of writing as a shape, a form, something that is more than all of its parts, something that is entire and is represented in his or her mind, and probably on paper, by a shape. (1982, p. 10)

Is this figure truly in the carpet, or only in our eyes? That's probably an unanswerable question. And it's the question raised by Gary Lindberg, Paul Mariani and others in this volume. Is our interpretation of the text really true, really out there in the text itself . . . or do we impose our own patterns on its surface? Can we know the text as it is, "in itself," or the past "in its own terms?" Misreading, Gary Lindberg and David Bartholomae suggest, may be an irradicable component of reading itself. Just so our reading of the past through the evidence which it has left to us. I prefer to look at the problem, both in literary criticism and in history, in terms of the self-other relationship. We know the text, we know the past insofar as we can know anyone, anything. Historical research is a kind of dialogue in which the result is probably neither wholly ourselves nor the other. We cannot examine the evidence without being changed by it; the evidence cannot be examined without being shaped by our perceptions of it. Finally, we work, as Paul Mariani concluded, for that "phosphorescent" moment of recognition when the pattern coalesces before our grateful eyes.

That moment, however, only ushers in another problem. The original anecdote suggests that once the sculptor has the elephant firmly in view, the stuff he carves away is meaningless: chips of anonymous rock. Supposedly this material says nothing about elephants, but in practice it has "elephant" written all over it. Poring over this heap of language about elephants, disconnected facts about elephants, disparate images of elephants, our student must seek her own figure. But if that figure is to come into focus, she must then resolutely discard, carve away, all irrelevant figures, however valid. To tell *her* truth she must suppress other truths.

This kind of arrogance comes hard to many writers, and seems to students, I think, uncomfortably close to lying. Hence their anxiety

about "bringing in their own opinions" or being "biased." And the
more seriously they take their research, perhaps the more anxious they
become. When my own index cards threaten to overwhelm me, I consult this passage from Henry James; it's pinned above my desk:

> Really, universally, relations stop nowhere, and the exquisite
> problem of the artist is eternally to draw, by a geometry of his
> own, the circle in which they shall happily *appear* to do so. He is
> in the perpetual predicament that the continuity of things is the
> whole matter for him, of comedy and tragedy; that this continu-
> ity is never broken, and that, to do anything at all, he has at once
> intensely to consult and intensely to ignore it. (Henry James,
> Preface, *Roderick Hudson*)

James's quotation shows, I think, how strong the connections are
between the writing of fiction, particularly the novel, and the writing
of history. The word *history* itself comes from the Greek *historia*,
meaning "learning or knowing by inquiry" (*Random House College
Dictionary*, p. 628). In its modern usage, the word is significantly ambiguous. It refers both to "a continuous systematic narrative of past
events" and to "the aggregate of past events." In other words, "history"
signifies both the narrative about the past and the past itself. This ambiguity, I think, is highly significant. It implies a recognition that in
some fundamental way the past does not become history until it is
narrated. Someone must question that aggregate of events, inquire into
them, then give them a form which renders them intelligible, humanly
significant.

There are few such words, I believe, in our lexicon. Words which
express so succinctly the dialectical relationship between the "reality"
of events, and the human construction of that reality. I suppose the
word *myth* aspires to that ambiguity—in the hands of phenomenologists "myth" strives to mean both the human story about our origins
and the "real truth" about those origins—but the word *myth* is for
most of us still too close to "fiction," even to "lie." Not so "history."
To discover our history is to compare our history.

And this leads me to the difficulties of historical research. We
tend to think of history as chronology—one damn thing after another.
We also tend to think of historical writing as linear narrative, telling us
exactly *how* one damn thing led to another. History both as event and
narrative appears to be diachronic, linear. However, an infinity of
events occurs simultaneously at every moment. The exact relationships
among these events, as well as the infinity of events preceding and
succeeding them, is problematic to say the least. Each event is over-
determined, shaped by a multitude of forces, rooted in complexity.
Further, even if their development does proceed according to a linear
scale, there are many scales and they are not necessarily synchronous:

geological history unfolds over gigantic spans of time, human history over smaller units, individual histories over even smaller ones . . . .

These particular problems have led to long-standing disagreements as to whether written history should be a narrative or an analysis. The narrative suggests that the historian tells a story: first this happened, then that. However, the analytic approach may give chronology secondary importance and search instead for the causal relations between events, the deep structures which determine their unfolding. Is the historian more like a novelist or a literary critic? Like a biographer or a psychologist? Is history one of the humanities or the social sciences?

However, the question is not, finally, all that useful. For as we know, a narrative often implies an analysis. To put things in their proper order one must select and emphasize according to their inter-relationships. The narrator's choices often reveal an implicit thesis, as, for example, numerous critics have noted about George Orwell's classic, "Shooting an Elephant." Further, analysis often demands narration: telling a story to make its patterns clear, or to move from one level of generalization to another. Thus Herbert Butterfield believes that the ideal history "would perhaps be 'structure and narrative combined,' a history which is both, 'a story and a study'" (Herbert Butterfield, p. 205; quoted in Kracauer, pp. 121–22).

To return to Henry James, the historian is only too aware that "relations end nowhere." It is the historian's "exquisite problem," just as it is the artist's, "eternally to draw, by a geometry of his own, the circle in which they shall happily *appear* to do so." Confronted with the roar of information, the noise of historical evidence, the historian must construct or discover (I feel they are two sides of the same process) a synchronic structure . . . a gestalt . . . which organizes its events and renders them intelligible. Claude Lévi-Strauss writes, "So far as history aspires as meaningfulness, it condemns itself to making choices. . . . A truly total history would neutralize itself; its outcome would equal zero" (Levi-Strauss, p. 340; quoted in Kracauer, p. 137). And as for the rationale governing these choices, Isaiah Berlin comments that, "Historical explanation is to a large degree arrangement of the discovered facts in patterns which satisfy us because they accord with life as we know it and imagine it" (Berlin, p. 24; quoted in Kracauer, p. 97). It seems to me that Isaiah Berlin and Don Murray are talking about the same process.

II

I'd like to look more closely now at the writing of history per se. In particular I'd like to focus on the theories of one writer, Siegfried Kracauer. Kracauer's primary specialty was film, but before his death in 1966 he completed a book called simply, *History: Last Things Before the Last.* The title reflects Kracauer's belief that history can never give us the "last word"; that word is reserved for some apocalyptic revelation at the end of time, should such moment ever come. Until we can see through God's omniscient eyes, history's totality will never be revealed. Human understanding then is always limited, always provisional. We are always writing, to use Frank Kermode's phrase, "in the middest," and never at the End.

Kracauer draws his conclusions not from theory—he turns away from philosophers like R. G. Collingwood—but from practice, from the reflections of those who have actively struggled with composing history: Isaiah Berlin, Marc Bloch, Arnold Toynbee, and others. The chapter of his book which concerns me here is called, "The Structure of the Historical Universe." It deals only with written texts, because for Kracauer the historical universe we are able to compose is the only historical universe there is.

Kracauer's analysis of the determining force of composition rests mainly on structuralist principles. As elaborated by de Saussure and Lévi-Strauss, these principles assert that the elements in a given structure derive their significance from their relationship to the other elements in that structure, from their place within the pattern as a whole. Shift the pattern and the meaning of each element shifts in kind. Remove an element from one structure, reposition it in another, and its significance must change accordingly. Meaning, therefore, is not essential, intrinsic to the individual element itself, but "arbitrary" in the sense of "arbitrated" or mediated.

Throughout this chapter Kracauer works with an analogy between film and historical texts. The basic premise is that both claim to represent reality, and to do so with a certain scientific authority. The photograph and the history, for the naive at least, appear eminently "objective." However, the photograph is deeply marked by its maker's subjectivity, revealed in such choices as the tonality and contrast of the colors, the grain and sheen of the paper, the cropping of the print, but most critically in the photographer's perspective or "slant" on the subject, the composition of its internal elements, and its depth of field.

An example which I use to get a class aware of these problems goes like this. You're on assignment for *Life* magazine. Your subject is an Iowa farm; you have just one shot to get your point across. How will you set it up? You've got a reasonably limited number of elements to work with: the family, the house, the farm machinery, the geometric forms of a silo or barn, the corn and soybean fields, some cows and pigs perhaps, the distant profile of some neighboring farm, the Great Plains themselves, the horizon line, the lowering clouds. Out of these a composition, a gestalt perhaps, must emerge.

Suppose you put the farm family in front of their Victorian house, showing the silo looming behind, a few pigs, and then distantly, the fields and horizon. Your composition says something now about the farm family as a traditional way of life. Turn around and set your camera up in the fields behind the house and we see endless rows of corn swallowing up the foreground, while in the distance a tiny house and barns come into focus under a ponderous mass of clouds. Now we're saying something about the importance of the land and the relative dependence of people upon the elements. Put the farm machinery up front and we're saying something else, perhaps about mechanization and change. Arrange the family so that the father dominates and we're talking about patriarchal values . . . and so on. Each choice encourages one interpretation and limits others. Even if you were limited to one spot from which to take your shot, you would still have to choose a focal point. Something must be emphasized while the rest must blur, fade, or disappear entirely.

This example illustrates Kracauer's first "law" governing the structure of the historical universe: "the law of perspective." You must choose a perspective, even though this choice necessarily excludes others. You must focus on something, and accept the inevitable blurring of the background. Every field creates a ground.

One of the most astute recent discussions of the practical problems this law creates for working historians comes from *America Revised*, Frances Fitzgerald's analysis of American history textbooks. Her chapter on ethnic bias begins with a critique of the Anglo-Saxon, Protestant, male perspective of most textbooks written before the nineteen-sixties. A particularly naive example is this passage from *America: Its People and Values*, by Leonard C. Woods, Ralph H. Gabriel, and Edward L. Biller:

> A friendly Indian named Squanto helped the colonists. He showed them how to plant corn and how to live on the edge of the wilderness. A soldier, Captain Miles Standish, taught the Pilgrims how to defend themselves against unfriendly Indians. (Quoted in Fitzgerald, p. 103)

According to Fitzgerald, The Council on Interracial Books for Children objects to this passage because "it is Eurocentric to characterize native Americans as either 'friendly' or 'unfriendly.' Squanto was actually assisting invaders, whereas the 'unfriendly Indians' were defending their communities." The Council's report concludes that, "All nations define a 'patriot' as one whose allegiance is toward his or her own people . . . . Consequently, true Native American heroes are those who fought to preserve and protect their people's freedom and land." (Fitzgerald, p. 103)

Given the Council's ideal of a truly "multiracial, multicultural" American history, Fitzgerald finds that their objections to this passage raise some serious implications for its fulfillment, despite her strong support for that very goal:

> To begin with, if the texts were really to consider American history from the perspective of the American Indians, they would have to conclude that the continent had passed through almost five hundred years of unmitigated disaster, beginning with the epidemics spread by the Europeans and continuing on most fronts today. Then, if the texts were really to consider the Indian point of view, they could not simply say this but would have to take the position of Squanto—if not that of his more patriotic fellows—and categorize Miles Standish as friendly or unfriendly. And ditto for the next four hundred years—while making sure, of course, to portray the diverse views of all the Indian nations, and their diverse relations with the white settlers. When you add to this, as the council would, the Chicano, Asian-American, African-American, Puerto-Rican, and women's perspectives on events, American history becomes unbelievably complicated—as does the whole issue of what constitutes balance and fairness" (Fitzgerald, pp. 103-4).

Here I can't resist recalling Kracauer's comment that the writing of history is theoretically so complex that if histories didn't already exist we might conclude they were impossible.

Fitzgerald also discovers another level of difficulty. Even if we are able to include multiple perspectives such as gender, ethnicity, race, and culture, these perspectives entail different levels of generalization which are not necessarily compatible nor fully inclusive. As she puts it,

> . . . culture, of course, is not the same as race, and (to raise a problem that neither the text writers nor their critics seem to have considered) some of the greatest cultural differences in the United States lie between Anglo-Saxon Protestant males. (Fitzgerald, p. 104)

Fitzgerald's point calls into question the explanatory power of generalizations. There is more to human experience than these perspectives can encompass. To speak of someone *only* in terms of race, gender or ethnic origin is to consign to background fuzziness other, equally significant, aspects of their experience, aspects which may even contradict the generalization we are trying to illustrate. Richard Rodriguez is more than a Chicano writer. Ralph Ellison is not fully described by the term "Black writer," nor Emily Dickinson by "woman writer." Such generalizations are important, oftentimes crucial, but their explanatory power is still limited.

To go back to my original example, the photograph for *Life* magazine, we are comparing, perhaps, the information contained in a Walker Evans close-up of a dilapidated farmhouse, eloquent with weatherbeaten detail, to an aerial photograph of the same farm, a photograph in which it is represented as only one square on a green and gold checkerboard. Or, we are moving from the analysis of one day in the life of one family to the study of five decades of farming on the Great Plains, or even, God help us, to the history of agriculture in the Western world. The second approach might be called macro-history, as opposed to micro-history, exemplified by the small-scale study.

Kracauer strongly distrusts the macro histories: the grand, sweeping syntheses of a Toynbee or Spengler, who offer interpretations of whole nations, peoples, and civilizations: " . . . all that is discernible at the very high altitude where universal history comes into view are vaguely colored giant units, vast generalizations of uncertain reliability" (Kracauer, p. 118). His suspicion of the bird's eye view is closely related to a central problem Kracauer sees in the writing of history:

> As a matter of course, the range of *intelligibility* of histories is a function of their width of scope. The higher their magnitude, the more of the past they render intelligible. But the increase of intelligibility is bought at a price. What the historian gains in scope he loses in terms of micro information. (Kracauer, p. 129)

Lévi-Strauss puts the problem even more drastically, "Depending upon the level at which the historian places himself, he loses in information what he is gaining in comprehension, and vice versa" (Lévi-Strauss, p. 347). The aerial photograph reveals the checkerboard of corn, soybean, and wheat fields; however, the human experience of those fields is drastically simplified. A demographic study of female life cycles in the Iowa farm population cannot give us the same richness of detail revealed in one farmwoman's diary.

This principle goes against a "basic tenet of Western thought": "the belief that the widening of the range of *intelligibility* involves an increase of *significance*" (Kracauer, p. 131). Kracauer would argue instead that "the traditional identification of the extreme abstractions— say, the idea of the 'good' or that of 'justice'—as the most inclusive and essential statements about the nature of things does not apply to history, or related approaches to reality" (Kracauer, p. 131).

To complicate matters even further, the greater the scope of the study, the higher the altitude, so to speak, the more subjective the analysis. For example, if we are going to tell the story of the life and death of a political institution over several centuries, we must synthesize such enormous amounts of information that finally we must give up any pretense to real intimacy with our evidence. Given the continuous and inexhaustible network of relationships which Henry James described, we will be forced to "intensely ignore" much more than we can "intensely consult." Thus a Toynbee or Spengler begins to merge with the mythmaker, the metahistorian, whereas those working on lower levels remain more forgiving of ambiguities and contradictions in their evidence . . . and hence remain more faithful to the texture of actual experience.

Confronted with these problems, the historian may indeed be tempted to seek salvation through specificity. Let's do a house-by-house computer-demographic study of every family in one Philadelphia neighborhood from 1800 to 1850; then, maybe we can say something about the effect of industrialization on urban family life, in the Northeast. The microhistorian, like the Tolstoy of *War and Peace*, believes that "God is in detail" (Aby Warburg, quoted in Kracauer, p. 106).

However, as we rush toward the smallest unit, hoping to find that crisp fact, to lose that fuzziness, we simply run into new problems. Thus Kracauer asks "whether [the historian] really [ever] hits rock-bottom in examining the psychological make-up of the individual," for "this alledgedly smallest unit itself is an inexhaustible macrocosm."? Just when the historian "is convinced he has come to grips with it," "reality again recedes" (Kracauer, p. 116).

In other words, try to tell the whole truth and nothing but the truth about anyone, even yourself, and you will possibly go mad. Will and Ariel Durant spent ten volumes on the History of Western Civilization and Leon Edel spent five years on the life of Henry James, and I don't think anyone would argue that the last word has been said on either subject. Whatever level, it is not a question of the whole truth, but which one. And as far as mythmaking goes, Kracauer aside, I suspect the biographer has as strong a claim as any.

Moreover, there is some information which can only be captured by the large-scale generalization. Indeed, Kracauer takes pains to show that there are ways in which we *are* only part of a crowd. Just as the composition of the essay or the photograph brings some elements into focus and blurs others, the structure of the group calls some aspects of the personality into play and inhibits others. We construct collective structures; then those structures construct us. For the practicing historian, the life-cycle study of Iowa women may reveal patterns of behavior underlying the everyday experience of our hypothetical diarist, patterns of which she may be only dimly aware and which may never rise to the surface of her daily journal.

Despite Kracauer's suspicions, then, he does acknowledge that the so-called macrohistories have a certain validity and purpose. They can describe regularities which might otherwise go unrecognized; they can sometimes reveal the forest despite the trees. In this case, a reasonable question might be: Why not incorporate several levels of interpretation in your history? Kracauer compares this strategy to a basic principle in film narrative: "the big must be looked at from different distances to be understood" (Kracauer, p. 122). According to Pudovkin's *Theory of Film:*

> To receive a clear and definite impression of a demonstration, the observer must perform certain actions. First he must climb upon the roof of a house to get a view from above the procession as a whole and measure its dimensions; next he must come down and look out through the first-floor window at the inscriptions carried by the demonstrators; finally, he must mingle with the crowd to gain an idea of the outward appearance of the participants. (Pudovkin, quoted in Kracauer, p. 122)

But what happens to information as it travels from the small-scale study up into the synthesis of the macrohistorian? Or, conversely, when the microhistorian zooms in on some detail of the grand synthesis? Equally important, what happens when the historian moves from one disciplinary framework to another? For example, our hypothetical diary reveals a different face to the literary critic than to the demographer. More complications arise when we consider the varied perspectives of literary criticism itself. Will the reading be feminist? Formalist? Marxist? The problem of scale is not the only problem the historian faces, merely the most clear-cut, the most paradigmatic.

These questions lead to a second law governing the structure of the historical universe, "the law of levels." Drawing on D. W. Griffith's film, *Intolerance,* Kracauer describes how Griffith shoots a crowd scene, then singles out Mae Marsh, then focuses on the actress's hands in an extended close-up. Taken out of their larger context, the significance of these individual elements begins to shift: "As we are watching the big close-up of Mae Marsh's hands, 'something strange is bound to happen: we will forget that they are just ordinary hands. Isolated from the rest of the body and greatly enlarged, the hands we know will change into unknown organisms quivering with a life of their own'" (Kracauer, p. 126; interior quotation from Pudovkin).

In a similar way, we may zero in on a section of, say a Renaissance painting, and discover in this close-up a new composition reminiscent of Japanese prints or abstract expressionism. Shift the framework and you don't necessarily get more meaning in relation to the old framework, but new meaning in relation to the new framework. You haven't solved your problem but rediscovered it in a new context:

> Imagine . . . three historical narratives, each of which includes a portrait of Luther—the first a history of the German people, the second dealing with the Reformation, and the third a full-fledged biography—I believe it to be highly probable that the

three portraits involve different sets of meanings and therefore are in a measure incommensurable. (Kracauer, p. 126)

Because each portrait suggests a framework of interpretation different from any other, to move from one framework to another is not to move around in the same world of meaning, exploring a consistent landscape, but to switch world views, literally.

Thus while interpretations made at different levels or from different perspectives may be linked to create coherent narrative, it is much more difficult to synthesize a consistent analysis from these separate investigations. Focusing on the relationship *between* levels—for example, the relationship between a novelist and her culture—does not solve the problem either. The "synthesis" does not reveal the totality of either one, but only those aspects relevant to their relationship.

Given Toynbee's suggestion that the historian try to merge the "bird's eye view" with the "fly's eye's view," Kracauer concludes that, "the resultant traffic difficulties are insurmountable. . . . Because of the 'law of perspective' part of the evidence drops out automatically. And because of the 'law of levels' part of the virtually available evidence reaches its destination in an incomplete state." Indeed, "the two kinds of inquiry may co-exist, but they do not completely fuse; as a rule, the bird swallows the fly" (Kracauer, pp. 127-8).

As for the dream of a "total," fully inclusive history, working historians must grapple with a "nonhomogenous" universe layered with "fields of varying density" and "rippled by unaccountable eddies" (Kracauer, p. 127). Finally, our strength depends upon recognizing our weakness: "To the extent . . . that historical ideas are generalizations they cannot be 'right' without being 'wrong' also" (Kracauer, p. 100). Telling *a* truth demands we forego *the* truth.

III

All very well, perhaps. But how do you bring such weighty matters into a college composition class? While freshmen do make unlikely recruits for modernism, I have gotten some to sign up. At the University of Minnesota in 1978, I designed a research assignment using some of the ideas I've just outlined.

The Composition Program in Minneapolis then emphasized analytical essays and carefully structured assignments. However, instructors were also encouraged to teach the writing process through small group conferences, extensive revisions, and prewriting exercises. This particular assignment, positioned toward the end of the two-course sequence, introduced students to academic research. I decided to make it a paper on architectural history. This may seem a very odd choice, especially since I don't know all that much about architecture, but then neither do I know much about nitrates in hot-dogs, a topic dear to many freshmen hearts.

I wanted a number of things to happen. First of all, I wanted to recreate some of the conditions under which research actually takes place. That is, real research takes place within a framework: a body of knowledge and a community which controls and shares that knowledge. It seems to me that this sense of an existing discourse is very important, and very difficult to get in a class whose emphasis is not on content but process. Without a structure to work within and against, students can easily be overwhelmed by data whose relative importance they are unable to determine. A student may then simply forego any attempt at creating order, or simply parrot the first authority whose thesis seems plausible.

In addition to a shared framework, I wanted a subject that was broad enough and immediate enough to get students interested. Not an event nor a document. Buildings are concrete. To use Henry James's phrase, they are examples of the "visitable past." They can be entered, touched, as well as researched and discussed. Since part of my intention was to make students aware of choices, even of conflicting choices, I wanted them to have as many perspectives on the past as possible, and for those perspectives to be as different as possible. Hence the pre-writing assignments ranged from describing a building's sensuous, even tactile, qualities to analyzing its architectural style.

Initially, there were some brief library assignments. The class read the "Prologue" to *The Architecture of America: A Social and Intellectual History* (1961) by John Burchard and Albert Bush-Brown. In addition to the American background, Burchard and Bush-Brown surveyed the questions which engage architectural historians. Their book stood for a whole discipline; it defined that discipline's vocabulary and articulated its world-view.

Next, they looked at *Architecture of Minnesota* (1977) by David Gebhard and Tom Martinson. Essentially a field guide to local architectural styles ranging from the Georgian mansion and Victorian cottage to the WPA Moderne post office and International-Style skyscraper. Better yet, it had photographs and capsule histories of important Minnesota buildings, many of which the students saw every day in downtown Minneapolis or right on campus.

I began the first classroom exercise with Kracauer's photography analogy and the imaginary assignment for *Life* magazine. Since many of the students had been raised on or near farms it was a felicitous choice. Next we tried to see a well-known landmark from as many perspectives as possible. The class chose the IDS Building, a Philip Johnson office complex which dwarfs downtown Minneapolis. We started with a bird's-eye view and considered the building within the whole sweep of the city skyline. Students asked as many questions as they could while I put them on the board without trying to answer them. How had this huge glass tower affected the image of the city? Was it a symbol of Minneapolis's power and prestige or an incongruous giant, a tribute to corporate folly? Whose money built it? Why? Who designed it? What kind of statement were they making? Why? What was this building's relationship to the history of architecture in general? To the history of monumental architecture? How did it compare to the Pyramids? (A bird's-eye view from dizzying altitudes.)

Next, we imaginatively moved downtown and narrowed our focus. We asked whether the change in perspective made us evaluate the building differently or raised new questions. Seen from the street the building's scale shifted. Instead of a massive, mirrored surface, visible for miles across the prairie, the IDS now offered a courtyard with small-scale shops under a glass canopy. We considered the design from various angles: aesthetic, functional, social. Did people like the building? Did shoppers enjoy coming into this courtyard from the fierce Minnesota winter? How about the workers? Did the building do what they wanted it to? Was it a good machine? Why were the escalators placed as they were? (Now we were down to the fly's-eye view.)

Throughout the discussion I tried to give students ideas about where to find answers to their questions and to show how their questions might be related, or not related. Most important, I tried to get across how a particular question would generate a related perspective on the building and a focus for an essay.

In the next classroom exercise we looked at some research sources. I brought in a variety of pieces written about another well-known building: the Coffman Memorial Union Building on the University of Minnesota campus. The main structure had been designed and raised in the thirties and was a grand example of WPA Moderne style. However, by the seventies the building was too small and needed mechanical updating. With a burst of aesthetic enthusiasm Coffman was redone in full-blown high tech: huge greenhouse additions, red and yellow air ducts traveling every which way, intricate traffic patterns outlined by theatre lightbulbs. Virtually all the freshmen in my class had been bewildered by this gaudy display as they struggled to find mailboxes, cheeseburgers, and dean's offices.

I made sure that at least two of the sources on Coffman were written from radically different perspectives. The first was a brochure put out by the Student Union describing their own building's history. It was, needless to say, pro-renovation. However, Gebhard and Martinson's *Guide to Minnesota Architecture*, published through the University's own architecture school, lamented the loss of Coffman's aesthetic integrity. They looked back nostalgically on the old thirties' style. According to them, the city had lost a treasure, comparable perhaps to New York's Radio City or Rockefeller Center.

We considered what the two histories left out, and why. The students could easily see how their different perspectives lead to different conclusions. Put most simply, Gebhard and Martinson were primarily concerned with the building as cultural artifact and aesthetic object, while the Student Union saw Coffman as functional tool and group symbol (the University swings confidently into the future, etc.). The important point was not to show that one source was right and the other wrong, but that if they were to use either source its perspective had to be taken into account. Moreover, the student had to construct a perspective and a judgment of his or her own, rather than accept another's blindly.

Finally, each student chose a local building. First, they had to visit it and write a description of their immediate impression. Then they had to do some basic research. When was it built? By whom? For what? In what style? If they couldn't find exact information they were to make educated guesses based on comparison with other buildings in Gebhard and Martinson's *Guide*. At first they were to work without a definite thesis. They were simply to explore their church or their house or whatever from as many angles as they could. And to ask as many questions as they could. One student, a hockey player, wondered why Williams Arena was so old and ugly and yet its fans loved it so. Another student wondered how her neighborhood ever found the money to build its extravagent cathedral, and why.

They were required to interview at least one person associated with the building. If it was recent, they could try to meet the architect. (Not all that unlikely since the University's Architecture School was just two doors away.) They could also interview people who worked in an office complex, like the IDS Tower, or someone who had attended a church for many years. A student investigating an old slaughterhouse in St. Paul talked to the planners who were deciding whether it would be destroyed or renovated.

The main thing was for them to gather a mass of diverse information, then, like the sculptor in my opening anecdote, find their elephant, their figure in the carpet. I wanted them to experience both the confusion of research and its exhilaration. To feel the dialectical play of discovery and construction. After students compiled information from the field, they brought their topics into focus. Then they went out for more information to develop a thesis, and then back to their desks to modify that thesis . . . all working toward that final figure. There were at least two conferences before a rough draft ever appeared. One brief example will have to suffice for the class's experience.

Victor Klosinski chose his own house to write about. He was Polish-American, living in South Minneapolis. The house itself, a bungalow, was built about 1920 in the Craftsman style which defines many of Minneapolis's older, middle-class neighborhoods. At first Victor was intrigued by the neighborhood's original character. It had been a fairground, and the legacy was still visible. The local Skelly Garage, for example, had once been a blacksmith shop for fairground horses and still kept "Earl's Market Fair" in its name. But the piece of information which drew his eye concerned the Bethany Lutheran Church, right down the street. He discovered that the church had financed most of the construction on the block, then made sure that houses were sold to congregation members in order, as he put it, "to have complete control over who could establish themselves as a resident there."

Now Victor's paper came into focus. He defined the central idea this way,

[The church's action] illustrates the influence individual churches had on their communities during the late 1800s to the early 1900s. People seemed to identify themselves through the church they belonged to rather than through their occupation and this was directly evidenced in the communities they built. (Victor Klosinski, p. 1)

With this thesis in mind, Victor reviewed the architectural composition from a new perspective. A gestalt emerged. He noticed things such as the extraordinary lack of privacy—evidenced by the large picture windows fronting the street, the contiguous backyards, the doorless rooms within the house itself. No place for a rowdy adolescent or a nonconforming neighbor to hide.

In the paper which followed Victor analyzed the social attitudes and moral values expressed by his own house and neighborhood. What Victor had to *forget* was much of his own experience. In the process of bringing his paper into focus he had to carve away virtually all his memories of growing up in that house. Those memories may have led him initially to ask the right questions. "Intensely consulted" at the outset, these connections now had to be "intensely ignored." Only those which illustrated his central idea—which fit within its formal "geometry"—were kept. The loss was painful, but these discarded chips implied another, different perspective, perhaps they promised another essay for the future. Like the histories Kracauer describes, Victor's success was only a momentary stay against confusion, but I suspect awareness of its limits only heightened his pride in the achievement. Freshmen writers, like all writers, are connoisseurs of chaos, but they too are equipped with fictive powers.

References

Bartholomae, D. (1986). Wanderings: Misreadings, miswritings, misunderstandings. In this volume.

Berlin, I. (1960). History and theory: The concept of scientific history. *History and theory* (Vol. 1, No. 1). The Hague, pp. 1–31.

Burchard, J. & Bush-Brown, A. (1961). *The architecture of America: A social and intellectual history.* Boston: Little, Brown.

Butterfield, H. (1959). *George the Third and the historians.* New York: Macmillan.

Fitzgerald, F. (1979). *America revised.* Boston: Little, Brown.

Gebhard, D. & Martinson, T. (1977). *A guide to the architecture of Minnesota.* Minneapolis: University of Minnesota Press.

James, H. (1967). Preface to *Roderick Hudson.* Baltimore: Penguin. (Original edition published in 1909.)

Kermode, F. (1966). *The sense of an ending: Studies in the theory of fiction.* London: Oxford University Press.

Klosinski, V. (1978). Untitled paper. Composition 1–002, Section 64. University of Minnesota, Minneapolis.

Kracauer, S. (1969). *History: Last things before the last.* London and New York: Oxford University Press.

Lévi-Strauss, C. (1962). *La pensée sauvage.* Adlers Foreign Books: Paris.

Lindberg, G. (1986). Coming to words: Writing as process and the reading of literature. In this volume.

Mariani, P. (1986). Lowell's turtles: Visions and self-revisions. In this volume.

Murray, D. (1977). Write before writing. Article developed from a paper given at the National Council of Teachers of English Convention, New York City, November 1977.

13

Framing Narratives

JUDITH FISHMAN SUMMERFIELD

Queens College

I want to break with narrative convention at the start by beginning twice.

Beginning #1 is an *ending*, not mine, but Paul Mariani's—I celebrate what he said at the end of his talk last night:

Isn't that what we finally write for, for that secret phosphorescence we call the revelations of the self, words framing the figure in the carpet, still dust shaping into the magnetic figure of the rose? Fictions we call our writing but they are the fictions by which we live . . . .

Beginning #2 is a fiction by which I live, a story that came to me from my father: for me, he is one of the great storytellers, and at 80, the stories of his childhood are just as vivid as the events of today. The story is about his mother, who died in the Ukraine long before I was born. The story goes that when she married my grandfather, on the day that the bride and groom stood at the marriage altar, they were both exactly the same height. And then, after that, she *grew*, and came to tower over her husband. And the villagers renamed her: Chana the Tall One. When my father first told me this story I cannot say. It had been told to him when he was a grown man living in America; it had been told by a villager who had been a guest at the wedding, and some time when I was old enough to listen, he began telling me stories of the old country.

I say that the story is now mine, for I have *framed* it: I reconstruct it out of the contexts of my own life, out of what John Dewey calls *funding*, and, for me, it is an open story. The kernel—the narrative core—is reducible to a few clauses: man and woman marry, and then the woman grows. But the narrative resonates in my mind: it is open for telling and retelling, for reading and rereading, and I read it through my life, as I speculate and wonder and imagine and try to enter the life of a woman living in the Ukraine at the turn of the century. How old was she when she married? 15 or 16? How tall did she grow? Am I tall like her? I know she gave birth to 11 children. How did she bear seeing some of them die young? I know she wanted to read. How did she bear not reading, herself, the letters from her son in America, whom she knew she would never see again? And did not. I know she died young, at 48. Was it better to have died then, and not to have known the ravages of revolution and civil war? What does *better* mean? I wonder about her dailiness, her dreams. I contrast my life with what I imagine of hers. I read histories of the time. I try to place her, to typify her—and to particularize her. I wonder if you can grieve for someone you never knew. Does one really grieve for oneself? I write about her. She wouldn't allow herself to be photographed: I see her only through the words I have, and so I construct and reconstruct her. I frame her through the stories I've heard, but there are so many gaps. I want to realize her—this grandmother for whom I was named. I fill in the spaces, the gaps, with my imaginings, my wonderings, with the fundings of my own life. I participate in her life, *virtually*; again and again I am brought in, compelled to reflect upon, to evaluate, to make sense of. She enters me as I enter her.

In the teaching of reading and writing at the college level, I am convinced that stories such as this, stories that make up our personal histories, stories of our own lives and stories we have been told, should play a significant part in our curricula; I believe, as well, that the writing and reading of narrative will lead us into a rich and varied pedagogy. And so I begin my courses by asking students to *tell* stories from their own lives, ones that have been passed down, or ones that come out of the actualities of their own lives. I ask them to imagine that we are sitting round the fire, relying on each other's words to keep us warm in an age without television or radios or v.c.r.'s. And so in a concrete windowless classroom in New York City, we pretend that we are villagers in the Irish ceili, like those in Henry Glassie's remarkable study, *Passing the Time in Ballymenone* (1982). We are all storytellers, and we tell stories to pass the time, to entertain, to share values and to make sense of the world.

We begin very quickly to form a ceili, a community of tellers and listeners, and we find that we all have stories to tell. Others have grandmother stories, stories from the old country—particularly in a college such as Queens, where half our population comes from the "old country," and we share in the wealth of our respective histories, and quickly see that we have stories that have been handed down—stories about how our parents escaped from Ireland, or Russia, or, how our parents met, or how we were named, and we have stories of the actualities of our own life, that we might pass on to our children. We introduce ourselves by telling stories, and become associated *to* our stories, and we begin to explore how much our lives are made up of stories, and reflect upon which of the stories are "unfinished," which are *open* and leave us with *gaps*, with wonderings, with questions.

We *tell* stories, first, because that is what we normally do in our lives—we tell our representations of events to others: story-telling is a social act—it involves teller and listener; we *tell* stories because in the lives we live outside the classroom, we spend much of our waking activity and much of our solitary activity representing events that have happened to us and to others, both those in which we were participants and those to which we were spectators. And so we begin to explore *why* we tell stories, and how we tell stories, how we construct our lives and compose our selves. And we begin to note how stories change—given the time and place and audience for the telling; we bring to the surface what students know unconsciously—that stories are reconstructions, and not retrievals.

There's a lot of interest these days in narrative; in many fields—from folklore studies to cultural anthropology to psychoanalysis to sociolinguistics, art history, film studies, literary history, to a new field calling itself narratology. Scholars and researchers generally agree that stories are the fundamental means by which we make meaning and value experience, by which we *frame* our lives and our histories. We tell stories because we need to put things that happen into words, to understand, to consider and reconsider, to take stock, to figure out, to analyze, to plan: and every story we tell draws upon and reconstructs the past—as it anticipates the future. Every story we tell is both old and new. We tell stories, says Henry Glassie, because we are always testing our fundamental values. We tell stories, say Paul Hernandi (1980, p. 203), both to assert ourselves and to transcend our selves. We can hardly take a step, says Barbara Hardy, without narrating:

> Before we sleep each night we tell over to ourselves what we may also have told to others, the story of the past day. We mingle truths and falsehoods, not always quite knowing where one blends into the other. As we sleep we dream dreams from which we wake to remember, half-remember and almost remember, in forms that may be dislocated, dilapidated or deviant but are recognizably narrative. We begin the day by narrating to ourselves and probably to others our expectations, plans, desires, fantasies, and intentions. . . . We meet our colleagues, family, friends, intimates, acquaintances, strangers, and exchange stories, overtly and covertly. We may try to tell all, in true confession, or tell half-truths or lies, or refuse to do more than tell the story of the

weather, the car, or the food. We may exchange silences or marvellous jokes. And all the time the environment beckons and assaults with its narratives. Walls, papers, mass-media, vehicles, entertainments, libraries, talks, slogans, politicians, prophets, and Job's comforters persuade, encourage, depress, solicit, comfort and commiserate in narrative forms. Such logicians tell stories. Humankind cannot bear very much abstraction or discursive reasoning. The stories of our days and the stories in our days are joined in that autobiography we are all engaged in making and remaking, as long as we live, which we never complete, though we all know how it is going to end (1975, p. 4).

Dreams, waking, talking to others, talking to ourselves—narrative is so much a presence, so much with us, in us and upon us, that we rarely take note; "it is simply there," says Roland Barthes, "like life itself" (1977, p. 79).

We barely notice it in its varieties and potentialities in the teaching of composition; in fact, if narrative is considered at all, it is seen as one of the "modes," and particularly as a simple mode—that we can use on the royal way to exposition or academic writing. Of course, narrative plays a major part in our "literature" courses, as we pay homage to great storytellers—Homer, Shakespeare, Milton, Tolstoy, Wordsworth—but we hardly ever call them storytellers: narrative is subsumed under genre courses—great works of fiction—or period courses—the rise of the modern novel. Storytelling gets lost within what we name "literature." "Stories," we may think, are for children. Personal stories we're suspicious of, and so our students' stories may get an airing during the week when we ask them to write a personal narrative or a narrative essay, and then we rush on to description or exposition or argument. Harold Rosen (1982) says it well:

> There is a persistent message of our society and in particular our educational system: stories are for children, the gullible, the naive. We have other kinds of discourse for the serious business of society. "We may start by telling stories but we must end by telling the truth," including the truth *about* stories which we call literary criticism or even narratology. In the literature of language education it is often proposed that the ultimate goal for the teaching of composition is academic prose, objective exposition or some such. No one tells us why language development should not include as a central component getting better at telling and responding to stories of many different kinds (p. 1).

I want to speak, along with Rosen, for narrative, for capturing the excitement, exhilaration, the possibilities of narrative that we find in other fields; I want to speak for redefining narrative, for seeing it as central to what we do as tellers and listeners and as readers and writers.

It is out of the social situation of telling and listening that I move my students to writing and reading texts. Students tell stories about each other, and then they write the stories they have told. They begin to observe differences between speaking and writing, between utterance and text: What happens to the tale when it is written? What is gained? What is lost? What happens to texts, to the audience, when expressive, attentive, questioning eyes of listeners are absent; when the blank page must hold all the gestures and intonations of body and voice? A student in class this semester said, "But where do I begin— now that I write? I could begin in a hundred places. How much background do I have to give my reader? Where is the beginning?" Nowhere, they quickly discover. And everywhere. And so they begin to learn that texts are composed—as Hugh Nolan says of the stories he and his friends tell in the ceili: "Stories . . . they're all composed; they're all fiction. Somebody made them up. And isn't it a very smart person, man or woman, that can frame a tale? It's wonderful, you know" (Classie, p. 37).

Students begin to see, very quickly, that there is no one story of any event—there are versions, and what you put down on paper now or tomorrow will undoubtedly differ from what you write next week. When Virginia Woolf (1976) sat down some two years before her death to begin her memoirs, she knew full well that the "past on which the identity of the present moment rests, is never static, never fixed like a fly in amber, but is subject to alteration as the consciousness that recalls it" (p. 12). "I think," she says, "I have discovered a possible form for my [memoirs]. That is, to make them include the present—at least enough of the present to serve as platform to stand upon. It would be interesting to make the two people *I now, I then*, come out in contrast. And further, this past is much affected by the present moment. What I write today, I should not write in a year's time" (p. 75). And so—when we say to our students—write of your personal experiences: so they *know* what that means? What possibilities are open to them? Do they know how the present infuses, shapes, changes, modifies representations that were already fluid to begin with and that are not ever static? And that all this holds for reading a text, as well. How we read a text tomorrow will differ from the way we read it last week, or last year. There is no one reading, there are *readings*.

Men, like poets, "rush 'into the middest,'" says Frank Kermode, "*in medias res* when they are born; they also die *in midiis rebus*, and to make sense of their span they need fictive concords with origins and ends, such as give meaning to lives and to poems" (1979, p. 7). The most definite mark of a life, the most concise narrative, is told *of* us—

on our tombstones: the date of birth and the date of death. ("We are born astride of the grave" says Beckett.) But, thank goodness for the gap in between.

Alive, we fill in the gaps: we select beginnings and endings for the actualities that make up our lives, in our tellings and in our writings. Beginnings and endings are not givens; they are composed, they are fictions. A story, then, is a "reading" of an actuality; it is not the event. It is language mediating and representing event. It makes up its own event. Our students need to know this—this fundamental epistemological fact, that they are freed from the illusion that they must represent things as they "actually" occurred. They need to know about the Freudian concept of *nachtraghlikeit*, usually translated as deferred action or belatedness, that "the past or indeed any object of memory or language comes into being only after a fact, as a function of the *place language or memory* requires it to hold" (Meisel, 1981, p. 25).

I recall, vividly, a student in a class where we were talking about autobiography—in particular Richard Wright's *Black Boy*. One afternoon, he blurted out, "I hate Richard Wright. In fact, he makes me so angry I feel like walking out of the room."

"Why so?" I asked, surprised, intrigued.

"Because," he said, "he can remember back to when he was four! And my earliest memory—I don't think I can remember anything before I was twelve, and that was only six years ago."

He was distressed that Wright could remember that the "wind was whistling," that the "coals were glowing," and the biggest blow of all, was that he could remember *exactly* what people said.

As we began to explore the problem, students expressed their convictions: writers have photographic memories; they're born that way; their brains are different, and they, the students themselves, loathe writing about their own lives because their memories are so poor. They have not yet realized that dreams, that events, that actualities, are mediated through language, and that writers—through the options of text—can create the *illusion* of presence.

What they came to see was that Wright didn't have a video machine hooked into the event that had taken place when he was four years old. He constructed a text; he framed an event—from a vantage point years later, when he was a spectator of his past life. And the entire autobiography moves between the I then and the I now; the "participant" *in* things as they are happening; the spectator—*out*—looking back and reflecting upon, evaluating: the *in* and the *out* became the frame for the entire text.

We need to do this epistemological spade work as students construct texts that represent their own lives, and as they react to the texts of others: we need to unearth the misconceptions that students have about memory, about representations, about language, about textuality, about fictions and "truths."

They need to know, as well, that there is no simple narrative, that no representation can be neutral, objective, value free, that every narrative is a verbal representation of an event—something happened—and that it is shaped and generated by *evaluation*, the answer in advance to the listener's always potential question, *So what? What does it matter?* They also need to know that they can take possession of a text, pry it open, react to it, interact with it, enter it by taking on a role suggested by it. In narratives—whether they be personal histories, fiction, news stories, film or histories—students can enjoy the possibilities; they can fill in gaps; they can write transformations—other versions—as spectators or participants, and they can see what options they have for evaluation.

I want to focus now on a single form of narrative that we and our students encounter daily—a type of story that is so much a part of our lives we hardly notice it: to newspaper people, they are *fillers*, those human interest stories that newspapers print to fill up space. "There could hardly be data," says Erving Goffman, with less "face value" (1974, p. 14). Yet he sees them as representative, as reported events that satisfy our demands—not for facts but for typifications. "Their telling demonstrates the power of our conventional understandings to cope with the bizarre potentials of social life, the furthest reaches of experience." They are a cross between an "experimentum crucum" and a "sideshow"; they are "frame fantasies" that encapsulate our interest, our dreams, our terrors, our nightmares, and they are open texts, precisely because they have been cut from a "stream of ongoing activity," what Goffman calls a "strip." They are, to use Edward Said's words, in the "always already begun realm of continuous human effort." They represent *a* point of view, an angle of vision. The newspaper reporter or editor has selected the bare bones of what we can readily imagine to be a richer, more resonant, more extended version of "the" story. They are the extraordinary, a moment when John Doe hit the news, a "once," that makes us laugh or cry or stop to think. Often these bits and pieces of daily life leave us wondering, speculating, reflecting on the world as it is reported to be—and we stand there—as spectators, thankful that we were not there, or sorry. Fillers—as all narratives—leave us spaces to fill up. And our students can *react*—as spectators, and as "virtual participants," and in so doing, see what happens to texts.

Here is a filler, entitled, "Class By Himself":

CLASS BY HIMSELF

BRADFORD, Pa. (UPI) — D. Edgar Cohn took all the door prizes at his 75th high school reunion — he was the only member of the class able to attend.

There are two other survivors from Cohn's class, but one was too ill to attend and the other couldn't be located, school officials said.

Being the lone classmate at the reunion didn't bother him too much, he said.

The Herald Journal Logan, Utah, Sunday, June 12, 1983-9

And here, now, is a student, Joyce Oldroyd's, reactive text. She is a "virtual participant," taking on the role of Edgar Cohn as he's getting ready for the event, the "do." She translates event into poem; her text is paratactic and unevaluated: the text sounds like utterance—like Cohn talking to himself:

Class by Himself

Shaky hands to knot my tie
Why won't the collar stay in place
I'll wear the vest — the weather's fickle
Is that Jenny drivin' up?

Reunion — umm — Sarah's gone
Why am I sprucing?
Walter's feeble — will he come
I'm exhausted with this fussin'
Is that Jenny drivin' up?

Friday — today is Friday
Have I missed the "doo"?
Lunch and pictures . . . reminiscing
Is that Jenny drivin' up?

Joyce Oldroyd

And here is a story of a goose that was cooked:

GOOSE IS COOKED

PITTSBURGH (UPI) — Charles Wood Jr. found out what a pet goose is worth in court —at least $140.

Wood, 18, of Pittsburgh, was found guilty of criminal mischief Friday, fined $40 plus court costs and directed to pay $100 restitution to Gary and Andrea Simpson, who owned the pet goose, Pebbles, which disappeared May 27.

Acting on a tip, Mrs. Simpson said she and a Humane Society officer found goose feathers in the basement of Wood's home down the street shortly after Pebbles disappeared from their backyard May 27.

Logan, June 12, 1983.

And a transformation: the police officer to whom the tale is told offers his reaction as participant/spectator:

As a cop, I've seen a lot in my time, but the day the lady came crying bloody murder was a dilly.

"Oh, I can't believe it, Poor Pebbles, oh Pebbles my baby!" She was sobbing about a baby.

I said, "Lady, calm down please. What about your baby?"

"Oh, officer, that Charlie Wood killed him!"

I immediately stopped everything, and took her arm.

"Step over here and tell me, please, what happened?"

"Oh, I can't believe it! He came to my house last night and took Pebbles and he killed him with an ax!"

I think to myself, "My god, an ax!" I buzz homicide and try to calm the lady.

"Please stop crying, now, it's important to get the facts."

She calms down a little and then screams, "And he ate him!"

By then my hair's standing on end, and I say to Detective Smith as he comes up, "We've got a bad one, Dave."

"What is it?" he says softly over the sobbing woman.

"Lady says her baby was murdered — with an ax, and then, so help me Dave, she says he was eaten."

Dave turns green; the lady looks up at me and says, "Goose! Goose! It was my pet goose, my baby!"

Hysterical women make me ill.

Adrienne Morris

We note that once the police officer *understands* the events being represented to him, once he can breathe easily, he *evaluates* and typifies, and frames the event by his observation: "Hysterical women make me ill." The spectator's stance is an evaluative one.

And here is a final one:

GARDEN INVITE — An 83-year-old great-grandmother convicted last year of growing marijuana in her Houston backyard thanked a judge for ending her probation last week and invited him to see her garden. But Laura Ethel Clark told State District Judge Michael McSpadden that one plant — the marijuana she said she used to relieve her arthritis — would not be there. "There won't ever be any more of that," Mrs. Clark said.

Daily Times May 15, 1983, B, p. 4

A story invites us to enter in, to identify with the characters and issues involved. By recasting a story into another form, we often come to see what we had not seen before—as spectators. As writers, we can become virtual participants, and we can understand—literally, *to step under*, and from the inside we can comprehend—seize or grasp or make meaning. As we enter the story, it enters us, and we make it our own. Here is Karen Dyrbala taking on the role of Mrs. Clark, writing to her great-granddaughter:

To my Great-grand-daughter,

I'm writing to you to explain my actions for growing marijuana, I hope that you will think of me as you always have and not as a criminal. Someday when the neighbor who turned me in gets old I hope they never had to deal with the pain of arthritis. I feel I must explain to you that I do not wish to cause you any embarrassment. Sometimes when a person is in pain, as I am, they resort to any method that will relieve that pain; that is why I was growing marijuana. I must tell you though that I have learned my lesson. Judge McSpadden will not see any more marijuana growing in my garden. My only problem now is making sure he doesn't go in the spare bedroom.

Your loving Great-grandmother,
Laura Ethel Clark

"We perform verbal acts as well as other acts," says Barbara Herrnstein Smith, "in order to extend our control over a world that is not naturally disposed to serve our interests" (1978, p. 85). The "world" has not, in Karen's eyes, served Laura Ethel Clark's interests; and her writing-in-response-to-reading allows her to stand in opposition, to be critical. The filler, what we might call the primary text, gives her opportunity to react, as writer. We've given her opportunity to enter what Langer calls a "virtual" experience; we've given what Goffman calls an "engrossable—engrossing materials which observers can get carried away with, materials which generate a realm of being." We've given her opportunity to enter a role, to step into someone else's shoes. Karen steps into Laura Ethel Clark's shoes and allows her to "speak" in a specific social context: a great-grandmother writing a letter of explanation to her great-granddaughter, about events that have been reported.

She takes the story and runs with it: she fills in gaps (what did Mrs. Clark *do* afterwards); and transforms the event, frames it from her own views, her own fundings, as virtual participant and spectator. What we have here are frames within frames. What I am interested in here are Karen's responses as a reader-turned-writer, and it is D. W. Harding (1937) and his views on the role of the onlooker that I find crucial. To Harding, the role of the onlooker is complex. As onlookers, as spectators, we do more than watch, we watch out of *interest*, and out of our systems of values. "Our hopes and anxieties for ourselves and other people," says Harding, "very largely depend upon what we have learnt, as spectators, of the possibilities that surround us." "Our interests are not merely intellectual; we are 'glad or sorry' about them on account of the significance they have for ourselves, for our friends or perhaps for people in general." The role of the onlooker, he argues, has a deep and extensive influence on our system of values. As participants, we have difficulty evaluating; our vision is blurred. The spectator, on the other hand, "often sees the event in a broader context than the participant can tolerate" or, indeed, know. Jimmy Britton, who worked with Harding for the first time at the Dartmouth Seminar in 1966, discovered that he and Harding were thinking along very similar lines, and he subsequently remarked: "I think it is no distortion of Harding's account to suggest that as participants we APPLY our value system, but as spectators we GENERATE AND REFINE the system itself." (1982, p. 51).

Karen's relationship with the primary text, the filler, is in that dual role of participant/spectator. She is an onlooker, an observer of events that have happened to someone else, but as she writes, she becomes a virtual participant. She enters the scene as if she had virtually been there. It is clear that her involvement is empathetic: she is sorry about Mrs. Clark, and in her fiction she sets things straight. She gives Judge McSpadden a sharp swift kick. In another version, Karen might allow Judge McSpadden to speak—to prepare a legal brief, to defend his reading of the law; or she might put McSpadden and Clark in dialogue debating about laws and people. And so on. There are gaps to be filled; the story, as Ted Hughes says, becomes a unit of imagination. For the mind to turn over, reflect upon, wrestle with.

The reader-turned-writer, by reacting to texts, has an opportunity to apply, and to generate and refine her value system, *and* to explore the options of texts. What I observe again and again is that virtual participants' texts—like Joyce's Edgar Cohn—as they attempt to represent events *as if* they are happening are primarily paratactic: coordinate structures predominate; the participant cannot see the forest for the trees and thus does not evaluate.

The spectator's texts habitually move toward hypotaxis to carry evaluation. Both the goose story and the Laura Ethel Clark story reflect the spectator remarking on or "doing something" to reflect those values. What we explore are the varieties of textuality that emerge from different frames of mind—and it is this conceptual frame, that of spectator and participant, that I have found most useful, most generative, in practice in the classroom and in theory in reflecting upon that practice.

The frames of spectator and participant allow us, as well, to consider the complexities of a reader's relationship with a text, as she reads and rereads, as she moves in and out of text, draws close and steps away, interacts, and reacts, agrees and opposes, or as William Stafford says, "You toss back and forth against a live backboard. And, particularly, if it is a congenial poem—or friend—you are reading or hearing, you furnish a good half of the life. The travel circuit of an idea or impression is a sequence of reboundings between you and the page" (1978, p. 6).

The clock has ticked away 45 minutes, and we've all moved along this inevitable, irreversible, chronological road our culture has chosen to live—for we live by clocks we have invented. Framing narratives, as I hope you'll agree, involves more than chronology: we can read any event—including this one—achronologically, evaluatively. And I can think of no better way of stopping time than through the reading and writing of texts, particularly of narratives. I suggest that we use narrative in many forms, many guises, as it appears in autobiography, biography, poetry, fiction, history, personal journals, film, dreams, psychiatric reports, and that we loosen what Jimmy Britton calls "the stranglehold that the expository essay has maintained over writing in American higher education." He notes, as well, that "if today's winds of change are any indication at all, narrative will be a candidate for a leading role among those forms of discourse that will replace the expository essay." (1984, p. vii). I suggest that students write stories of their own lives and of others' (their grandmother stories), of their individual histories and of collective histories, that they see that there is no one version of life or of an event, that there are versions of the Viet Nam War, of Kent State, of the 1890s, of what we call history; there are versions of Frost's life, versions of a news story, versions of a fairy tale, versions of Genesis. A text is never complete, never closed; every time a story is told or written, it is new. "History," says Ted

Hughes, "is really no older than the new-born baby." And a story engages: it is a unit *of* and *for* the imagination.

References

Barthes, R. (1977). The structural analysis of narrative. In *Image/ music/text*. New York: Hill & Wang.

Britton, J. (1982). *Prospect and retrospect*. Montclair, NJ: Boynton/ Cook.

_____. (1984). Foreword. In *Courses for change in writing: A selection from the NEH/Iowa Institute*. Montclair, NJ: Boynton/ Cook.

_____. (1984). Viewpoints: The distinction between participant and spectator role language in research and practice. *Research in the teaching of English, 18*, 320-332.

Fishman, J. (1981). Enclosures: The narrative within autobiography, *Journal of Advanced Composition, II*, 23-30.

Fishman J. and Summerfield, G. (forthcoming). States of mind, acts of mind, forms of discourse: Toward a provisional pragmatic framework. In D. McQuade (ed.), *Linguistics and Stylistics*.

Glassie, H. (1982). *Passing the time in Ballymenone: Culture and history of an Ulster community*. Philadelphia: University of Pennsylvania Press.

Goffman, E. (1974). *Frame analysis: An essay on the organization of experience*. New York: Harper & Row.

Harding, D. W. (1963). *Experience into words*. Cambridge: Cambridge University Press.

_____. (1937). The role of the onlooker. *Scrutiny, 6*, 247-258.

Hardy, B. (1975). *Tellers and listeners: The narrative imagination*. London: The Athlone Press.

Hernandi, P. (1980). On the how, what, and why of narrative. *Critical Inquiry, 7*, 201-204.

Hughes, T. (1976). Myth and education. In G. Fox, G. Hammond et al. (Eds.), *Writers, critics, and children*. London: Heinemann Education Books.

Kermode, F. (1966). *The sense of an ending: Studies in the theory of fiction*. New York: Oxford University Press.

_____. (1979). *The genesis of secrecy: On the interpretation of narrative*. Cambridge, MA: Harvard University Press.

Labov, W. (1972). *Language in the inner city. Studies in the Black English vernacular*. Philadelphia: University of Pennsylvania Press.

Meisel, P. (Ed.). (1981). *Freud: A collection of critical essays*. Englewood Cliffs, NJ: Prentice-Hall.

Rosen, H. (1982, April) *The nurture of narrative.* IRA Convention, Chicago.

Said, E. (1975). *Beginnings: Intention and method.* New York: Basic Books.

Smith, B. H. (1978). *Margins of discourse: The relationships of literature to language.* Chicago: University of Chicago Press.

Stafford, W. (1978). *Writing the Australian crawl: Views on the writer's vocation.* Ann Arbor: The University of Michigan Press.

Woolf, V. (1976). *Moments of being: Unpublished writing.* New York: Harcourt Brace Jovanovich.

14

Reading While Writing

DONALD M. MURRAY

University of New Hampshire

The writer writing. The writer reading. The writer hearing from the page what the writer does not expect to hear. The writer hearing (reading through the ear?) the line passing through the mouth before it is thought, read, accepted, known. The line changing as it is read. The purpose of the line adapted to the expectation of the reader *or* the text, the need of the reader *or* the text. The writer surprised by the given line, learning to read surprise, possibility, unexpectedness. The writer learning to accept surprise, possibility, unexpectedness. The writer reading what is there, what may be there, what isn't there until it is placed there by the reading. The writer reading other writers, hearing what their texts did not intend, did not need to say, did not need to know. Writing by reading, writing in the ear a text that belongs to neither writer. The writer learning, stealing, adapting, accepting, using, seeking to hear in the line passing out through the mouth, passing through the eye, something that is not there until the act of writing/reading, reading/writing.

One evening after a day's writing, numb from my own words, the writing going on, refusing to stop, we went to the Mall to eat, too full of writing to eat well. Afterwards, we allowed ourselves to be drawn into the anonymous current of mall walkers. I resisted the too bright bookstore with the light glinting off the plastic book covers; this week's talk show best seller, last month's non-seller reduced. Then I saw Jayne Anne Philips' *Machine Dreams* and took it down automatically, as if to weigh it. A peck of words, a half peck?

It opened itself to the first page. Journalism gave me an obsession with leads—first words, the first line, sentence, paragraph, page that establishes the authority, voice, direction, pace, meaning, music of the

241

book. My own leads direct me toward my own discoveries and I am both fearful and respectful of leads. I have learned that few books survive a poor first page (but that many books don't live up to a good one). In bookstores I am a taster of first lines, just a quick sip, cupped on the tongue, tasted, tested.

I can still feel—not remember but refeel—the physical impact—not intellectual but physical—of the first page of *Machine Dreams*. I felt the same way when I opened the door of the coal furnace and was pushed back by the red heat, white at the center. I didn't read the page so much as receive it. The experience *of* the text was more powerful than the experience reported *in* the text.

I couldn't handle such a book right then. I wanted to escape writing and I forced the book shut, pushed it up and into its place on the shelf. I wanted casual reading while writing. I wanted reading that wouldn't intrude on my own writing. We drifted out of that Mall and into another and passed another shining bookstore where, as if sleepwalking, I went in and bought *Machine Dreams.*

Let's look at that first paragraph but don't get your critical scalpels out. I think this is a fine lead to a significant piece of work by an important writer. This novel is, in my opinion, a major, significant work but that isn't what we're dealing with here. What I'm trying to explore is the impact of that text on one writer who is writing while reading.

It's strange what you don't forget. We had a neighbor called Mrs. Thomas. I remember racing up a long way to pull the heavy telephone—a box phone with a speaking horn on a cord—onto the floor with me. Telephone numbers were two digits then. I called 7, 0, and said, "Tommie, I'm sick. I want you to come over." I can still hear that child's voice, with the feeling it's coming from inside me, just as clearly, just as surely, as you're standing there. I was three years old. I saw my hands on the phone box, and my shoes, and the scratchy brown fabric of the dress I was wearing. I wasn't very strong and had pneumonia twice by the time I was five. Mother had lost a child before me to diptheria and whooping cough, and stillborn twins before him. She kept me dressed in layers of woolens all winter, leggings and undershirts. She soaked clean rags in goose grease and made me wear them around my neck. Tommie would help her and they'd melt down the grease in a big black pot, throw in the rags, and stir them with a stick while I sat waiting, bundled in blankets. They lay the rags on the sill to cool, then wrapped me up while the fumes were still so strong our eyes teared. I stood between the two women as they worked over me, their hands big and quick, and saw nothing but their broad, dark skirts.

(Having written—read—my second draft to this point, I drove to a nearby town to get a newspaper and a cup of coffee [and, yes, a doughnut]. I needed to step away from her text and my text to read without a written text, to half remember, to dream the text that may be written or read. Driving, I am free to read, to write, to image [imagine] a text. I am purposely purposeless, and by allowing my thoughts to drift I have, by the time I return, read several interesting unwritten texts, texts I wouldn't yet want to record. My reading away from the text told me that there really was a text of this article to be written. I had caught a glimpse of a misty middle section and an even more unclear final one, and that was all I wanted right now. I would not want to read too clearly at this time. I might prevent surprise. I return to the previously written text.)

Reading Off the Page

When I read—scanned—Jayne Anne Phillips' opening paragraph for the first time, I received at least three texts from that text, almost simultaneously, overlays, each ignited by her text.

It is an August afternoon, just after lunch. The air is heavy, humid, and the sunlight is so bright it hurts my eyes when it glints through the broad maple leaves. I have escaped the dark, cool house to sit on the granite curb and play in the wonderful, black stinking tar I watched a crew of sweating men cook and spread that morning. I press my feet into the heat of the tar that almost burns and roll small, satisfying mashed potato balls of tar with my fingers. I do not hear the truck but see its green snout with M for Mack on it, growing larger, larger, larger and the great wheel, a swollen tire of the trucks in the funny papers, growing larger and larger. All silent, even when the truck shakes the curb and veers away so close I can see the great greasy naked drive chain passing almost over me and feel my grandmother yanking me back.

That is what I read in her text, that is what her text said to me. I read her words and passed back to that moment and then forward through a sickly childhood and teenage years marked by fever and delirium. The worst vision in the delirium was the great cartoon wheel growing larger and larger. I can dream it today, and I see it standing in that Mall store. And I read another text of my own in her text.

My grandmother, strength of my childhood, is on the floor and her arm has a bruise the size of a muffin and it is growing as I stare at it, and she tells me, who is not allowed to use the telephone, to use it to call Dr. Bartlett. And I do, and he comes in his Packard, and I let him in the front door. He puts a splint on Grandma's arm, and before he leaves he tells me what I knew, that I am grown up, growing up at least. I learned that the fear of something happening to Grandmother was greater than the happening. I could do what I had to do.

And still another text.

I sneak into the pantry which is filled with the purple smell of grapes cooking and reach up to see in the great crockery bowl when the flood of molten jelly pours over me and across the floor into the kitchen where Grandma is screaming. And I hear those screams, hers and mine, today and that dreadful feeling at what can never be undone.

Behind those paragraphs stand the ghosts of hundreds of other paragraphs waiting to be read before they are written. This reading off the text, away from the page or through it, is a tribute to the writer and her text. When I attend a poetry reading, for example, a test of its success for me is how much I write in my daybook, fragments of what may become poems. They are not the poems being read and not the poems I would have written without the reading. They are something in between, created in the air between the poem floating towards me and my lines floating towards it. In reading how often I stare into that middle distance, remembering, imagining, reading a text that is neither the author's or mine. These imagined texts are in a very real sense readings of the original text. They would not occur without that text.

Having crept this far out on thin ice let us speak for a moment with respect for non-comprehension, for encouraging our students not only to understand the text they are reading, but to allow that text to spark other texts, ghost texts (bastard texts?) that are born because of the communion between the written text and the experience of the reader. The writer reading the writer's own pages or the pages of another writer is often reading an unexpected text that has only minimal relationship to the text on the page, but would not exist without that text. Perhaps these texts are fathered by a traveling man, but once they are read, conceived, they can be written down and revised into their own reality, and then read with care as well as with stimulating uncare.

Reading Within the Page

Writers do not only read off the page, however, they read within the page, bringing their own experience with their craft to illuminate the hidden craft of the writer. I am impressed by how quickly Phillips drew me into the whirlpool of her story. One sentence, just six words— "It's strange what you don't forget"—and she has made connection with me, has prepared my mind for the remembering that will accept and reinforce her story. She has begun a dialogue with me. I ask what is strange that she can't forget, and she begins to tell me. In effective writing, the writer involves the reader in the creation of the full text.

Immediately after that we have a switch—or a refinement—of point of view. As a writer I am impressed by her smooth move, which puts me within the narrator's (the rememberer's) experience, reaching up a long way to pull the phone down. At the same time Phillips has begun to hint at a time and place: years ago in a rural area. And in the same sentence I have been drawn back into the narrator's mind, and then put within her childhood. I become the child.

And yet I am moving back and forth within the experience of remembering. I am remembering simpler, older telephone numbering systems with the narrator. I am also feeling the importance of the experience: I am sick and in need of help.

Now there is another nice twist that I can appreciate the way an old basketball player appreciates a head fake to the right and a move to the left. Phillips' narrator stands apart from herself, and we hear her grown-up narrative voice, with a touch of dialect (West Virginia?) hearing her own childhood voice. And I read on and off the page simultaneously, bringing depth and density to her text. I am projected into my own life, where I so often these days see myself both young and old, experiencing life through a series of double and triple exposures, seeming to be, for example, father, son, self, all at the same time. I want to discover how Phillips can spark that reaction. The good writer is always forcing the reader to contribute to the text. What is published is only half—or less—of the text of the book.

I notice that Phillips uses the second person for the second time and gets away with it. That is something the young writer rarely gets away with and I wonder how she makes it work.

I'm also intrigued by the double narrative Phillips establishes. The writer is telling me a story, and in that story a character is telling me a story. She is establishing a technique that will be used again and again in different ways as she allows the people in her book to reveal themselves to the reader.

We are only a third of the way down the paragraph and the narrator takes us back through the opening scene, seeing it again, hearing it again, filling it in with detail, making it more a believable reality. Phillips uses the technique of the oral storyteller, who moves forward and then back and then forward again, making sure that the listener understands. One of the greatest problems for the writer is moving back and forth in time, and I'm impressed how Phillips moves me to the time when the narrator was three, and then forward to when the narrator was five, and then back to before the narrator was born—in two sentences. Only a writer who has seen his or her own prose become twisted and tangled in problems of time can appreciate how gracefully this writer moves back and forth in time.

The writer reading this paragraph appreciates that intangible—voice—which is the most important element in writing. In a matter of lines the author has established that her strong voice, heard previously in her stories and poems, will be adapted to the book. The text, in other words, will possess its own voice. And then within that voice we will hear the voices of the characters themselves. Speech in this paragraph is not real, it is better than real. It gives the illusion—the authoritative, believable illusion—of real speech.

And finally, in this one paragraph, the author plunges me back into childhood, and I experience the childhood of the narrator, and I must read on to discover what happens to this child. This is not suspense, but inspired curiosity. The writer has instilled in me a need to know what will come next.

How conscious am I of this kind of detail while I read? Very conscious. But not an articulated consciousness all of the time. And yet when I read a good writer—Jayne Anne Phillips, William Kennedy, Toni Morrison, John McPhee, Robert Caro, Ann Tyler, Raymond Carver and so many others—I find myself laughing out loud with sheer delight when a move is made that I know can't be made or I hear myself say "Go, go, go," as I become cheerleader to a text that is working.

I've been reading and writing for more than half a century, and I do not often need to articulate what my teachers, my editors, and my own writing have taught me. I must, however, pay particular tribute to Mortimer B. Howell, who taught me the difference a word can make in that critical year before World War II. I still have his marked-up copy of Hardy's *Return of the Native*. It took us weeks to get off Egdon Heath we so carefully attended to the text. And after the war I studied with Dr. Sylvester Bingham of this institution, who so carefully analyzed a text that a classmate of mine who later went into the CIA said our course was the best training he had for military intelligence. My reading of craft may now be instinctive, but it was taught and learned from those two instructors, and many others.

I also believe that in my continual reading I am storing away far more than I am aware of, and that those texts off and within the page are stored in the brain, waiting to be recovered during the act of writing. What seems spontaneous to me is probably high-order plagiarism.

Writing While Reading

The writer, of course, never stops writing. The writer goes to the writing desk for an hour or two, or sometimes a heroic third hour a morning, but continues to write all day and night away from the desk. Many writers believe the most important writing takes place away from the desk, and most writers try to live a life—mostly unsuccessful—that protects the writer from those interferences that invade the secret territory in which writing is taking place. Those who live with writers must grow accustomed to the blank stare, the unhearing ear, the sudden "huh?" or "What did you say?" or even a bark, "Can't you see I'm writing?" when the writer is apparently staring out a window, watching television, walking down the street, eating a meal, or reading. The writer reading your novel is reading his or her own. I pay close attention to Phillips' lead, but standing around within my peripheral vision are all the other leads I have written, the lead on my own novel, the lead to the chapter I am trying to discover. It is as if all previous lovers, wives, husbands, friends, and family have shown up at the same party. I do not want to measure my love against a present new one, but . . .

A kind of comparison does take place. My lead competes with Phillips' lead. And so writers become very careful about what they read while writing. These are writers whose voices distract or force imitation. Few writers are defeated by this competition, even when they should be. The better the material writers read, the more it stimulates their own writing. I publicly denounce competition and intellectually do not believe in it, but secretly I practice it. And Phillips has defeated me in head-on competition. But it does not matter. She is better than I am. So what? I am writing my book, she is writing hers.

This paper could stop here, and perhaps it should, for I am less sure about what comes next, less sure about the relationship between her text and mine. I hope there is none. I do not want to imitate her text, and if I were conscious of doing this in any way I would do something else. But this paper is about the relationship of reading and writing, and as I write, I read. We can not separate the two acts, and so I must try to show you something about one kind of reading I do of my own texts.

I shall reread the opening paragraph of a novel I am working on after having read and analyzed Phillips' opening paragraph. I am in no way conscious of imitating her, but I am certainly conscious of being inspired by her to make my own text better.

I read the following two paragraphs quickly without a pen in hand, forcing myself just to absorb the text and not to make any changes in it. I wanted to hear the text, see what was shown to me by the text, to attempt to be a reader seeing the text for the first time and then I go to work.

                    (2)

1. It is dark but I am awake and I must not allow myself to drift into the

morning sleep of nightmares remembered.

                    (2)   (2)
            (2)   to   as (2)
    I will rise ∧ and steal the early morning from the day ∧ I first learned

(2)
the importance of early morning during those four summers in Maine before I

                    (3)   (3) (2)
            (2) now-then   leaning my   (3)
    was 12., when I ∧ would slide out of bed and, barefoot, allow the weight to
    (3):   then-now

(3)   (2)
rest on one foot, then the other, sneaking down the outer edges of the stairs

        (3)
    boards do (2)
so they ∧ would not squeak.
                                        (5) from a boy's knowledge,
                                (4) from summer camp, from Boy Scouts, ∧
    ↪In the Army, I was taught the ∨ tricks ∨I already knew ∧ and combat seemed,
                                (5) such (5) as

at first, hide-and-go-seek without the mothers calling us in just as the game

got good.

                            lifting up (2)
        (2)   ed   leaning down on the handle to keep it quiet
        ↪ I learned to open/the front door, ∧ever so slowly and raced across

                                    (4) then,
            (2) into   (3) I felt it ∧ name it now.
the dunes until I entered ∧ the great loneliness of the beach. ∧ If I sail

east I will see nothing but the mountain waves until Portugal. The sand

                                        (4)   (4)
stretches so far south the houses on the headlands shrink to miniatures and

                                        (4)
even the great resort hotels to the north grow tiny. enough to fit inside a

(4)
even the great resort hotels to the north grow tiny. ~~enough to fit inside a~~

(3)
(3)   overhanging green blue
~~dollhouse livingroom~~. The Atlantic, an ~~always differing~~ shade ~~of blackgreen~~ ,

(4) always   (2)
                                       south to
is ~~ever~~ on my right as I run north and on my left as I run ∧ home. My feet

(5)   I
hurt from the ice cold sand at the tide's edge, ~~as~~ my toes ∧ dig in and toss a

(3)
Going out,
comet's trail of sand behind me. ~~At first~~, the morning sun is so pale I have

no shadow to race, and I look back to see the Robinson Crusoe trail of

(2), dark brown, hard and level,
footsteps, the only marks on the waveswept sand ∧ . I run again, then stop to

take inventory of driftwood, mussel shell, boat splinter, bottle without a

(4)   (4)
note, seaweed, crab shell, sneaker, and, one morning, my first dead body, a

(3)
purple, (5)
woman, naked, ∧ scarlet, swollen, her tongue so large it cannot fit back into

her mouth.

Having read Philips' lead, mine does not seem immediate enough. It seems to stand back a bit, to instruct the reader, to get in the way. I'd like my lead, in its own way, to be as immediate as hers. I uncap my pen and make the changes marked by the number 2 for the second reading. There are few delights to compare to the joy of taking a sharp pen to your own text, a text that you feel needs work, but that is capable of working. As Bernard Malamud says, "I work with language. I love the flowers of afterthought."

I strike the first paragraph and move closer to the real text. The prose becomes more immediate and active, and that's the main contribution of that reading. I have made the text cleaner, cutting out what might get between the reader and the text. In a sense, I am eliminating myself, the writer, even though this is a book in the first person in which the narrator, the writer, is simultaneously telling and experiencing the story.

I stand back from the text overnight and then read it again, making the changes marked with 3. I begin the third reading by putting in, "now then," and taking it out; putting in "then now" and taking it out. Whenever such changes are seen on a text we must realize that they are but one or two of the dozens of readings that may take place consciously and possibly unconsciously by a writer who is paying close attention to the text. The changes of this reading continue to make the text more immediate, until we come to the insert and the line "I felt it, name it now," where that line seems to me to deepen the book and put it into a more effective context. I wasn't conscious of moving back in time the way Phillips did, but perhaps I was inspired by her. The other changes are simply efforts to make the text honest.

Readings four and five are the writer fussing, reading what should be put in, reading what should be taken out.

Now the text reads:

I rise to steal the early morning from the day as I learned those four summers in Maine before I was twelve. I slide out of bed and, barefoot, lean my weight on one foot, then the other, sneak down the outer edges of the stairs so the boards do not squeak. In the army I was taught such tricks as I already knew from summer camp, from Boy Scouts, from a boy's knowledge, and combat seemed, at first, hide-and-go-seek without the mother's calling us in just as the game got good. I open the front door, lifting up on the handle to keep it quiet and race across the dunes until I enter into the great loneliness of the beach. I felt it then, name it now. If I sail east I will see nothing but the mountain waves until Portugal. The sand stretches so far south the houses on the headlands shrink, and even the great resort hotels to the north grow tiny. The Atlantic, an ever-changing greenblue, is always on my right as I run north, and my left as I run south to home. My feet hurt from the ice-cold sand at the tide's edge. I dig my toes in and toss a comet's trail of sand behind me. Going out, the morning sun is so pale I have no shadow to race, and I look back to see the Robinson Crusoe trail of footsteps, the only marks on the waveswept sand, dark brown, hard and level. I run again, then stop to take inventory of driftwood, mussel shell, boat splinter, bottle without a note, seawood, crabshell, sneaker, and, one morning, my first dead body, a woman, naked, purple scarlet, swollen, her tongue so large it cannot fit back into her mouth.

There was, of course, before I had read Phillips, a similarity in the technical problems we both faced and that may have been one reason I was struck by her book. I am trying in my novel to achieve the kind of time within time that she is establishing. I am concerned with the multiple levels of experience we live in middle-age, experiencing and reexperiencing life simultaneously, and I am particularly concerned in the novel with how the images of war in this military nation create particular realities for all of us, but especially for veterans.

While I write my first drafts and my later drafts, my early notes and my revisions, my plans and my final edits, I am reading the text I intended to write, the text I am writing, and the text I hope yet to write, a kind of triple vision or triple reading that is made possible by all the other readings of my own texts and the texts of others that have come before, the few texts I remember (with a memory that is distorted by the need of the moment) and all the texts that I have forgotten but that are somehow there.

Researching Writing/Reading

My own revelations, perhaps better called confessions, are merely the speculations of one writer and they should be suspect. They are not conventional research findings. Perhaps this whole subject can not be explored by our traditional research techniques but, in any case, I am not a researcher. I am a writer and a writing teacher, who looks within to try to understand my subject matter. I realize better than my critics how eccentric this may be, but I hope it can be a starting place for more authoritative research into how we read while writing and write while reading. I think this relationship is the most significant research frontier in our profession at the present time, and I would like to pose some obvious questions that apparently haven't been obvious as we have attempted to keep our discipline divided into separate camps of reading and writing.

- How does the writer, other than by direct modeling, make use of other texts in creating his or her own texts?
- In what ways does the experience of writing increase the act of reading?
- How does the writer cause the reader to write a text while reading?
- How can this off-the-page or ghost text be described?
- What is the relationship of this ghost text to the written text?
- Does the writer create a ghost text that is different from the written text the writer produces?
- How does the writer read to see the possibility of an entire text in fragments of writing—code words, phrases, lines, sentences, paragraphs, notes?

- Does the writer create a pre-text in the mind that is read during the act of writing? If so, how can it be described?
- What are the different ways the writer reads the unfinished text of another and the unfinished text of his or her own?
- What are the reading skills the writer needs at different stages of the writing process?
- What are the reading roles a writer may play at different stages of the writing process?
- How does the text control or direct both its reading and its writing?
- How much of the text is heard and seen?
- How does the reader's voice affect the reading of the text?
- How much does the personal experience—and feelings and opinions—of the writer/reader affect the writing and reading experience?
- How can the interaction of reading and writing during both the reading act and the writing act be described?
- How do different writing and reading tasks change the description of the writing/reading interaction?

These are a few of the questions to which I would like answers. Wouldn't we all? The implications of those questions are, for me, that we need new research methods so that we can attempt to capture the complex idiosyncratic nature of the reading/writing interaction. Today we recognize that it is impossible to separate reading from writing. Every writer reads at the moment of writing. It has appeared possible for the reader to read without writing, but I wonder if that is really possible. Does the reader while reading actually write a text that is quite different from the one written?

I hope that this conference, which is part of a national trend towards increased examination of the integration of reading and writing, will play a role in sponsoring a new, intergrated reading/writing research that will focus primarily on the reading/writing interaction.

Teaching Reading/Writing

When I first became a teacher of writing at this university I was told that I could never become an Associate or Full Professor because I was a writer. I didn't realize the theological importance of those ranks, and so that didn't bother me. I was also told that I could not serve on committees, and I am forever sorry they broke their word on that one. I was also told that writing courses couldn't count for major credit. I wasn't surprised. When I attended this school American Literature courses couldn't be counted for literature credit.

I naturally responded to such snobbery with a reverse snobbery of my own, and succeeded in being as petty and pompous as any of my colleagues on the other side of the aisle. But things changed, and we have moved closer and closer together. The writers in the department got promoted; we serve on committees—unfortunately—and we believe in the interaction of reading and writing.

In recent years my own conference teaching has changed so much that I see myself as a reading teacher as much as a writing teacher. My students make the first appraisal of their texts, because I must know how they read their own text. I monitor their reading and try to help them read more effectively, for they can not write better unless they read better. That is only one of the ways we can bring the teaching of writing and reading closer together. Some others may be:

- To encourage and take seriously the text students write in their heads while reading, especially if those texts seem eccentric to us and do not match the text we have created (written in our own heads) while reading the same pages. Am I speaking in favor of non-comprehension? Perhaps, at times, as a higher comprehension on the part of the teacher.

- To work with our students, in conference and in workshop, to develop the skills of reading fragments that may inspire a text and to read an unfinished text so that it evolves into increased purpose and meaning.

- To give our students more experience in reading the early drafts and evolving texts of publishing writers within and outside the classroom.

- To encourage increased writing of parallel texts within writing classes, texts that are not so much about what has been written by another but texts which allow the student to approximate the writing experience of the writer.

- To listen to our students (and to published writers?) as they tell us how reading affects their writing and writing affects their reading.

- To design courses in which reading and writing share equal emphasis. This should not mean a return to the traditional Freshman English course in which the student was assigned an essay and expected to produce a formulaic response in writing to that essay. In such a course both honest writing and reading, as I practiced it as student and instructor, was often not tolerated. I am imagining classes in which reading and writing texts evolve in a contrapuntal interaction in the way I speculate that writers work.

I know that I am always reading while writing and writing while reading and that if we encourage and study this challenging, complex relationship we will be blessed with a problem we can never solve. We can, however, learn much that is significant in the attempt, and that is what we want, after all, isn't it? Not answers so much as important questions and there are few questions more important than: What is the relationship of reading and writing?

15

Lowell's Turtles: Visions and Self-Revisions

PAUL MARIANI

University of Massachusetts at Amherst

PROLOGUE

Consider a series of fictions, analogues, a fable, a grid of expectations, something statistically "proven," or—in the language of the scientists—the mapping of groups, what we once called a marshalling of the evidence. As if we could actually *prove* our case, indisputably, beyond a doubt. Whatever strategies we as writers assume, we must know that we are tracking out a fiction, hoping—like Whitman—that what we assume, for the moment, the reader too will assume. Even as I write this I am aware not only of linguistic irritants but of the world around me in the form of an untypological fly walking and jerking its hypertensive, wary way across the page with the distrustful motion a million years of genetic programming have fed into its jellied mass, too too happy, perhaps in its own unpuzzlement, before it vanishes from my more simply-faceted perspective and is gone.

But the fly only makes matters worse, for he reminds me, staring at the blank page before me, that I am writing these words for a weekend conference to which, monklike, we come, by plane, train, bus, by car, by foot, to examine the word, the very thing, the medium, the currency, I see myself exchanging with you now in my imagination, the hall empty as I write, the hall full as I read, becoming more fully aware of that initial petrifying fear of the writer's exacerbated self-consciousness staring into inner or outer space. As here at Murkland*— and may that onomastic gesture not stand as sign for this weekend's proceedings—in a hall of self-reflecting mirrors, each of you as a multi-

---

*The conference was held in Murkland Hall—an appropriate place to speak about turtles. (Editor's note.)

faceted eye, seeing in the text what we think we see and what, given
the liberating constraints of any particular now, as *now*, on an evening
in October in New Hampshire, what we desire too to see.

And yet, and yet, and yet . . . we keep returning to the texts, as
if from them we might find the truth we need and, as writers, remake
it in our own image. Excluding the pure music of mathematics for the
moment, if such music really does exist, all writing seems to me finally
autobiographical, self-referential, and—finally—fictive. If my own work
as critic, as biographer, and as poet has taught me anything, it is that
all writing is a fiction. If, then, Pilate's gibe was true and we cannot
know the truth even if we stare it in the face, then I suppose writing
is a matter of rhetoric, the persuasion of the other to our point of
view. In this sense, at least (though we do not often say so in a free-
wheeling democracy such as ours), writing is a source of power, a visible sign of the self's ineffability, a revelation and a concealment, a
continual remaking of what we take to be our truest faces, a palimp-
sest of self-portraiture, like Rubens' hundred faces, all his own, yet
each one different, except that our self-portraits are done not only in
pen and pencil but with typewriter and—in this age of machine roman-
ticism—with the ultimate la machine, the electric, terrifying processor
of our words.

Can we ever uncover the parts of a given text to say what went
into it at the moment of creation? I do not think so. And yet one goes
on trying, fascinated by the attempt to see into the deep well of the
self. We stare and stare, Frost tells us, but most days we see only our
faces wreathed in fern or watch the clouds behind us reflected in those
black waters. But then, rarely, a sign is given us, an irritant, a prelin-
guistic matrix, if you will, a something. Truth? or just a piece of quartz
lying on the bottom of the mind? Who can say? Except that, out of
the search itself for something, out of that irregular process, random,
chaotic, like a bee stumbling against a glass pane insanely for escape,
we touch on something, the words, the words, the words, as if they
were the tracks of sub-atomic particles across an X-ray plate, never
seen themselves but for their tracking. Is not the writing itself a fictive
space enclosed or open-ended, a thing with flying buttresses or atrium
or porch, a shell to say the white hot mind lived here once before it
cooled to language? Call it, this writing, a house on a hill, a woodpile,
a design. In the fictive landscape a writer makes his or her own over a
lifetime's labor, we will find perhaps many houses, each made out of
a special need to keep warm and out of wind and rain, a place one
might domesticate and even hang with pictures, if for no other reason
than to remind us of our love for order, the order we make against the
chaos we fear. We write, at last, I think, because we must. Otherwise,
as William Carlos Williams once said about the despised poem, we die

each day for lack of what we find there. By which he must have meant that there are many small losses the imagination suffers—perhaps needlessly—before the final overwhelming blank. And against that there are the words.

Having said all this, then, having sufficiently forewarned and forearmed you, as it were, I want to examine a very great contemporary poet's poems by looking at one seemingly simple and straightforward image as one writer rediscovered its import in his writing: the image of Robert Lowell's turtles in four poems written over a fifteen-year span. One of the things I have noticed in writing about writers is how often they keep coming back and back to the same preoccupations, the same lyrical irritants, often the same images. "We had the experience but missed the meaning," Eliot tells us in his *Four Quartets*, but he must mean "meanings," which is why the writer keeps coming back to the image which sits unperturbed upon its black log in the still waters of the mind, writing, sixty years and more if necessary, until at last the imagination's sun goes down and the current, for all we know, ceases then forever.

Reading the letters of a very young Robert Lowell to his maternal grandfather, I was struck with the unintentional poignancy of his description of hunting turtles while he was at St. Mark's School in Marlborough, Massachusetts. I suppose I saw this particular image because a young William Carlos Williams had once had stationery made up for himself which carried a small drawing of a turtle with the French beneath it: *j'arriverai*—I will arrive. It is the old fable Aesop tells of the tortoise and the hare. For Williams, of course, the turtle represented a sign of hope, of delayed but imminent springtime, a reminder to himself that eventually he would reach the artistic mark he had set for himself. But for Lowell the turtle would come to take on a different set of meanings as he continued to return to his image, each time coming to understand it in more sympathetic and at last in more terrifying ways.

On April 20, 1928, an eleven-year-old Lowell wrote a chatty newsletter to his grandfather, a letter filled with misspellings and weighted with a humdrum narrative. He speaks of catching turtles:

> After launch I filled my canteen with ginger ale and went into the woods to the place were [I] catch turtles. When I got there I saw a turtle on the other side of the pond. Then I poked him and he whent into the water. Then I whent around to the other side of the pond and caught him.

And three years later, to his grandfather again:

On Sunday I caught two turtles which I've got now and on Monday a snake which I let go. Mother [is] sending me a globe to put the turtles in.

(23 April 1931)

It is a characteristic gesture of Lowell's, something no doubt repeated many times, this hunting after painted turtles in the springtime ponds of eastern Massachusetts and southern New Hampshire. But in his mid-forties, an older Lowell returns to this childhood scene, what he recalls now as his "season of joy," remembering how he had swooped down on those unsuspecting turtles, stashing them in a garden urn filled with water and raw hash, until the urn had begun to ferment as his turtles began turning into a fetid stew. The poem is called "The Neo-Classical Urn" and is collected in Lowell's 1964 volume, *For the Union Dead.* Reading it one is struck by the echoes there to Keats' "Ode on a Grecian Urn," especially in Lowell's evocation of such pastoral images as the "cylindrical / clipped trunks" of bleaching pines and the pale eroticism and dynamic stasis of the "cast stone statue of a nymph, / [with] her soaring armpits and her one bare breast." So the older, crippled Lowell remembers himself as a boy who could not rest, a boy who would race off the pathway by the pond "to snatch / the painted turtles on dead logs" before they could flee.

But even if the body of the poet must move slowly now, the brain still cannot rest, for its "juice [is] alive / with ferment" while the fermenting bubbles "drive the motor." This complex image of electric fermentation Lowell doubles in his poem, as we watch the dead turtles begin popping up on the "stale scummed / surface" of the white urn, and the urn assumes once more its primary funerary significance. By extension, then, the poet's own skull becomes a white urn, a vessel dredging up from the silt of the past the image of dead turtles rising with the ferment of decay. So the poem ends where it began, but with a difference, as Lowell watches himself rubbing his skull and taking in the "dying smell" of the turtles he had unwittingly killed, aware now that he holds within himself the killer's instinct to maim, including the maiming of himself, one of the "crippled last survivors" he finally freed: Like them, he too hobbles "humpbacked through the grizzled grass," his own body the implied victim of its own too-manic fermenting brain, that "poor head" that cannot rest and that has now—at forty-five—lost forever that earlier Wordsworthian season of joy.

In *For Lizzie and Harriet,* Lowell's collection of sixty-seven unrhymed sonnets published nearly a decade after *For the Union Dead,* Lowell comes back once again to his turtles. Here, in two sonnets which form part of the book's closing sonnet sequence entitled "Late Summer," Lowell seems to have created an analogue for the collapse

of his own twenty-year marriage to Elizabeth Hardwick. The place is
Maine: Lowell's summer home in Castine, the road to Bangor. The
loose and tight couplets and interconnecting rhymes which had roped
"The Neo-Classical Urn" together are gone in these later poems, to be
replaced by a loose blank verse line which approximates beautifully
the prose rhythms of the contemporary American idiom. So much is
implied here in Lowell's evocation of two cultures, two worlds: the
culture of the rich up from New York to vacation in Maine, gods for
whom "culture without cash isn't worth their spit," a race of people
whose laughter is always breezy. Call this image the image of Lowell
at his dinner table, entertaining as the public man at his home in
Castine. And then there is the painted turtle: an emblem of the lowly
and the despised, of those like Lowell himself who are at bottom "out-
of-power," the stone dome upon the turtle's back a sign literally of its
petrifying fear which, over millenia, has resulted in the stone fortress
it carried with it wherever it goes.

But there is something more. For it is fascinating to watch
Lowell's bicameral vision with regard to the turtle, on the one hand
seen from the Darwinian perspective, the turtle as comic "understudy"
to the dinosaurs which as a species it has managed to outlast, and on
the other hand the turtle as "a stone of stumbling to God." *A stone of
stumbling to God.* Does he mean by this epithet that the turtle is a
stumbling stone to a belief in the God of Genesis, contrary proof of
the apparent randomness by which some organisms survive and others
do not, proof as well against anything like a hierarchical chain of being
in the universe? Or does the turtle become, perhaps, in terms of the
typological vision of Lowell's Puritan forebears, a type of the stony
soul still thirsting after God, stumbling after that ontological pressure
like the turtle stumbling after the water which it needs and craves? We
can not be sure, for the syntax of the poem will not provide us with
the certitude of either answer. But it seems clear that Lowell's turtle
has been filtered through a complex series of texts and rhetorical
models which include—among others—the typological strategies of a
Cotton Mather as well as both the fiercely denotative language of a
Darwin and the stylistic signatures of Flaubert, Whitman, and Henry
James.

"Returning Turtle" completes the two-part cycle, a comic dimin-
uendo of the great procession out from and back to God and nature,
in this case identified with the "sleazy surface" of the Orland River.
Lowell begins the sonnet with an image of the vagabond quester in
search of a grail of sorts, in this case water. Like so many of Lowell's
poems, this one is also in part about the problem of naming. What, for
example, to call the painted turtle beyond painted turtle itself? So
Lowell tries on a phrase like "faded savage, / the last Sioux," captured

and imprisoned by the white man, imagined here as saying, as Chief
Sitting Bull in his weariness had said:

Why doesn't the Great White Father put his red children on
wheels, and move us as he will?

Which is what the poet does, in the old belated gesture of once again
freeing the turtle, after having kept it captive, this time in his bath-
room tub for a week, using his ten-year-old daughter as his excuse.
Now father and daughter watch the turtle as it rushes

for the water like rushing into marriage,
swimming in uncontaminated joy,
lovely the flies that fed that sleazy surface,
a turtle looking back at us, and blinking.

The simile strikes us first as somewhat odd, bourgeoise, and comic—
this turtle rushing for water like someone rushing into marriage, free
at last, or thinking itself free, as it swims in the "uncontaminated,"
unalloyed joy of its new existence. And yet the river is surely not uncontaminated to the onlookers. In fact, it is downright sleazy and fly-
blown, and the turtle itself is not sure of what is happening to it as it
finds itself unconstrained by its domestic prison and turns now to look
back blinking. Lowell's syntax, as well as the weight of the simile, does
not, finally, insist upon a corresponding or necessary analogue between
the turtle's state of being and the unnamed one who rushes into marriage. Rather, what Lowell gives us here is an allegory for his own belated third marriage: a man in his mid-fifties and a "faded savage,"
driven by contrary impulses he himself does not seem to understand,
as he rushes into a marriage after a season of uncontaminated joy not
unlike the joy he says in "The Neo-Classical Urn" he felt hunting turtles as a boy. But very early on into that marriage something in Lowell
seems to have known he had acted too hastily in leaving his second
marriage, metaphorically positioned here by the summer world of
Castine. So it is Lowell, then, watching himself as he swims out into
the waters of a new life like the poor turtle, as much acted upon by
forces he cannot understand as he seems to act, and turning now to
blink back uncomprehendingly, wondering how it is he ever wound up
here in a too too happy earthly paradise he fears as much as welcomes.

Lowell's final turtle poem—and his finest—was written less than
two years before his death. It is called, simply, "Turtle," and it is
placed strategically at the beginning of the last section of his last—and
arguably his best—collection of poems, *Day by Day*. This poem, inter-
estingly enough, seems to pick up exactly where "Returning Turtle"
left off, with an old turtle wading out amorously into that dubious
river of joy. By now the marriage predestined to failure because it was
built on a dream has indeed failed. The painted dream has not held fast,

these poems say, anymore than poetry itself alone could secure the poet's happiness. In the long run, Lowell tells us at the end of a lifetime's writing and revising, the writing makes nothing happen. Rather it tells us only, if we are honest, what *has* happened. Now Lowell sees himself as an old turtle become "absent-minded, inelastic," unsure even of what has happened, having re-invented and rethought the past too often, "kept afloat" only "by losing touch" with reality.

An old painted turtle, a half-frozen fossil moving towards its death, a quixotic, pathetic, heartbreaking figure wading out into the depths "in a foolsdream of armor," the armor of his dream of love, the dream of the poem. No, it is not enough, he sees now as he wakes on a winter's morning, and surely no defense against the killer who has waited for him all these years. What killer? Why, the snapping turtles that were also out there in the ponds he stalked so many years before. For, unlike the blinking, amorous, painted turtles, snappers do not wade out. Instead, they submerge, ready to rip a finger or a toe off the unsuspecting. For Lowell knows that snappers have not survived for so many thousands of years merely "by man's philanthropy."

Once more in memory Lowell goes back to re-examine his boyhood scene. Till now he had written of the scene as if he were a god, dispenser of the fate of painted turtles, capturing them and setting a few last survivors free as his conscience worked its way on him. With time, he had come to share in their vulnerability, to see himself as one of those grizzled survivors even as he watched his friends die. But what of the killer snappers, kept out of sight in the dark waters of his own subconscious? In "Turtles" Lowell wakens into an unfamiliar world. Yes, it is a winter's tale, morning, it is his bedroom. And yet, all is strange. One recalls, perhaps inevitably, a story like Kafka's "The Metamorphosis," where the narrator finds himself transformed one morning into a huge insect. So Lowell wakens to see "three snapping turtles squatted on my drifting clothes" across his bed: two adults and a squeaking, mewling infant. Do they represent his parents and himself? Or his wife, Caroline, his son, and himself? Or are they palimpsests of the same family group, himself young, himself an old man?

They are hungry, he understands, and they have set themselves to feed on what is already dead in Lowell himself, a process the poet sees has been underway for some time, three-fourths iced over already, as another poem informs us. So it has been his own bent towards self-destruction, that patient will towards death which he had once misread as freedom and as simple joy but which now turns out to have been the will for oblivion itself. In "Ulysses and Circe" he had defined himself approaching sixty as a shark, "a vocational killer / in the machismo of senility, / foretasting the apogee of mayhem." So all it has taken is time, he sees now, time to see what was out there waiting to take him